Social Skills for People with Learning Disabilities

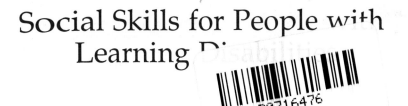

THERAPY IN PRACTICE SERIES
Edited by Jo Campling

This series of books is aimed at "therapists" concerned with rehabilitation in a very broad sense. The intended audience particularly includes occupational therapists, physiotherapists and speech therapists, but many titles will also be of interest to nurses, psychologists, medical staff, social workers, teachers or voluntary workers. Some volumes are interdisciplinary, others are aimed at one particular profession. All titles will be comprehensive but concise, and practical but with due reference to relevant theory and evidence. They are not research monographs but focus on professional practice, and will be of value to both students and qualified personnel.

Social Skills for People with Learning Disabilities

A social capability approach

Mark Burton

Head of Development and Clinical Services, Manchester Joint
Learning Disability Service, Manchester, UK

and

Carolyn Kagan

Principal Lecturer in Psychology, Manchester
Metropolitan University, Manchester, UK

with

Pat Clements

Member of Additional Support Team, Mancunian
Community NHS Trust, Manchester, UK

CHAPMAN & HALL

London · Glasgow · Weinheim · New York · Tokyo · Melbourne · Madras

Published by Chapman & Hall, 2–6 Boundary Row, London SE1 8HN, UK

Chapman & Hall, 2–6 Boundary Row, London SE1 8HN, UK

Blackie Academic & Professional, Wester Cleddens Road, Bishopbriggs, Glasgow G64 2NZ, UK

Chapman & Hall GmbH, Pappelallee 3, 69469 Weinheim, Germany

Chapman & Hall USA, One Penn Plaza, 41st Floor, New York NY 10119, USA

Chapman & Hall Japan, ITP-Japan, Kyowa Building, 3F, 2-2-1 Hirakawacho, Chiyoda-ku, Tokyo 102, Japan

Chapman & Hall Australia, Thomas Nelson Australia, 102 Dodds Street, South Melbourne, Victoria 3205, Australia

Chapman & Hall India, R. Seshadri, 32 Second Main Road, CIT East, Madras 600 035, India

Distributed in the USA and Canada by Singular Publishing Group Inc., 4284 41st Street, San Diego, California 92105

First edition 1995

© 1995 Mark Burton and Carolyn Kagan

Typeset in 10/12pt Palatino by Best-set Typesetter Ltd., Hong Kong
Printed in Great Britain by St Edmundsbury Press, Bury St Edmunds, Suffolk

ISBN 0 412 43380X 1 56593 194 7 (USA)

A catalogue record for this book is available from the British Library

Library of Congress Catalog Card Number: [to follow]*

∞ Printed on permanent acid-free text paper, manufactured in accordance with ANSI/NISO Z39.48-1992 and ANSI/NISO Z39.48-1984 (Permanence of Paper).

For Doris and John

Contents

Preface

Sometimes people . . . take the mickey, they tease you. I say "excuse me, I'm a human being like you". They still laugh. Don't turn your back on us. We wish you'd treat us like human beings. Sometimes you treat us like zombies, as if we're from another planet. You're human beings and so are we. Treat us like human beings.

Mary, Jackie, Elizabeth and Valerie, Islington Elfrida Rathbone, 1985 p. 68

This book is intended chiefly for those people who are working to support adults with learning disabilities take their rightful place in society. It is for those who are seeking to (i) find better ways of helping to strengthen communities so that they are able to include all their citizens in local life, and (ii) help people with learning disabilities participate in and contribute to their communities. The people involved in this work come from an increasingly varied set of disciplines, and employing organizations, and occupy various roles and job titles. The book is aimed at both students and professional staff from different therapy professions, community nursing, social work and care management, and those involved in further and community education. It is also meant for those working in the new generation of supported living services (whether these are based on dispersed residential or domicilary support models), day services, and those working in detached community support roles.

Such disciplinary boundaries are, quite rightly, increasingly fluid, and the approach presented here cuts across the traditional territories of these occupational groups: there are now several courses training "hybrid" workers for dual qualifications in social work and learning disability nursing, and these workers will need comprehensive frameworks for organizing their practice of supporting people in actual community settings rather than in one kind of service or organizational setting, labelled "health" or "social services". While not written specifically for them, we hope the book will also be of some interest and usefulness for other allies of people with learning disabilities – their families, and those involved in volunteer or advocacy roles.

The emphasis and illustration, throughout, is on adults, but many of the ideas are directly relevant, or can be adapted, to work with younger people.

The approach offered in this book has evolved through our work in the North West of England over a number of years. We mention the North West of England, not just as a means of locating us, geographically, but because services for and with people with learning disabilities in the North West have developed in a distinctive (if not entirely unique) way. In 1982, 11 social service authorities and 19 health districts signed up to *A Model District Service*, a policy document which was to shape the direction and nature of services for people with learning disabilities. This, as you can imagine, was some achievement. Today, in 1994, the same authorities still adhere to a coherent and shared set of positive and constructive values and service principles across the North West. This has not happened without the commitment of all those involved in delivering services, from sessional contact staff and volunteers right through to directors of social services, chief executives of health authorities and regional managers. People with learning disabilities and their families have been strong advocates for the *Model District Service*, which envisages the development of community services that enhance people's life experiences and fulfilment, while at the same time closing the large institutions.

The Regional Advisory Group has brought together different stakeholders in improving the life circumstances of people with learning disabilities throughout this period, and it is likely that, had it not succeeded in this task, there would be far fewer examples of good and innovative practice and positive outcomes for people in the North West. The Regional Advisory Group successfully mixed campaigning at all levels with coordination of provision at regional, district and local levels. Within its brief, the Advisory Group supported the deployment of two small, interdisciplinary teams – the Regional Training Team and the Regional Development Team (now combined to form the North West

Training and Development Team) to stimulate and catalyse service development and professional practice.

Both of us have worked closely with the Regional Advisory Group. Mark has been a member of the group for nearly ten years, and has led a number of initiatives, supported by the group, which are directly relevant to the work of this book. In particular, Mark developed an approach to quality assessment that focused on the experiences of people using the services as well as the coherence of the services themselves (Burton, 1992). He also coordinated some work on people caught in the "competence trap", whose needs are not well met by any of the existing services and for whom the method of working outlined in this book is particularly appropriate (Burton, 1990). Since 1982, Mark has worked with people with learning disabilities in Manchester as a psychologist and as manager of learning disability services.

Carolyn has been a part-time member of the Regional Development Team since 1987. This has involved working with people with learning disabilities, family members, volunteers, contact staff and their managers, as well as people from a variety of other agencies who have a stake in bettering the futures of people with learning disabilities. Sometimes assistance is given via advice or consultancy, sometimes through evaluation, and sometimes through "trouble shooting" when particular problems and difficulties arise (see Kagan, 1991 for a description of the work of the Development Team). Carolyn is a social worker and also teaches at Manchester Metropolitan University. The courses she teaches are those concerned with understanding interpersonal and social change, from the perspectives of people themselves, as well as the groups and communities to which they belong. She has written extensively about the development of professional interpersonal skills.

Both of us have been involved in stimulating different communities' capacities to include disadvantaged people in different ways. We were both involved in establishing a voluntary organization to help people with learning disabilities extend their leisure opportunities (Kagan, 1987). Mark has also been involved in the youth movement for many years, whilst Carolyn has been a member of a community health council and local council for voluntary service as well as being involved with community development in inner-city areas, with particular reference to police–community relations.

In 1984 we received a research grant from the then Manchester Polytechnic for a piece of action research on "Social Rules and Social Skills of People with Mental Handicaps" *sic*. We were fortunate in being able to employ Debbie Thorpe and then Pat Clements to work on this project. It was in the course of this work that many of the ideas and practices suggested in this book were developed and piloted. Since then we have tried and tested the ideas in the course of our work and, over the last decade, have refined the process, alongside many other colleagues who have also tried out different aspects of the approach. We are grateful to Pat Clements, who not only challenged our assumptions but also managed to transform our aims into practical possibilities. Pat spent many hours with us discussing the format the book should take and how the process of working might be made most accessible to those who might use it, and she must take some of the responsibility for the final version of the approach. Tim Lister also helped us formulate our ideas early on the process, and we are indebted to him for providing personal, professional and financial support for the research: Tim employed Pat to work within the service he managed, field testing the approach we had developed.

We were greatly encouraged in the writing of the book by practitioners who attended a session we gave at the annual British Institute of Mental Handicap Conference, in 1989. Many people there made it clear to us that there was, indeed, widespread and enthusiastic interest in the approach. People attending a number of courses we have run over the years have tried some of the ideas and methods, and helped us refine the aproach. In particular, those who participated in regional workshops on interpersonal skills and relationships, the University Diploma in Community Care, community nursing courses, and the many colleagues who have participated in short courses, have not only helped us clarify how we have presented material, but have also helped us maintain our own commitment to making the approach more widely available to both students and experienced practitioners.

However, the book is more than a transcription of training materials. Practical suggestions emerge from elaboration and discussion of key concepts and the linking of ideas derived from different perspectives: the approach is firmly underpinned by both theoretical analyses and by previous research. The practical activities we have included are those we have used on many occasions. Some we have made up and others are adaptations of familiar and unfamiliar exercises whose original sources are unknown. We think we have arrived at our own adaptations of these exercises, including some previously published in Kagan, Evans and Kay (1986). However if any reader feels that we should have credited her or him with an original idea, and that we have failed to do this, we apologise. In the text, we have responded to feedback from practitioners in the field and from students who have tested the approach, and have written the book in a non-academic style, omitting references to the literature. The readings supplied at the end of each chapter should lead the critical reader to relevant material, carefully chosen, not for its recent publication in erudite journals, but for its relevance to contemporary thinking and practice. In our discussions we do not seek to describe, adopt or evaluate particular models and approaches offered elsewhere. Instead, we seek to use ideas and practices and adapt them for our own purposes.

The book has been a long time in the making. Just as we were about to embark on writing it, the health and social services as well as higher education were thrown into even greater disarray than usual. We have been caught up in massive changes in the organizations in which we work. Nevertheless, with the support of many people we have managed to complete the task. Tom McLean has chaired the Regional Advisory Group and has shown us the effectiveness of "networking". Peter Hewitt, Director of Salford Social Services, and Eileen Waddington, Director of Community Care at the North Western Regional Health Authority, steered the regional strategy in the face of many threats to it from the health service reforms and introduction of community care. Peter has also given Carolyn constructive and supportive supervision for her work with the Development Team. The Development Team has always been a small resource, but Carolyn has been lucky enough to work with Tom McLean, Chris Gathercole, Alan Coates and Mildred Austin as the other team members. All of us have shared ways of thinking that are mirrored in the approach we are suggesting here, and Chris and Mildred have both been constant sources of validation for the approach as well as sources of information about best practice throughout the world: the profound changes in how we try to support people with learning disabilities and strengthen the capacities of communities have taken place simultaneously, and quasi-independently across many countries. Sue Canavan has helped considerably in the efficient and high quality administrative support she gives to the team – we apologise for not organizing ourselves well enough for her to type this manuscript for us! The humour and good working relationships within the team are greatly appreciated. Mildred and Sue Lewis, from the Metropolitan University, have been tremendous sources of encouragement and support and have helped Carolyn prioritize both her work and her temper.

Mark has spent the last 12 years working with the local community services for people with learning disabilities. He is grateful to the many colleagues who have tried various ways of working on both the personal and community competence fronts. These colleagues have been based with health, social services and the voluntary sector, primarily in North and Central Manchester. These contributions have been so many that it would be invidious to select names. It has not always been easy: learning what does not work has been as important as learning about what can work, and often the work has been frustrating, especially when the organizations themselves have got in the way of creating better outcomes for those who rely on them. These colleagues, therefore, have been an essential source of strength throughout these years.

Many people with learning disabilities have also made their contributions. We have tried to use this way of working with them, in partnership, as a means of helping them gain greater opportunities and enriched experiences. In doing this, we have been reminded of everyone's enormous potential for growth and development, through opportunities to develop social competence and to make the most of social opportunities.

We are grateful for the patience and encouragement shown by Jo Campling as commissioning editor in the Therapy in Practice Series, and by Catherine Walker and Lisa Fraley from Chapman and Hall. We really do appreciate their friendly assistance and prompting.

Last, but certainly not least, we offer our thanks to our daughters Amy Kagan and Anna Kagan. Not only have they done more washing up and prepared more meals than usual, but they have shown tolerance and consideration beyond that normally expected. They are quite right when they protest that "weekends are meant to be for your family".

Mark Burton and Carolyn Kagan
November 1994, Manchester

Burton, M. (1992) *Roads to Quality: A sourcebook for improving services to people with major disabilities*, Regional Advisory Group on Learning Disability Services, Manchester.

Burton, M. (ed.) (1990) *Caught in the Competence Trap: A review of provision for adults with moderate learning difficulties*, Regional Advisory Group on Learning Disability Services, Manchester.

Islington Elfrida Rathbone (1985) *The Friday Afternoon Book: By Us Lot, The Young Women's Group at Elfrida Rathbone, Islington*, National Children's Bureau and Islington Elfrida Rathbone, London.

Kagan, C. (1987) *Evaluation of Blackley Leisure Integration Support Services. Final Report to Mental Health Foundation*, Manchester Polytechnic, Manchester.

Kagan, C. (1991) *Looking to the Future: A discussion paper about regional development and training for services for people with learning disabilities in the North West*, North West Training and Development Team, Whalley.

Kagan, C., Evans, J. and Kay, B. (1986) A Manual of Interpersonal Skills for Murses: An experiential approach. Harper and Row, London.

A NOTE ON TERMINOLOGY

As we note later on, the words used to refer to the people who are the subject of this book are full of problems. We have followed the current British Department of Health usage which is to talk of "people with learning disabilities". In educational contexts the term "learning difficulties" is used, but, while this is preferred by some self-advocacy organizations, we believe that for many people it implies that the problem is less real or more easily overcome than disability might imply.

The identification of the disability or difficulty as one of "learning" is also problematic. For a North American audience the term "learning disability" has a different meaning, corresponding to our terms "moderate learning disability" as well as "specific learning disability". Perhaps we should not worry too much about the other side of the Atlantic: they still talk about "mental retardation". The Australians have favoured "intellectual disability" and, while not finding favour in the UK, this would appear to identify the fundamental problem more accurately. The difficulty is not simply one of learning (although it may be manifest through difficulty acquiring new skills), but may be in one or more intellectual or information processing functions. If we define the problem too narrowly as a problem of learning we risk prescribing a lifetime of being taught, and, as we argue throughout this book, people with "learning disabilities" need rather more than this.

Trying to reform terminology is a thankless task (Mark Burton's 1988 piece, for example, attracted a series of counter arguments and protestations), and it can divert us from the real issues of life opportunities and experiences, which stem from the commitment to full social and civil rights for all (Foley and Pratt, 1994). We have been pragmatic in this book in following the current British terminology.

Burton, M. (1988) Who has the learning difficulty? *Community Living*, **2**(1), 7.

Foley, C. and Pratt, S. (with the British Council of Organisations for Disabled People) (1994) *Access Denied: Human rights and disabled people*, Report 7, Liberty – National Council for Civil Liberties, London.

1

Social skills and social capability

Mary is a quiet, rather reserved woman of 34 years, with a warm sense of humour. She is short and a little overweight. Her clothes and hairstyle make her seem older. Mary lives with her stepmother and their dog in an established inner suburb of an industrial town. Although there had been suggestions that Mary was "slow" from an early age, she did attend a mainstream school until age 11, transferring to what is now termed a school for children with moderate learning difficulties. Going to that school led to ridicule and bullying by children in her neighbourhood. On leaving school at 16, Mary attended an Adult Training Centre and then an annexe where she did contract work, putting instructions in the lids of home-brew beer kits. She attended a college course for people with special needs and was found employment (half-time) as a cleaner by the employment service for people with learning disabilities in her area. She is not very keen on this work which is largely solitary (except when she cleans the ground-floor areas), and says she would rather work where there are children. Mary's stepmother used to take and control all of her money, and there were suspicions that she spent most of it on drink for herself. Now that she is getting older and more infirm Mary is assuming greater autonomy. Unfortunately the two women have never really got on well, and Mary's role was always subordinate, to the extent that she has had few opportunities to learn how to manage a house.

Mary's social life is also restricted, as this typical week's schedule suggests.

Monday	Cooking class for people with learning difficulties
Tuesday	Mencap club (fortnightly)
Wednesday	Swimming session for people with learning difficulties
Thursday	Home – TV
Friday	Home – TV
Saturday	Home – TV
	Shopping for Food
Sunday	Home – TV
	Occasional visit to local pub for 30 minutes.

Mary has been denied opportunities to learn how to do many ordinary things and, apart from her employment (itself not very rewarding), her life is restricted. She has also, from time to time, been unnecessarily grouped with people with severe learning difficulties which has damaged her own image of who she is.

Bill is a tall slim man of 57 years old. He is a very gentle person, although, like most of us, he can lose his temper when treated unfairly. He has rather long, grey hair that can look unkempt, and he also tends to choose clothes that look strange for a man of his age. He recently moved into his own flat in a working-class suburb of the town that he originally came from. His neighbours are all elderly and many are infirm, since his flat is in a sheltered block. Bill enjoys chatting and will offer descriptive anecdotes about his life in the hospital which was his home for 41 years. He also expresses interest in politics, religion, space and technology, and places he has recently visited with a social services support worker.

Most of Bill's weekends are spent alone, either listening to records, or watching TV. Sometimes he sees his only close friend Pam, whom he has known for several years. She is Bill's only non-service contact, and he has become quite dependent on her, holding her in some awe. Pam can demand friendship on her terms, which often includes sharing his food, tobacco and money with her. Sometimes Bill does not have food left towards the end of the week. Friendship with Pam also demands loyalty, forgiveness, and tolerance despite severe temper outbursts.

From the age of 7 to 54 Bill lived in a large mental handicap hospital. His life in this paternalistic environment was dictated by rules, regulations, and the authority of staff. He never had the opportunity to do his own budgeting and shopping, cooking or laundry, nor to decide what he should wear. Neither did he have the opportunity to handle money, travel independently, or build relationships. As he explains, he learned to live in the institution but needed a lot of help to learn how to live outside where so many things are different. Having said this, Bill learns new things readily. Bill has lived in a flat before, but trouble with the neighbours led to a return to residential care, prior to moving to his present home. He lost some possessions during this period. He spends some days at a local day centre for people with mental health problems, although he does not have such problems himself.

After Bill's return from the hospital, his brother was reluctant to make contact with him, although more recently the social worker arranged a meeting on neutral ground that seemed to go well.

This book is for those who are working in collaboration with people like Mary and Bill in order to improve their situation. It may also be of use for those concerned with other dependent and devalued people, but our experience and the examples used here are based largely on contact with people for whom we have yet to find a better description than "learning disability". Later in this chapter we indicate some cautions about using the framework with certain people. Throughout, our emphasis and examples are on and about adults, although the approach is also relevant to adolescents and, with some adaptation, to children.

STARTING WHERE PEOPLE ARE

Before we can help to improve the situation of people we must know what that situation is. As we will show later, it is essential that we establish each person's current situation prior to trying to make any kind of intervention or there is a very strong chance that the intervention will be irrelevant to the interests or needs of the person. However, there are some common themes in the typical experiences of people with learning disabilities, and it is an understanding of these common experiences that forms the basis for our approach to social skills and social capability.

Having a learning disability (or other impairment) makes it likely that the following things will happen:

- segregation from the ordinary life of those in the mainstream of society;
- being grouped together with others on the basis of impairment, dependency or stigma;
- isolation;
- loneliness;
- having a negative reputation;
- being treated in ways that are dehumanizing;
- poverty;
- a lack of power, choice, autonomy, self determination;
- limited opportunities or help to grow or develop;
- insufficient help in getting important things done;
- threats to health or personal integrity;
- vulnerability to exploitation or ill treatment;
- an identity that is dominated by the role of "client".

What would it look like for people if all this was reversed? People would have autonomy and control over their lives, respect accorded to them whoever they were, and resources (relationships, qualities, experiences, roles, interests, money and other material resources) on which to base that respect. They would have ordinary social experiences for growth and development together with whatever help (practical, thinking or emotional) was required to make the best use of these opportunities. They would be safe, while also taking reasonable risks in the pursuit of these very ordinary expectations.

In a nutshell, they would be part of a real social world (rather than marginal bystanders to it). And they would be supported to take part in it. They would change and the things around them would change.

It is no coincidence that some social philosophers have equated our humanity, or our distinctive human nature, as inseparable and arising from the web of social relations of which we are part: suggesting that people with learning disabilities might aspire to be part of this real social world is to do no more but no less than to suggest that they have been systematically excluded from ordinary human life and been given an identity that is less than fully human. To some extent services have supported this dehumanizing stance, but things may be changing.

A CHANGING CONTEXT OF SERVICE PROVISION

In the past, the main ways in which people with learning disabilities were seen by service providers emphasized their impairment. Because options were limited, people were seen in terms of their level of dependence, which corresponded to the types of provision available. People were fitted to services rather than vice versa. Furthermore, they got what they were given.

We should be honest and recognize that this will still be the reality for most people with learning disabilities, most of the time. Now, however, there is recognition that disabled people belong with the rest of us and, as a result, the possibility emerges of services taking on a different kind of role, supporting the person in ordinary places to have ordinary experiences with ordinary people. As thinking and provision change in this way so does our understanding of people with learning disabilities and, hence, of what it is that they need from organized services. Disability still exists, but it is more likely to be seen in its proper place, as a consequence of environmental and social barriers which restrict opportunities and experiences. Impairment still exists, but it is more likely to be seen in its proper place, as an additional fact about people which may need special attention if ordinary experiences are to be had.

This historical shift in the theory and practice of service provision provides us with a context that is more conducive to working with people with learning disabilities in ways that are relevant to them. Unfortunately, however, there are still plenty of pressures that can drag us back into less helpful ways of working. These include the continued existence of institutions (big and small), economic constraints, lack of knowledge and skills in those offering support, the limited experiences of people with learning disabilities (and their families and ourselves) of living an ordinary life, and the expectation held by people, without either a family or work interest in people with disabilities, that disabled people will be cared for away from the ordinary places that they themselves frequent.

It is because of this constant danger of slipping into a disabling and handicapping way of working and thinking that we need frameworks that keep the experience of people with disabilities central to our decision making. These frameworks are to help us to see, to think, and to practise in ways that are responsible to the interests of those who rely on our services. In using them we must recognize that they are not infallible. Further experience, particularly as the world changes around us, can mean they need refining or redesigning (as, for example, in the evolution of the principle of normalization from the late 1950s to the present day). The use of frameworks can also degenerate, so that they no longer set the occasion for the quality of thought and action they were intended to engender (for example, the degeneration of individual programme planning into a bureaucratic paper chase): they do little to meet people's needs in any meaningful way.

NEEDS

At many points in this book we use the term **needs**. The concept of need is one which has been associated with a great deal of confusion, but is nevertheless one that is necessary if we are to make any kind of principled change with people who rely on our

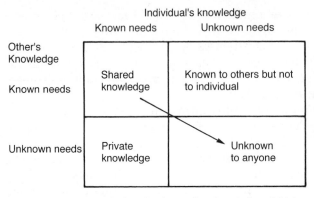

Arrow indicates increase in shared understanding of needs through joint process of learning

Figure 1.1 The CAROMA window: shared understanding about needs. (Adapted from the 'Johari Window' (Luft, 1969; Pfeiffer and Jones, 1974). Luft J (1969) *Of Human Interaction*. Palo Alto, CA: National Press Books. Pfeiffer, J.W. and Jones, J.E. (1974) *A Handbook of Structured Exercises for Human Relations Training*. La Jolla, CA: University Associates.)

assistance. One problem that a lot of people have with the concept is that it is very difficult to know what another person really needs. Similarly, it is very difficult to know what we ourselves need (try making your own list of needs!). We can combine these two problems to help us understand how we can actually make some sensible decisions about needs. Figure 1.1 describes a framework in which we can understand how it is that we can increase our own understanding of our needs and that other people may be able to identify needs we did not realize we had. When working with people with learning disabilities, we should be aiming to increase the amount of shared knowledge we have with the person about what her or his needs might be. This means we have to do two things: firstly we have to listen to what they, themselves, say about their needs (find out about needs which have hitherto remained private); and secondly we must communicate our understanding of their needs (share information we may have of which they may be unaware).

In other words, our task is to help people understand more about what they need, **and** to learn more about their needs. We start out from a position of **mutual relative ignorance** and over time become more knowledgeable. This approach to understanding need can help us avoid the two common traps: assuming that as professionals we have access to some kind of objective truth about what people need (we know what they need), and, on the other hand, surrendering to a simplistic view that self-determination is all important and that people who have missed many experiences can necessarily tell us what they need ("they know what they need, even if they do not know what could be possible"). What we are trying to discover is the particular combination, at this time, of those basic human needs and any extra need for assistance for the person with whom we are working. How impairments affect the fulfilment of needs and interests requires careful description of the person and the situation. We provide some frameworks for doing this later in the book.

In our approach, we try to avoid the following two typical errors of formal human services:

- Thinking about people in unrelated chunks, with different workers working on different bits, often with little effective coordination or communication about what we are trying to achieve with and for this person can have the effect of "people fixing" – of depersonalizing our services and treating users as passive recipients of doses of various bits of "therapy".
- Many possible forms of assistance can be missed, such as the involvement of friends, neighbours, co-workers, families, as well as the imaginative use of other resources that are not human services.

SOCIAL SKILLS

In the past, social skills analyses and training have fallen foul of both these errors. In North America and in Britain, the social skills of people with learning disabilities have been seen in terms of their behaviours. Little account has been taken of recent developments in the social skills field which recognize cognitive aspects of social skills, or of approaches that emphasize the context in which the skills are used. Social contexts not only constrain the effective use of social skill, but they are also necessary to understand as part of skilled social behaviour. Social skills training has been largely directed at the "fixing" of suitable behaviours.

Social skills training has also largely been confined to working with people with learning disabilities, either alone or in groups with other people with learning disabilities, in artificial settings. Social situations are simulated, and the thinking goes that once people have grasped the behaviours in a safe and protected setting, they can be set free to use their skills in real situations. Not surprisingly, a great deal of time has been spent training behaviours that do not generalize to real social situations and that make very little difference to the overall life experiences of people with learning disabilities.

Our approach broadens the thinking about social skills from a narrow focus on behaviours to personal and social competence which incorporates cognitive and situational aspects of social skill. In so doing we use the terms social skill, social competence and personal competence more or less interchangeably. Furthermore, social skill and competence is only one part of the approach, which emphasizes social capability. Social capability, as we shall see, embeds social skill and competence within the competence of communities and opportunities available to people with learning disabilities.

If we are to help people be included in the social worlds in which we all live, we will have to overcome the errors of traditional ways of thinking and working with people with learning disabilities. Explorations of social capability attempt to do just this.

SOCIAL CAPABILITY

Being part of a real social world implies having appropriate transactions with it. This means gaining the cooperation, assistance, and participation of others and responding effectively to the legitimate demands of others.

Neither of these things is just about social competence: gaining assistance might be done through somebody else noticing the need for it and making the necessary arrangements. Responding to the demands of others might involve another person explaining these demands in simple terms or negotiating with others to alter their demands. The capability to go to a party might rely on having someone to arrange transport, make introductions and keep the conversation going. It also depends on having been invited to the party in the first place (in other words, having been given the opportunity). Our distinction between capability and competence is important in putting the responsibility where it really lies, with all of us, not just with the person who has a disability. Capability, then, is made up of the person's social skill or competence and the competence of the community in the light

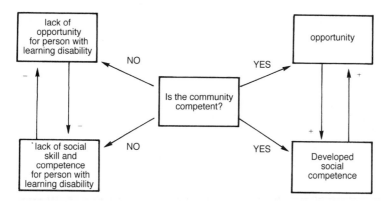

Figure 1.2 Social capability: competence of the community, social skill and competence in relation to opportunity.

of opportunities. Those of us who are highly competent are also likely to be highly capable, by virtue of our effectiveness in recruiting the assistance of other people, as well as in using machines and other devices. We are also likely to have and to have had a range of opportunities.

If our communities lack competence we may be denied opportunities and may have poorly developed social skills and competencies: the fewer opportunities we have the less social competence we will develop. On the other hand, if we live with and within a competent community, this may enhance our opportunities as well as our levels of social competence: the more opportunities we have the greater will be our social competence. Figure 1.2 shows how social capability arises from social competence and community competence with respect to opportunity.

Because people with learning disabilities will not all become immensely skilled or competent personally, it is important to take into account the non-competence aspects of social capability, and look to increasing opportunities and enhancing the competence of people's communities. We should not lose sight of the fact that our own social skill or competence is a result of our relationships with others: remove the competence of those around us (our communities) and we will all become socially incompetent.

To focus excessively on social skill or competence in people with a learning disability is to impose standards that we do not apply to ourselves. Yet this is what often happens. It is what leads to the kinds of statements and restricted practices with which we are only too familiar: "Grace cannot go shopping until she learns to manage her money"; "Kajal cannot go into town until she can use the bus"; "Nigel may not go out with his friend on Saturday unless he stops pestering staff about the time today (Tuesday)"; "Chris may not go into pubs until he stops eating cigarette butts"; "Ali cannot go to the Christmas Fair without the staff because he never listens to people" and so on. What if Grace is never able to manage money; Kajal is never able to use the bus independently; Nigel continues to badger staff for the time; Chris continues to eat cigarette ends; and Ali will never listen properly to people? How competent are those around them to teach them these things, to tolerate them or to assist them in doing what they wish to do despite their lack of social skill or competence?

We do not mean to disparage the importance of improving social skill or competence. For many purposes, competence is either the preferred means to capability or is a major component of it. A systematic and focused effort must be made to increase social competence, but this cannot be done in isolation from either a consideration of alternative means or a clear understanding of what the person needs to learn for what reason. People with learning disabilities often have their time wasted by others: we need to be confident that what we are doing is relevant to them and is an effective use of their time.

Figure 1.3 summarizes the nature of social capability and how it can be enhanced. Improved social capability, then, means parallel and linked improvement for the reason in three things:

- pattern of social opportunity
- pattern of social competence
- competence of the community.

It is a basic assumption of this book that these are all necessary, interlinked, and that none will happen without focused effort. This book includes an analysis of both the nature of "social skills" and of patterns of social life, in order to identify ways of making positive changes in both simultaneously.

However, because of the close linkage between social skills and social opportunities, we cannot know what social skill and competence is needed until we have understood the person's need for social opportunities: we cannot know how the community might become more competent until we know of a person's need for social opportunities. None of us can be skilled or competent in isolation; competence implies an end. Likewise we cannot

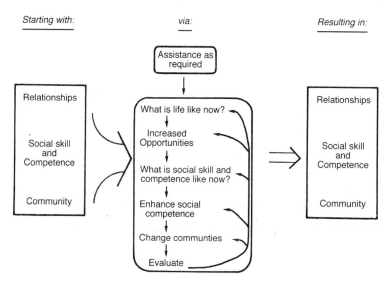

Figure 1.3 Model of enhancing social capability.

improve social skill and competence in isolation. It is for this reason that our model (as illustrated in the above diagram) nests social competence within social capability, connecting social competence with opportunity and the competence of communities.

This has a fundamental implication for how we work with people with learning disabilities. Rather than taking a predetermined training curriculum and working through it, often in a group, we define priorities and methods of working, as well as goals to be achieved, through individual need. This is in keeping with the emphasis of the recent British legislation on community care. As we have seen above, "need" is a tricky notion, and we must try to be very clear exactly what we are talking about when we claim to be starting from the identification of individual need.

USING THIS BOOK

The model of social capability, shown in Figure 1.3, provides the framework for this book. We will look at the nature of relationships, social competence and communities, before going on to explore practical issues to do with working with people with learning disabilities to enhance and improve their social capabilities. This work follows a process which takes people towards inclusion in their communities. The different steps in the process are:

1. understanding what life is like now for a person with learning disabilities;
2. increasing opportunities for a person with learning disabilities;
3. understanding what a person's social skill and competence is now;
4. enhancing a person's social competence;
5. increasing the competence of communities;
6. evaluating progress.

The steps provide a basic strategy for carrying out work with a person who has a learning disability, together with her context of people, resources and services. They incorporate three things:

- a value base: that is, a set of assumptions about the rights and legitimate expectations that people with learning disabilities (like the rest of us) should have;
- a means for analysing what is happening in the context, experience, and behaviour of the person; and
- some suggestions of practical methods for working with the person and the context.

It is our belief that all three components are vital and that much of what is on offer as guidance to practitioners misses out at least one of them. These three components interplay at each step in the process that we might simplify as one of narrowing down from the general to the specific (Figure 1.4).

This model provides a structure for the book, which is divided into two parts. Firstly we present a more theoretical section, where we establish the concepts that we will use to fully understand the nature of social capability and how to go about enhancing it. Following on from this, we offer a more practical section, where we take the reader through the process for working to improve a person's social capability.

Throughout we use examples. These all draw upon our work in the North West, but we have made identities anonymous, by changing names and sometimes by changing one or more features of the story, and in a few cases we have written composite examples, drawing on more than one person's experience. With these reservations, however, everything that we present, good and bad, is based on something that has really happened.

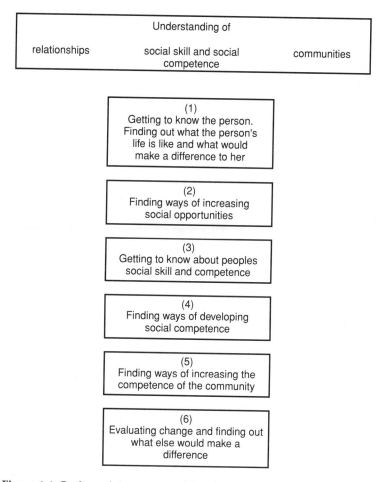

Figure 1.4 Outline of the process of developing social capability.

Where do the ideas come from?

The ideas we present in this book come from a variety of places: our experience working with people with learning disabilities and their supporters; from the work – published and unpublished – of other people; from many conversations with others, within the learning disability field and from outside it; from practical everyday reality and from the world of academic discourse. As practitioners it can be difficult to identify where all of the concepts, ideas and beliefs that we use in our work have come from. After each chapter we have listed reading material that can help readers develop their thinking and practice further, for example by understanding more of the background to the concepts, by seeing their application in a related area, or by comparing the perspectives of writers who may be covering much of the same ground, although sometimes from a different perspective.

However, this is not an academic text, and while we have both written in the academic mode elsewhere, here we have not broken the flow of text by substantiating every point with a reference to another publication. Nor have we sought to explain other people's ideas and models, or to evaluate the strengths and weaknesses of previous work. Instead, we have incorporated other ideas and practices into our own thinking and practical suggestions. Readers who wish to explore linked and contributing ideas in more detail, can follow up the further readings given at the end of each chapter.

SOME LIMITS TO APPLYING THE MODEL

Are there some people with whom the model outlined here would not be appropriate? Broadly our answer would be that the approach has general applicability to work with anyone who relies significantly on others to have basic needs met, and who runs the kinds of risks outlined at the start of the chapter, as a result of the combination of their disabling condition and society's typical response. However, there are some circumstances where the emphasis will need to be rather different from that taken here.

People who display dangerous behaviour

Most essentially, risks must be assessed and managed rigorously, and specialist professional help sought, if the approach is to be applied to people who display "dangerous" behaviour, such as arson, serious sexual offences, serious violence to others or self. We distinguish between people who can be described in this way and people (see below) who are simply responding to an intolerable situation, or who behave aggressively or irresponsibly because they do not understand the consequences of their actions or the context in which they find themselves.

People who display challenging behaviour

Any behaviour is "challenging" that is likely to seriously limit or delay access to and use of ordinary facilities. This might include violence or aggression to others, self-injurious behaviour, destructive behaviour, disruptive/antisocial behaviour, severe and persistent withdrawal, and high frequency stereotypic behaviours. In many cases, a pattern of challenging behaviour is no more than a person's response to a situation that they find intolerable. The general approach outlined here is appropriate to people who currently display such behaviour patterns, but it will need combining with a thorough analysis of the causes of the behaviour, again by appropriately experienced, knowledgeable and supervised staff. Without this it would be possible to exacerbate the behaviour problems, for example through too fast an introduction of demands or complexity to a person whose reaction to these is to engage in one or more of the behaviours described above. However, the detailed analysis of the person's behaviour should suggest ways in which opportunities could be opened up and competence increased. In other words, the starting point and the methods may be somewhat different, but the aim is still to enhance the person's social capability through methods rooted in a sensitive understanding of that person in context.

People with autism or similar impairments

Autism is characterized by impaired language development, impaired development of social relationships, and "the pursuit of sameness" through rituals, obsessions and/or repetitive self-stimulation. Various theories have been suggested, and there has been considerable progress in recent years. Our preference is to see it as a continuum of impairment stemming from a specific difficulty in understanding certain aspects of complex environments, including self and others. Again the considerations mentioned in relation to people displaying challenging behaviour apply: a significant proportion of those users of learning disability services who present behavioural challenges appear to be people with autism who are responding to the anxiety and stress of an environment that to them is difficult to comprehend and, hence, unpredictable and threatening.

We also find that most people with autism like contact with, and company from others, but on their own terms. Once the world is made predictable (for example, through a structured routine of activities and by the establishment of clear boundaries) and anxiety can be kept to a reasonable level, then the process of extending social capability can take place, again with sensitivity as to how the person can assimilate the change inherent in new opportunities and new learning, and with careful monitoring of how they are responding to any changes. We will not be more prescriptive than that, since people with autism are all different as are their social and interpersonal needs and difficulties.

People with mental health problems

Some people with learning disabilities also have mental health problems. Broadly speaking, there is no reason why the approach outlined here should not be used. The only caution would be during states of acute distress or confusion, when it would in any case be difficult to apply the approach. Otherwise the approach can be used, with due caution, in cases where additional stress might lead to an exacerbation of the person's condition.

People with very great disabilities

Our work on social capability began with people with mild and moderate learning disability: people we describe elsewhere as being in a "competence trap". Through the course of the work it has become clear that the general model is applicable to people with more severe difficulties, but not all the nuances of social skill will be necessary or appropriate Again, it is important to avoid making generalized assumptions. We have come across people with hearing and visual impairments who, having spent many years in services for people with severe learning disabilities, when given appropriate aids, showed no measurable learning disability at all. Other people have been credited with much greater ability to understand others than they actually have. Yet others have no clear communication, and little is being done to enhance their interactions at the most basic of levels. In none of these cases are people's needs being met. In one way our approach is particularly suited for work with people with multiple and complex disabilities. Even if personal competence is limited, social opportunities can always be enhanced. Thus people's overall capability will increase. Our approach does not rest on people being able to demonstrate their skills **before** social opportunities are opened to them.

Central to people's experiences in the social world and to their social capability are relationships with other people in their many different forms.

FURTHER READING

American Association on Mental Retardation (1992) Chapter 2, Theoretical basis of the definition, in *Mental Retardation: Definition, Classification, and Systems of Supports*, 9th edn, American Association on Mental Retardation, Washington, DC.

Baldwin, S. and Hattersley, J. (eds) (1990) *Mental Handicap: Social Science Perspectives*, Routledge, London.

Bulmer, M. (1987) *The Social Basis of Community Care*, Allen and Unwin, London.

Burton, M. (ed.) (1990) *Caught in the Competence Trap: A review of provision for adults with moderate learning disabilities*, North Western Regional Health Authority: Advisory Group for Learning Disability Services, Manchester.

Burton, M. (1994) Toward an alternative basis for policy and practice in community care: with particular reference to people with learning disabilities. *Care in Place: International journal of networks and community*, **1**(2), 158–74.

Carpenter, M. (1994) *Normality is Hard Work*, Lawrence and Wishart, London.

Cocks, E. (1994) *Encouraging a Paradigm Shift in Services for People with Disabilities*, Social Research and Development Monograph No. 9, Centre for the Development of Human Resources, Edith Cowan University, Joondalup, Western Australia.

Donnellan, A.M., La Vigna, G.W., Negri-Shoultz, N. and Fassbender, L.L. (1988) *Progress Without Punishment*, Teachers College Press, New York.

Edgerton, R.B. (1967) *The Cloak of Competence: Stigma in the lives of the mentally retarded*, University of California Press, Berkeley.

Ellis, R. and Whittington, D. (eds) (1983) *New Directions in Social Skills Training*, Croom Helm, London.

Flynn, M. (1989) *Independent Living for Adults with Mental Handicap: "A place of my own"*, Cassell, London.

Frith, U. (1989) *Autism: Explaining the enigma*, Blackwell, Oxford.

Greenspan, S. (1992) Reconsidering the construct of mental retardation: implications of a model of social competence. *American Journal on Mental Retardation*, **96**(4), 442–53.

Hobson, R.P. (1993) *Autism and the Development of Mind*, Erlbaum, Hove.

Hollin, C.R. and Trower, P. (eds) (1986) *Handbook of Social Skills Training (2): Clinical Applications and New Directions*, Pergamon, Oxford.

Illich, I., Zola, I.K., McKnight, J., et al. (1977) *Disabling Professions*, Marion Boyars, London.

Jupp, K. (1994) *Living a Full Life with Learning Disabilities*, Souvenir Press, London.

La Vigna, G.W. and Donnellan, A.M. (1986) *Alternatives to Punishment: Solving behavior problems with non-aversive strategies*, Irvington, New York.

Leonard, P. (1984) *Personality and ideology: Towards a materialist understanding of the individual*, Macmillan, London.

Murphy, G. and Holland, T. (1993) Challenging behaviour, psychiatric disorders and the law, in *Challenging Behaviour and Intellectual disability: a psychological perspective* (R.S.P. Jones and C.B. Eayrs, eds), British Institute of Learning Disability Publications, Kidderminster.

Nind, M. and Hewett, D. (1994) *Access to Communication: Developing the basics of communication with people with severe learning difficulties through Intensive Interaction*, David Fulton, London.

O'Brien, J. (1990) *What's Worth Working For? Leadership for better quality human services*, Responsive Systems Associates, Lithonia, Georgia.

Sparrow, S.S., Balla, D.A. and Cicchetti, D.V. (1984) *Vineland Adaptive Behavior Scales: Expanded Form Manual*, The construct of adaptive behavior, American Guidance Service, Minnesota, pp. 6–7.

Trower, P. (ed.) (1984) *Radical Approaches to Social Skills Training*, Croom Helm, London.

Wolfensberger, W. (1992) *A Brief Introduction to Social Role Valorization as a High-Order Concept for Structuring Human Services* (rev. edn), Training Institute for Human Service Planning, Leadership and Change Agentry (Syracuse University), Syracuse, NY.

Zarkowska, E. and Clements, J. (1994) *Problem Behaviour and People with Severe Learning Disabilities: The S.T.A.R. approach*, 2nd edn, Chapman & Hall, London.

2

The nature of relationships

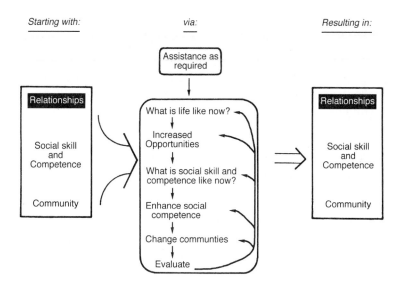

Starting with: via: Resulting in:

Assistance as required

Relationships

Social skill and Competence

Community

What is life like now?

Increased Opportunities

What is social skill and competence like now?

Enhance social competence

Change communties

Evaluate

Relationships

Social skill and Competence

Community

Relationships are central to any notion of social skills, competence and capability. Without relationships we are not social beings, and there would be no meaning to the concept of social capability. In one way or another, we spend most of our lives in the company of others, whether this be home lives, work lives or leisure lives. The development of a range of relationships is essential to the achievement of social integration and inclusion, and just as people with learning disabilities may need assistance and support in other spheres of their lives, so they may with the development of relationships. In order to offer this in any meaningful way it is necessary to understand something about the purpose and diversity of relationships, how they come about and how they develop over time.

THE PURPOSE OF RELATIONSHIPS

Not many of us experience physical isolation. However, there are lessons to be learnt from other people's experiences of isolation that highlight some of the purposes of relationships. Accounts by people held hostage for long periods of time show how being isolated leads to a loss of sense of time and place; distortions in thought processes occur and it is difficult to concentrate on any one thing; and, perhaps most importantly, people begin to lose a sense of "self" – who they are and where they fit in their own social worlds. Of course the hostage situation was an unusual and scary situation, but, nevertheless, we can see that relationships with others help us locate ourselves in the world and retain our optimal functioning and sense of "self".

Even if we have not been physically isolated for long periods, we may well have been lonely. These are times when we long for meaningful companionship, for joint activity with people we like, or for some sign of acceptance and liking. We can be lonely when there are lots of other people about. The experience of loneliness depends on our expectations for social contact and on the explanations we give for why we have no contact. So, if we see our lack of social contact to be because we have just moved to an area where we know no one, we will probably not feel lonely. However, if we have lived somewhere for 10 years and still have no contact with anyone, we cannot rest on this explanation and may feel lonely – that is if we do not have another reason for it that is personally acceptable. Again, if we do not expect to get to know anyone near where we live, we may not feel lonely if we do not know anyone after some considerable time.

Loneliness can lead to feeling unwanted, sad, even depressed and worthless, with a sense of purposelessness in life. Understandably, perhaps, we may not want to take advantage of the few social contacts that arise, as we may be afraid that we will feel even more lonely when they cease. This, then becomes self-perpetuating, as building on casual social contacts is an important stage in the development of a range of different relationships. Some of the signs of loneliness are that we find it difficult to make friends, often wait for people to call or write, find it hard to meet people, are frequently excluded by other people and know few people with whom to do things. It is not hard to see these signs in many of the lives of people with learning disabilities who are not always as able as the rest of us to go out, meet people and take the initiative in forming relationships. Some people will, therefore, need help in doing this if they are to avoid feeling lonely.

Relationships, then, do a number of different things for us: they give us a sense of acceptance and of being liked. This, in turn, contributes to our sense of "self" and of identity. To see the extent to which relationships contribute to our sense of identity, try Exercise 2.1.

Exercise 2.1 Relationships and identity

Write down 20 answers to the question "Who am I"?

Look at your list and:

☐ mark all the answers you have given that define yourself **in relation to someone else**. You might have included, for example "my daughter's parent", "captain of the tennis team", "a popular person";

☐ mark all the answers you have given that define yourself **in relation to a social group**, for example "Asian-British", "female", "resident of Manchester";

☐ mark all the answers you have given that define yourself **in relation to a social role**, for example "a friend", "a care assistant", "a jumble sale organizer".

What is left on your list? Would you have had the same list 10 years ago? How does identity change over time? Can other people "see" your identity? If so, how?

There is probably not much else left on your list other than descriptions, such as "fat", "bad tempered", "caring", and these types of descriptions are, in one sense, descriptions of social groups. By saying you are "fat", for instance, you distinguish yourself as similar to others who are fat and different from those who are not fat.

Exercise 2.1 shows the importance of relationships with others and belonging to different social groups for our sense of identity and "self". Doing a similar exercise with people with learning disabilities often highlights the limitations of their networks of relationships, the groups to which they belong, the roles they fulfil and, thereby, the extent to which their sense of "self" may be impoverished. Most of us have complex and multifaceted self-concepts, due largely to the complex web of relationships we have.

In addition to contributing to our sense of "self" and identity, relationships enable us to evaluate ourselves in relation to others – to locate ourselves in the social world. If we did not have a range of relationships, all of which provide points of comparison for us, it would be difficult for us to know if we were tall or short, old or young, religious or non-religious, happy or not, likeable or not, helpful or not, and so on. Of course, if we do not have a range of different relationships and points of comparison, we may get a very distorted view of how we fit in the social world.

> Duncan lives in a staffed house. He is 26 years old. His support staff are all women in their fifties. He cannot move about without help and, because there are other people who need a great deal of assistance living with him, he does not get out much. One of the other men in the house is very mobile and independent. He gets out a lot and talks about all the people he knows when he gets home. He helps Duncan in the house. The staff get frustrated with Duncan because he is very passive and shows little interest in meeting other people or in going out. A lot of their conversation with him is in order to motivate him to show an interest in various activities. It was suggested that Duncan needed some social skills training, and he was introduced to a social skills group run by the community health team. The nurse and occupational therapist running the group were lively and enthusiastic, but Duncan seemed to draw more and more into himself.

What is going on here? Firstly, Duncan knows very few people, even casually. When he compares himself with those people he does know, he comes to a number of conclusions. Looking at the staff, he sees himself as a young person who is being cared for. He is different in every way from them and sees no points of similarity, leading him to believe he cannot do what they do, care for others or help others do things. Looking at his independent house-mate, he sees someone similar in some ways to himself (sex, age), but living a very different kind of life and also caring for others, not being cared for as he is himself. So Duncan feels distant from him, and he is convinced that this house-mate is much older than him. He sees a great deal of similarity between himself and his other house-mates; he identifies strongly with how they behave, even though they have more complex disabilities than he has. Nevertheless, Duncan sees they are unable to do much for themselves, to go anywhere, do not receive visitors and receive a lot of help from staff. The strong comparison he makes between them and himself reinforces Duncan's own passivity.

At the social skills group, Duncan sees no similarity between himself and the lively and enthusiastic group leaders and so withdraws from them, conveying the strong message that he is a passive recipient of other people's care, rather than someone who can change some aspects of his life. In other words, Duncan is getting a very distorted view of himself in relation to others that is in great part due to the restricted opportunities he has for different social contacts. Most of us are able to compare different facets of ourselves with different people in different circumstances and thereby gain a complex understanding of who we are and how we fit in the social world.

> Beryl lives in a staffed house with three other women, who are also in their fifties. They all returned to their home town from a large hospital three years ago. Beryl has frequent temper outbursts which seem to be sparked by jealousy about staff giving time and attention to the other women – something they strive to do as equally and fairly as possible. When she returned from the institution, Beryl lost contact with her boyfriend who went to live in another town. She has also not heard from her mother for the last year. Her mother actually died 10 months ago and Beryl's uncle has maintained a pretence that she is still alive, a state of affairs that the service has only just discovered.

For Beryl there is nobody for whom she is "special". The staff understandably have a policy of impartiality in their dealings with the four tenants, and Beryl has lost the two people who meant most to her, without even having the loss of her mother confirmed properly. It is hardly surprising that she attempts to reconstruct "partial" (special) relationships with those most available to her, the staff.

Relationships, then, give us a sense of acceptance and of being liked; they contribute to our sense of identity by providing us with social roles and membership of social groups, as well as a point of comparison with others. They can be fulfilling and help us to feel good about ourselves, reinforcing our positive qualities. Equally, they have the potential to be unrewarding and even damaging, and can contribute to negative feelings about ourselves, reinforcing our negative qualities.

Perhaps most importantly, relationships can provide us with support and comfort, without which we stand in danger of being miserable and unable to withstand the pressures of everyday life.

WHOM DO WE LIKE AND WHY?

Most of us encounter very many people in the course of our lives. Yet these are only a small proportion of all the people it could be possible for us to meet. Furthermore, only a fraction of these develop into any kind of relationship. Exercise 2.2 helps us map our own relationships.

Exercise 2.2 Mapping relationships

How many people have you encountered today? Think back and try to estimate how many people you have come across in the following categories:

People you know intimately
People you know well
People with whom you are friendly
People you know vaguely
People with whom you are acquainted
People you recognize
Family
Known for any other reason
Now add people you have encountered this week.

What links are there between the different categories of people you have identified? Would your list have been different 10 years ago? If so, in what ways? Would you expect your list to be different in 10 years' time? In what ways?

It can be very illuminating to compare our own estimates of people we have encountered in any one day or week with those of people with learning disabilities. Try it.

Time and place

On the whole, superficial relationships are not within our control: they arise by our being in the same place and at the same time as other people. Of course we may deliberately set out to be in places at the times we know lots of other people will also be there, but in the course of our day-to-day lives, we do not try to exert this kind of control. Look at the more superficial relationships in the list you produced for Exercise 2.2, and think about which of these occur because you share time and place with them (for example because you stand at the same bus stop, work in the same building, shop at the same supermarket, attend the same gym, etc.). Clearly, opportunities to encounter lots of people, in relatively superficial relationships, depend on our being out and about in a variety of different places. A presence in the community is the necessary precursor to getting to know people. If we spent all our time in particular places with the same group of people, self-evidently we would not get to know many people. Yet this is the situation in which many people with learning disabilities find themselves.

Anne lives at home with her family. She is 19 and just about to leave special school and go to college. Over the years her parents have lost contact with most of their friends, and very few people visit the house. Anne attends school every day. She goes to Gateway club every Thursday where she meets the same friends as she sees at school. She goes on holiday with the school, again with the same friends, to a holiday camp which caters for people with disabilities at designated times. Her family go away for a week at Easter on a canal boat. Sometimes Anne has a school friend with her on the boat.

At the meeting to decide on a suitable college course, Anne's teachers, parents, social worker and Anne herself, agreed that segregated courses which she could attend with her friends would be the most suitable, as it was important Anne retained the friendships she had. No one thought to point out that Anne's friendships may be due, in large part, to the fact that she spent all her time with the same group of people and had very little opportunity to meet anyone else. Being in the same places at the same time as each other would have made it most likely that Anne would have become friends with her school mates. Anne has not had the opportunities to encounter other people, and thus has not had the opportunity to develop a variety of different friendships.

Whilst sharing time and place with people is important, we do not get to know most people we encounter in this way more than superficially. Many of the people we get to know better have some kind of **role** relationship with us.

Social role

Many of the people we meet on a day-to-day basis, we meet for a purpose and because of the role relationship we have with them. We know the postman or postwoman because he or she delivers the post to us; those who deliver the milk because they request money from us, the customers; the minister because we are the parishioners; the bus driver because we are the passengers; the GP because we are the patients; the client because we are community support workers; the care manager because we are day-service managers, and so on. Generally, we will get to know people with whom we have a role relationship better than those with whom we simply share time and space.

The kind of relationship we develop with "role partners", however, may not extend further than the particular role relationship. So, we may not get to know the manager of our service except in their role of manager. Even with those roles that have built in intimacy, such as family roles (father, mother, daughter, son, aunt, etc. are all roles), there may be limitations to the relationship between any particular role partners. Nevertheless, looking at the list produced in Exercise 2.2, it is probable that there are a number of important role relationships in your life. People with learning disabilities frequently know a lot of people who have different role relationships with them, yet they themselves fill very few social roles.

Kathleen spent her childhood in a residential school. For the last 20 years she has lived with her mother in a small house near the centre of town. Kathleen likes to copy large chunks out of books in beautiful copperplate handwriting, and spends most of her evenings doing this. During the day Kathleen attends a day centre which recently stopped contract work, replacing it with various leisure activities. Kathleen went swimming, horse riding and rambling, the latter two activities in segregated groups. It was sometimes difficult to get Kathleen to attend her leisure activities. The roles that Kathleen played were those of "handicapped person", "dependent daughter", "day centre member (who, in this capacity, took part in a number of activities)".

Five years ago Kathleen's mother got to know some other parents of adult children with learning disabilities, and heard of people like Kathleen who were doing all sorts of things for their local communities. Kathleen's mother began to take an active part in the planning of Kathleen's week. Amongst other things, she insisted that Kathleen should pay for her own swimming sessions at the entrance to the pool (role of leisure centre customer); she encouraged Kathleen to enter riding competitions (role of competitor); she got in touch with the local ramblers group and took Kathleen along (she now goes rambling at weekends with the group, unaccompanied by family or staff) (role of member of rambling group); and she arranged for Kathleen to write out the menus for two local hotels which changed their menus every two months (role of graphic artist).

As a result, Kathleen got to know the cashier at the leisure centre, other riding competitors and several people in the hotels for whom she did work. Kathleen does not talk or show any active interest in other people, but they now talk to her and include her in other conversations and sometimes in other activities. One indication that she notices a difference in how she is treated is that Kathleen is always keen to do the different things and, unless she is ill, is never difficult.

Kathleen may find interacting with people difficult, but these roles help make interactions predictable and understandable to her.

Social roles enable people to meet with other people for a particular purpose and to make some kind of contribution to social life. It is on the basis of these contributions that relationships are often formed. As we have said, role relationships do not necessarily extend beyond the context in which the role is played. More is needed if relationships are to develop further.

Similarity and difference

The reasons we get to know some people better than others are complex, and there are some characteristics of friendships and intimate relationships that are useful to highlight. We often like people with whom we have something in common. We may have similar interests or hobbies (and get to know them in the first place because we belong to an interest group, and thereby share time and place with them). The deeper the friendship, the more important is similarity of beliefs, values and attitudes. Sharing a common outlook on what is important in life (including, perhaps, political and religious beliefs) will often be important. Laughing at similar things and liking the same foods or activities – even the same television programmes – can be crucial components of friendships.

To make matters more complicated, we may also get on well with people who are dissimilar in many ways from us. It might be that we get on better with people who like doing different things, although if we never did anything together it would be difficult to sustain the friendship. We will often get on better with people who are different in character from us: two very talkative people may not get on very well together as they may both want to be talking all the time; two dominant people may constantly be arguing. Many of our relationships will be formed because the people involved complement each other.

If you think about the people you are friends with, or look at the close relationships included in your list for Exercise 2.2, you may well be able to see that some relationships are founded on the basis of similarity, some on difference, some on complementarity and some on a mixture of things, so you are similar on some things but dissimilar on others. Most of us will know a selection of different people and get on with them in different ways. Our web of relationships will contain people with whom we have similarities and differences. This is not always the case with people with learning disabilities, in part because they may know relatively few people, and in part because central relationships in their lives may be engineered by professionals rather than developing along a more natural course.

Miriam is noisy and demonstrative. She is easily frustrated and finds it difficult to control her temper. She lashes out when annoyed and, although she does not set out to hurt other people, has caused some injury to others if they happen to be close to her at the time. She has lived in hospital for 25 years and two years ago was resettled into the community with minimal support in her own flat. She was not able to support herself and returned to the hospital. She is to be resettled again within the next three months.

Miriam's planning conferences are guided by a psychiatrist who insists that Miriam should be placed in a staffed house with other people who "will be able to give as good as they get", because, the argument goes, Miriam forms relationships with people who can stand up to her outbursts, and what was missing from her last placement was firstly company, and secondly people who were similar to Miriam. In this example, it is being assumed that Miriam will not only be compatible with those who are similar to her in behaviour, but that she will develop supportive friendships with them. What do you think the likely outcome would be?

It is the opportunity to develop a range of relationships based on similarity of interests and possibly attitudes, values and beliefs, as well as differences in interests and personal qualities, and complementarity or similarity of personality and behaviour that we should be seeking in helping people with learning disabilities develop relationships. However, even this may not be enough when we consider the outcomes of relationships.

Reward and exchange

When a person does or says something that we like or that makes us feel good, we will probably like that person. We have derived something positive from the relationship, or the relationship has been rewarding in some way. Not many of our relationships, however, are one-way in the sense that only one person gets something out of it. Most of our relationships are rewarding for both people, and can be looked at in terms of what is exchanged between the two people. It might be as little as the exchange of conversation. We may like talking to a person because that person can tell us things we did not know: the person may like talking to us because we are good listeners. Both parties get something out of the relationship, although it is different in kind (knowledge for one person, feeling valued by being listened to for the other).

More may be exchanged over time in the course of other relationships. For example your mother may help look after your children when they are small and, in exchange (although not formally agreed as such), you will offer her a home when she is no longer able to look after herself in later years. Some role relationships have a very clear basis of exchange: a taxi driver will exchange driving you, the passenger, for money. Indeed, we can see that it is the exchange that gives many role relationships their purpose. It can be argued that so it is for all relationships. There is always something in the relationship for both parties and exchanges take place between them. The exchanges involved in relationships are explored in Exercise 2.3.

If one person in the relationship ceases to get anything out of it, or appropriate exchange (often called reciprocity) fails to take place, the relationship may dwindle. Many people with learning disabilities are placed in the part of "receiver" within a relationship and do not get the opportunity to reciprocate directly within the relationship or indirectly in kind. They are often part of

Exercise 2.3 Exchange in relationships

Look at the list of different kinds of relationship you produced in Exercise 2.2. (Complete this list now if you have not already done so.) For one relationship in each category, try and identify what each of you gains from the relationship. Identify what is exchanged between you and people in the more meaningful of the relationships on your list.

Category of relationship   What is exchanged?

People you know intimately
People you know well
People with whom you are friendly
People you know vaguely
People with whom you are acquainted
People you recognize
Family

What different "things" are exchanged between you and people in different kinds of relationships? Do you think these things would be similar for other people? Would they be the same things if your partner was of the opposite or same sex? Do older and younger people get different things out of different kinds of relationships? If so, in what ways?

imbalanced, one-way relationships which do not, unsurprisingly last any length of time.

Sophie is a young woman with multiple and complex disabilities. She has no speech and little muscle movement. She lies in an incline chair in the children's hostel where she lives. She has to be turned every two hours. Her shirt is changed at the same time as it gets very wet because she dribbles. Toni, a 19-year-old volunteer with a local leisure integration project has been spending time with Sophie, getting to know her to see if there might be any interest they had in common that they could share. Staff at the hostel were suspicious of Toni. They wanted to know what she wanted from Sophie and were fearful that she would exploit her in some way.

One day Toni's boyfriend, Dave, picked her up from the
Accidentally, the cable from his Walkman came unplugge
heavy metal music blared out. Sophie smiled. The staff th
this were surprised. Gradually, over time, Toni played more heavy
metal music to Sophie in the hostel and then was able to take her
home with her to listen to it in her sitting room. They had found
something in common they both enjoyed. Sophie got company,
listening to music, trips to Toni's home, as well as contact with
Dave and Toni's family out of the relationship. Toni got the joy of
seeing Sophie respond to the music, enjoyment in sharing her
music collection with Sophie, knowledge about some of the things
that are possible despite a person's multiple disabilities and satis-
faction that she had made a difference to Sophie's life from the
relationship.

Unfortunately, the hostel staff did not know how to enable Sophie
to further reciprocate within the relationship. Toni would make
arrangements to take Sophie home and staff would not ensure
she was ready to go; Toni would send Sophie birthday and Christmas cards but received none in return; Toni would visit only to find
staff had taken Sophie to a long-standing hospital appointment
without telling her, and so on. The effort Toni was putting into the
relationship could not be reciprocated by Sophie unaided, and staff
did little to enable it. Increasingly the relationship became too
one sided to continue – all the effort was put in by Toni and the
rewards were not sufficient to sustain it. Gradually Toni stopped
seeing Sophie.

This illustrates the important role that staff and carers can play
in helping people with complex disabilities sustain relationships,
particularly in the way of helping the relationships become reciprocal relationships. They cannot always be left to themselves to
develop: if relationships between people with learning disabilities
and other people always took a natural course there would be no
problem, and yet we see people with learning disabilities with a
very restricted web of relationships and few opportunities to
make casual acquaintances, never mind more meaningful friendships and relationships.

THE DEVELOPMENT OF RELATIONSHIPS

As we have seen, some relationships will not progress from
casual acquaintances, whereas some develop over time – sometimes considerable periods of time. In some relationships time
deepens our understanding of each other and strengthens
the relationship, whereas in others time weakens relationships

as we move into new and different areas of our lives, and we arrive at a point where we have ceased to have anything in common or to share mutual outlooks and interests. Some relationships begin and stay compartmentalized in one area of our lives, whereas others spill over into different areas of our lives. Whatever the course of a relationship, it cannot even begin to get started unless we have chances to meet other people.

Levels of relationship

There is some suggestion that there are three levels of relationships. The first is one of unilateral awareness. These are one-sided relationships wherein we may be aware of the other person but she or he is not aware of us. These relationships can be very strong and meaningful to us, as in a teenager's crush on a pop star, but they rarely lead to direct contact and are not fulfilling in any way. The second level is that of surface contact. These are our casual acquaintances, our role partners and people with whom we are familiar but know little about. The third level is one of mutuality, which includes those wherein we have a degree of personal involvement, possibly intimacy, reciprocity or give and take. Whilst it may be useful to think about the different levels of relationships and the extent to which we have a large number in our own networks, especially from levels 2 and 3, the levels do not give us any idea about how relationships actually develop. Level 1 relationships rarely turn into level 2 relationships; whereas level 2 relationships may move into level 3 relationships, the two types may be quite separate.

We understand intimate relationships, then, in terms of the same general framework as we understand other relationships. They are just as important for people with learning disabilities as for other people, and the same considerations apply with regard to sexual diversity, sexual health and sexual etiquette as for other people. Whilst there has been considerable attention paid to sex, sexuality and the development of intimate relationships, these are only a small (albeit important) part of our complex webs of relationships. Without a range and diversity of relationships none of us will be able to form meaningful and stable intimate relationships.

Cultural similarity

A number of features additional to those already mentioned above may help us understand the development of relationships more fully. Most of us tend to be friends with others from similar socio-economic and cultural backgrounds – the more intimate our relationships, the more this seems to be so. We are more likely to come across and take notice of people whose background, religion, occupation, status or financial position is similar to our own. Sometimes this fact is patently obvious for people with learning disabilities, especially those who only ever meet other people with learning disabilities in segregated settings (as in Anne's case above). Sometimes, however, this feature is overlooked by professionals, who consider that the only meaningful relationships people with learning disabilities can have are with people without learning disabilities and who share no personal history or experiences in common.

> James and Patrick are middle-aged, mild mannered men. They were good friends in the hospital both had lived in for over 20 years. Despite their preference to live together when the hospital closed, they were resettled to their districts of origin, 60 miles apart. Their social workers and support staff all considered it best that James and Patrick put their hospital lives behind them and start their new lives with a clean slate. Neither Patrick nor James had any photographs of each other and very little in the way of personal belongings to remind them of their hospital days. Both shared houses with other former hospital residents they did not know. For three years Patrick became very agitated at Christmas and in the middle of April. On 12 April in the fourth year of being resettled Patrick was caught shoplifting. When he returned home he set fire to his bedroom. Before long he was admitted to the medium secure unit, and it was only then that one of the unit staff who had been redeployed from the hospital mentioned the coincidence of his "breakdown" with his good friend James's birthday. James and Patrick were reunited and are now living together in a house in James's district of origin.

Physical attraction

Physical attraction is important for most of us, especially in the forming of intimate and sexual relationships. Again, the similarity factor is evident – we seem to end up with people similar to ourselves in terms of attractiveness (as judged by both ourselves and in terms of characteristics that are valued by our culture at this point in history). For most relationships, however, physical attraction is not so important as appropriate self-disclosure.

Self-disclosure

Self-disclosure refers to the revelations we make about ourselves to other people. As we get to know people better, we begin to

---

Exercise 2.4 Self-disclosure

Give two examples of self-disclosures to fit each of the categories in the chart below. Each category differs in terms of the intimacy of the disclosure (from intimate to non-intimate) and value of the disclosure (positive, neutral or negative).

	Intimate		*Non-intimate*
Positive	e.g. Other people really value my friendship. 1. 2.	e.g. I find it easy to talk to older people. 1. 2.	e.g. I enjoy rock climbing. 1. 2.
Neutral	e.g. I don't like discussing food at work. 1. 2.	e.g. I value friendship over money. 1. 2.	e.g. I never laugh at dirty jokes. 1. 2.
Negative	e.g. My best friend lied to me and I couldn't forgive her. 1. 2.	e.g. I get annoyed when people put their teaspoon back in the sugar bowl. 1. 2.	e.g. I hate crowds – I get dizzy when there are lots of people there. 1. 2.

Are there cultural differences in the use of self-disclosure? What are they? What are the dangers of self-disclosing? How important is reciprocity in self-disclosure? What are the advantages of self-disclosure? How does the context affect self-disclosure?

make disclosures about ourselves. However, we do not just say anything about ourselves to people, whatever the context. What we disclose to whom at what stage of the relationship is governed by finely tuned rules and expectations. We readily disclose certain topics to most people (what we think of the weather, television or radio programmes, food, etc.); other topics we disclose to people we know fairly well (interests, attitudes, tastes, work, etc.); some topics we only disclose to people with whom we are on fairly intimate terms (such as financial matters, sexual preferences, political beliefs, etc.). There may be some things we would only disclose to close family members and some things we would never disclose to close family members. There may be some things we would only disclose to women friends and some things we would only disclose to men friends.

Self-disclosure often plays an crucial part in the development of relationships. As more disclosures are made by both parties, our relationships may move from surface level to the level of mutuality. In any particular relationship we may have an optimum level of self-disclosure: gradual increases in this level from both parties helps to deepen and develop the relationship. However, major and non-reciprocal disclosures may have the opposite effect. Thus, if we tell someone something highly personal to ourselves and of great importance to us on first meeting, the person may well feel extremely uncomfortable, feel threatened, and be likely to avoid us in the future. The tricky part of giving self-disclosures is balancing disclosures with those other people reveal to us. Exercise 2.4 provides the opportunity to clarify different kinds of positive, neutral and negative disclosures.

The role of other people

Other people can have a much overlooked part in helping us develop relationships. Sometimes another person may be directly responsible for introducing us to a particular person or set of people. We get to know people our friends know, or who share activities with people we know. Sometimes we know of people from our friends and have formed an impression of them before ever meeting them. If our friends like them we may decide we too like them before we have met them. On the other hand, if our friends dislike them we may decide they are not for us, again before ever meeting them. It is not only via direct introductions that our friends and colleagues can help us develop relationships. We may simply accompany someone we already know to another event where there are lots of people we have never met. This opens up all sorts of chances to meet new people.

Friends, in particular, can play a part in helping relationships develop. They can act as go-betweens, carrying messages to and from other people. They can be sources of advice and support when relationships seem to be declining or it seems that we are not getting as much out of a relationship as we had in the past. Whilst this applies to strong and intimate relationships, it can also apply to more superficial relationships. On the whole, we do not manage all our relationships on our own: we have assistance from family friends and other people to get them started, to help them develop and to sustain them when they falter. People with learning disabilities need assistance, perhaps for longer and more often than the rest of us, in forming, developing and sustaining relationships. We have to find ways of opening up opportunities for them to meet a whole range of different people so that they can experience a similar complexity of relationships as the rest of us. Social skills, social competence and social capability can then help the relationships along, but they are no use at all if people do not have the chance to meet many different people in as many different capacities as possible.

Exercise 2.5 brings together a number of issues covered in this chapter.

Exercise 2.5 The development of relationships

With respect to (a) yourself and (b) someone with a learning disability, consider one intimate relationship, a friendship, a colleague and an acquaintance. How have these different relationships developed? Think of one example in each category and answer the following.

	An intimate relationship	A friendship	A colleague	An acquaintance
1. How did you meet?				

Continued

	An intimate relationship	A friendship	A colleague	An acquaintance
2. Did anyone else play a role in helping you meet? What was your relationship with this person?				
3. How long have you known him or her, or how long did the relationship last?				
4. How has the relationship changed over time?				
5. If a third person was involved in the relationship at the start, what is her or his involvement now?				
6. How similar or dissimilar are you?				
7. In what ways do you complement each other?				
8. How much "spill-over" is there between different areas of your life and this person?				

Continued

	An intimate relationship	A friendship	A colleague	An acquaintance
9. What sorts of things do you know about each other?				
10. In what ways do you differ in the different relationships?				

How did the different relationships differ from each other? Do you think people from different cultures develop relationships in different ways? If so, how? Does the development of relationships differ at different stages of our lives? If so, how?

In order to understand social skill, competence and capability, it is not enough to understand the nature of relationships. We form relationships within the communities in which we live. The understanding of communities is as important as the understanding of relationships.

FURTHER READING

The suggested readings cover the variety and functions of relationships in general, as well as those with people with learning disabilities in particular. We have included recent work on family and professional relationships, as well as work that highlights classic insights into relationships with neighbours. Sometimes the frontiers of our understanding are best pushed forward by reading fiction, and we have included one fictional account of strong and positive relationships formed by and with people with learning disabilities.

Amado, A.N. (ed.) (1993) *Friendships and Community Connections Between People With and Without Developmental Disabilities*, Paul Brookes, London.

Argyle, M. and Henderson, M. (1985) *The Anatomy of Relationships*, Penguin, Harmondsworth.

Brechin, A. and Swain, J. (1987) *Changing Relationships: Shared action planning with people with a mental handicap*, Harper and Row, London.

Brown, H. and Craft, A. (eds) (1989) *Thinking the "Unthinkable": Papers on sexual abuse and people with learning difficulties*, Family Planning Association, London.

Bulmer, M. (1986) *Neighbours: The work of Philip Abrams*, Cambridge University Press, Cambridge.

Craft, A. and Craft, M. (1983) *Sex Education and Counselling for Mentally Handicapped People*, Costello, Tunbridge Wells.

Edgerton, R.B. (1967) *The Cloak of Competence: Stigma in the lives of the mentally retarded*, University of California Press, Berkeley.

Finch, J. and Mason, J. (1992) *Negotiating Family Responsibilities*, Routledge, London.

Firth, H. and Rapley, M. (1990) *From Acquaintance to Friendship*, BIMH Publications, Kidderminster.

Fischer, C.S. (1982) *To Dwell Among Friends: Personal networks in town and city*, University of Chicago Press, Chicago.

Flynn, M.C. (1989) *A Place of My Own: Independent living for adults with mental handicap*, Cassell, London.

Horwood, W. (1988) *Skallagrig*, Penguin, Harmondsworth.

Perske, B. and Perske, M. (1988) *Circles of Friends: People with learning disabilities and their friends enrich the lives of one another*, Abingdon Press, Nashville.

Richardson, A. and Ritchie, J. (1989) *Developing Friendships: enabling people with learning difficulties to make and maintain friends*, Policy Studies Institute, London.

Rogers, C. (1961) *On Becoming a Person*, Houghton Mifflin, Boston.

Schwartz, D. (1993) *Crossing the River: Creating a conceptual revolution in community and disability*, Brookline Books, Cambridge, MA.

Tyne, A. *et al.* (1988) *Ties and Connections*, Kings Fund Centre, London.

Walmsley, J. (1993) It's not what you do but who you are: Caring roles and caring relationships, in *Health, Welfare and Practice: Reflecting on roles and relationships* (J. Walmsley, J. Reynolds, P. Shakespeare and R. Woolfe eds), Sage/Open University Press, London.

The nature of communities
and social networks

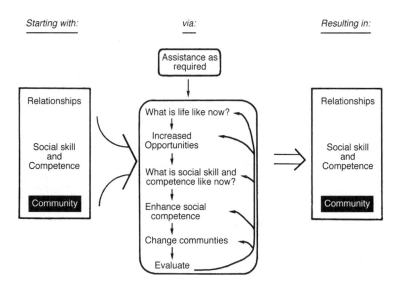

We have argued that an understanding of social skills, competence and capability must extend beyond what we, as individuals, are able to do. In order to do the things that really matter to us, we must be able to create and support continual opportunities to engage in a variety of activities and to develop networks of relationships in the community. In this chapter we will outline different ways of looking at "community" and "social networks". We will also consider some aspects of social situations that may make it difficult for people with learning disabilities to participate in their communities and develop social networks.

COMMUNITY

In order to explore the meaning of community, complete Exercise 3.1.

Exercise 3.1 The meaning of community

What does it mean to you to say you are part of a community? Jot down a few notes about different communities you would say you belong to and what you get from each of them.

Community	What do you get from this community?

What sorts of different communities did you identify? Would your list have been different ten years ago? In what ways? How similar do you think your list is to those produced by other people? Why might there be differences?

For most of us, having a sense of community makes us feel close to other people; it gives us a feeling of belonging, of identity and of purpose. We also live in communities that may be defined by their geographical location. Certainly, if you look at the notes you wrote in Exercise 3.1, above, you will probably see that your communities give some kind of meaning to your life, contribute to your identity and provide the place for a wide range of activities and relationships.

Community as place

We often refer to communities when we mean geographical localities, even neighbourhoods. Yet it will be a weak community if the only thing we share with other people is the area in which we live. The more things we have in common with our neighbours, the more contact we have with each other and the greater our sense of loyalty towards each other, the stronger we will be as a community. In some localities we can see the role that geographical features play in defining the community, largely by making it more or less likely that we will meet and get to know some people rather than others. A river, railway, a major road, sometimes even a public park, for example, can divide us from people who live nearby. These physical divides can be overcome, particularly if we have something more in common. Contact between, and loyalty to each other arises in part from shared interests.

Community of interest

When we share beliefs, interests, activities and so on with others, we belong to communities of interest. These may be organized around, for example, hobbies, leisure pursuits, local action campaigns, self-help groups, religions or cultural activities. We may be part of communities of interest within our local area or these communities may extend beyond. So, we may be involved in a national political party with regional meetings; we may go cycling with a club that draws people from all round the area, and so on. Certainly, the growth in postal, telephone and electronic communications has meant that widely dispersed communities of interest can be supported. Communities of interest give us opportunities to meet with or link up with like-minded people with whom we have something in common. Thus, part of our social identity is made up by the communities of interest to which we belong. These communities may be strictly limited to a particular interest and exist for a short length of time, in which case they may be communities of "limited liability".

Eileen's mother was Irish and had a lot of Irish friends, although none of them lived close by. Every month Eileen and her mother would go to the Irish club across the other side of the town. Eileen was particularly fond of Irish folk music, which she heard at the club. Although she could not talk and was confined to her wheelchair, Eileen felt happy and relaxed when she heard the music. A local befriending scheme had started up in the locality and Eileen's social worker had suggested to her mother that she would probably benefit from having a "friend". She agreed it would do Eileen good. When Claire arrived, Eileen's mother was relieved to find she was in her mid-twenties like Eileen. Claire spent several evenings in the house with Eileen, listening to her records of Irish folk music.

Eileen's mother suggested to Claire that she take Eileen over to the Irish club on Friday nights. However, Claire said that she did not think she should as the project to which she belonged was supposed to encourage local activities and relationships, and the Irish club was outside the area. So, instead, they went walking about Eileen's neighbourhood, to the pictures, to a live band at the local pub, playing Country and Western songs. Whilst Eileen went along with these things, she did not seem to enjoy them much, and the only person who talked to her was Claire. Eventually, Claire was persuaded to take Eileen to the Irish club. She obviously enjoyed herself and Claire saw a side to her she had not seen before. Lots of people came talking to them and Eileen was obviously pleased to see them. Claire began to get to know some of the people at the club and before long she had found out that some of them visited a pub in a nearby village that also had live Irish music. She and Eileen went along with them one day and there met someone who said he thought he could teach Eileen to play the tin whistle. He did.

The project Claire worked for had a simple notion of **community and relationships equals locality.** When Claire began to take Eileen's community of interest into account, although she went out of the locality, she was able to involve more people in Eileen's life, doing things that Eileen enjoyed and in which she, herself, began to take a part.

Communities of "limited liability"

At different stages in our lives, we may have particular interests in common with other people at a similar life stage; when we have young children we may get to know other parents in a similar position, and share baby-sitting and collection of children from school. Our attachments are for a specific reason, and unless we become friends with others in this community our responsibilities for other people may be limited to those connected to young children. When the children are older, the community disperses, even though we may all still be living in the same neighbourhood. Such communities of "limited liability", then, involve a very narrow range of responsibility for other people, rather than any system of broad and universal attachments.

These different types of community have two things in common. They each provide us with relationships and attachments to other people, and they contribute to our sense of identity. Exercise 3.2 helps us clarify different types of communities.

Exercise 3.2 Nature of communities

Take any local paper. Look through it for indications of different types of communities. Include the articles, news, pictures, advertisements, classified advertisements and sports reports, all of which might give indications of different kinds of communities. Complete the chart below.

Type of community	What is this community like?	What is it that reveals this in the paper?

Which parts of the paper revealed most about the different communities in your locality? Would this be the same of all local papers? Were there any parts of the paper that were irrelevant to community? If so, which?

We each have our own sense of the boundaries around our communities and these may or may not be linked to geography. It is, therefore, impossible for us to define the size of other people's communities without knowing how they, as insiders, see them. To do this we either have to be insiders ourselves or we have to talk with other people about how their meaningful links with other people are made up.

Sometimes, of course, our communities of interest and of place will coincide or overlap considerably. If we live in a place with a lot of local groups and activities, all of which have overlapping membership, we will be a part of a strong community. Some of the things that make this more likely are when our locality is cohesive in terms of social class and income; most people have lived in the area for a long time; members of our families live near to us; there is local industry in which many of us are employed;

we shop at local shops; we actually want to get to know each other; there is either a history of local collective action (such as tenants groups, park action committees) or there is an external threat to the locality that leads to the formation of campaigning groups (such as the proposal to build a bypass). Furthermore, the more geographically isolated we are, the more we are likely to develop close attachments to our neighbours.

Jeremy had lived in a hospital, way out in the countryside, for as long as he could remember. He had lots of jobs there: helping with the painting; working in the print shop; doing furniture restoration; working on the farm; looking after the bees. You name it, he had done it. Nearly everyone there worked within the hospital. He went to the social club along with other people, took part in the Christmas pantomime and bought presents for his brother and his family at the hospital shop. His brother used to visit him regularly and knew most of his friends. Some of them had even been with him to stay at his brother's house. Many of the nurses lived in the hospital, and lots of them used to muck in alongside him and his friends in the work groups, the social club and for things like the summer fête and the Christmas show.

Jeremy felt a real part of his community. He was appreciated for the contribution he made to hospital life and he looked forward to coming home whenever he had visited his brother. The hospital closed. Jeremy went to live in his brother's town where he knew no one except the three men with whom he now shared a small house. He quickly got used to the staff that worked with them in the house, but they went home as soon as their shifts ended: he never felt he really got to know them. Jeremy did not have a job. Instead, some "community" support workers used to take him to some classes at the local college or to the local leisure centre. These were interesting but there was always a different group of people there and hardly anyone ever spoke to him. The rest of the time Jeremy stayed at home, encouraged to cook for himself and the other men, which he did not enjoy, and to do housework and washing. Jeremy did not feel he was appreciated or that he belonged anywhere now.

In the hospital Jeremy lived in a socially isolated place. He did lots of different things with different combinations of the same people, with whom he had lived for a long time. Everyone was in the same boat – no one had much money to spend, and when they did it was in the same shop. All in all, Jeremy lived in a close and cohesive community that gave him a sense of worth and of belonging. He lost all this when he moved out and, to date, the community he lost had not been replaced.

Whatever the make-up of our communities, they all involve networks of social relationships of various sorts.

SOCIAL NETWORKS

Personal relationships with friends and acquaintances, neighbours, relatives and colleagues are crucial to us. They make us feel appreciated and worthwhile, liked and loved. It is through relationships that we learn about ourselves, other people and the world at large, as well as gaining information and skills. Relationships are our most important sources of advice, support and practical help. Through relationships we share ideas and develop new experiences. Most of us can describe our relationships in terms of patterns of who we know and of who knows whom. These patterns are called social networks.

Structure of social networks

There are many different patterns of relationships making up social networks, and these patterns are explored in Exercise 3.3.

Exercise 3.3 Structure of social networks

On a large piece of paper, draw a circle with your name inside in the middle. Now draw lines out from this circle, each line representing a different person you know well. The finished picture will be the simplest way of describing your social network: it consists of the different people with whom you have a good relationships. Now look at your picture and link up people who, themselves, have connections. Represent weak connections with a thin line, strong connections with a double line, connections characterized by conflict with a wavy line, and so on.

How different would the network pictures look for people we did not know well, or for people with whom we work? Who knows whom in your network? How enmeshed are you in your network? How might you strengthen this network? Are there any parts of the network that would benefit from being weakened? If so, why?

A more complex way in which we can think about social networks is to consider who knows whom and what kinds of relationships they have with each other. You may have found that most people in your original picture knew each other, but when you went on to say how well they knew each other, or how much time they spent with each other, you could see that the links are weak. In other words, the network is "loose-knit". On the other hand, you may have found that the people in your picture were all good friends who did a lot of different things together and spent a lot of time with each other. In other words the network was "close knit". Different networks to which we belong may be either loose-knit, close-knit or a mixture of the two.

Types of social networks

Most of us have a number of distinct social networks from which we receive and contribute different things. First and often foremost are our family networks. Some of us may have close-knit and extensive family networks, whereas others may have loose-knit or minimal networks. Several things make family networks unique. Firstly, we generally have closer contact with family members over a longer period of time than with any other networks of people. Secondly, families may be more likely to give us certain kinds of help and support than other people: we may, for instance, feel it is easier to receive financial help from family than from friends. Lastly, family members may be more willing to help out at times of particular difficulty, such as the birth of a child, illness, increasing infirmity in old age, and so on. We may feel a shared obligation with members of our family that we do not with anyone else We are usually more likely to fulfil these obligations if we live close by. Even if we do not like members of our family, they may still be important to us in these ways.

Generally, we like members of our friendship networks. There is a greater likelihood that friendship networks will be loose-knit than will family networks, as different friends may not know each other. However, the longer we have known a particular network of friends, and the more our contact with them extends across different areas of our lives, the more close-knit it is likely to become. Friends may give us day-to-day help if they live near, advice, emotional support at times of distress, and so on. We may el the sense of direct and personal obligation to friends that we feel for family. However, we may still receive and offer help in kind across our friendship network – the more close-knit the network, the more "trading" within the group for help and support there will be. Over time, each member of the network will have contributed and received help and support in a variety of different ways.

Networks of neighbours, however, may be close-knit in the sense that we all know each other, if only by sight, and loose-knit in the sense that we do not know each other well or share many activities in common. Nevertheless, we can be a source of mutual aid and support. This is particularly so in respect of minor services, such as taking in the post if we are on holiday, holding house keys, feeding pets and lending tools. We can usually rely on neighbours to help out in emergencies, even if we do not know each other very well. Neighbour networks may continue over long periods of time, particularly if not many people move in and out of the area.

Networks of work colleagues, on the other hand, may be close-knit for the narrow activity they share but not extend beyond the workplace. Although colleagues can be valuable sources of support, advice and information, unless we become friends with them out of work these shared activities will be very much task-related. These networks may not contribute much over our total life course. Similarly, contacts we make at evening classes, meetings and such, will usually be limited to that setting, unless the contacts develop into friendships. Whilst many friendships may develop from shared interests or hobbies, certainly not all interest groups give rise to friendships.

This is not to say these relationships are unimportant to us, but we should see them in the context of all our other social networks. The fewer networks we have, and the less important membership of these networks is, the more important will be contacts we make with anyone in any setting. If all our contacts are one-off, in this way, when we draw our network maps (as at the beginning of this section), we will see that there are very few interlinkages, and the people we know will not form a network as such. Most of us, however, would find that we could not get the complications of our social networks on one piece of paper. Not only do we have linkages between people we know within different networks, we also have considerable interlinkages across networks: our friends know members of our families who know people we work with who are also our neighbours and so on.

Imran lived at home with his mother, father and five brothers. His cousins lived next door, and another set of cousins lived in the neighbouring street. Every week he and his family either went to a different aunt and uncle's not too far away, or they came to his house. All the children and young people ate with the women and the older boys ate with the men. Imran's mother was a dinner lady at the primary school at the end of the road. Although Imran went to a special school, he knew a lot of other children nearby because his mother knew them all. Imran used to help his older brother, Hassid, do his paper round, and got to know a lot of his neighbours this way. One of Imran's other brothers, Asad, would walk two different neighbour's dogs, and Imran liked to help. Imran lived within a set of close-knit relationships which interlinked family, neighbour and cultural networks.

Michael lived with his mother; his sister, Joy, worked in Hong Kong. Although she had a family of her own and wrote about twice a year, enclosing photographs, she had only been back once in the last three years. Michael was picked up by the day services bus every morning, taken to the day centre and dropped off again at 4.15 every day. Michael's mother worked part-time in the hospital laundry. She did her shopping during her lunch break. She usually got home just as the bus arrived to drop Michael off. Michael spent the evenings and weekends watching television with his Mum or sitting upstairs in his bedroom. Sometimes they would go shopping together. Michael knew and liked the newsagent round the corner and the fishmonger. On Sundays the two of them would go to church, although they rarely spoke to anyone except the vicar. Michael and his mother spent the long summer holiday in a caravan in Wales. As they had been going there for many years, they knew the local post-mistress, who was always very friendly towards them. Over the years, Michael's mother had lost contact with most of her friends and was so tired she saw very few people. Michael knew quite a few people but they were not closely linked. He had a very loose-knit network of relationships.

Simple, loose-knit networks contribute to our identities and feelings of belonging. The more complex our networks and the more close-knit they are, the stronger will be the communities of which we are a part, as well as our own sense of community with other people. It is only with a range of different kinds of networks to which we contribute, both in terms of offering something to other people in the network and in terms of strengthening the network, that we feel a part of our community and society at large.

SOCIAL SITUATIONS, COMMUNITY AND SOCIAL NETWORKS

People with learning disabilities may need help in forming, contributing to and supporting social networks. Some of this must be done by working with different communities of which they are a part. Sometimes, though, particular social situations can make meaningful participation in communities and social networks difficult.

Situations make it difficult for people to be competent members of their communities in a number of ways. Their physical design may make positive interactions difficult; situations may be difficult to penetrate and, once penetrated, may be difficult to participate within.

Environmental design

Physical features of a setting may guide, determine or block particular ways of behaving. In some situations, the design of the setting makes it relatively easy for us to use it for the reasons it should be used. In others, though, the physical design makes it very difficult for us. Take, for example, a shop that appears to be self-service. We can be thrown into some disarray if we go in and find that some of the goods we want are behind the till. As customers, are we allowed behind the till? In this case, the particular shop has a poor "fit" between the physical aspects of the setting and our behaviour. If, as we stand looking bemused, the shopkeeper tells us that things behind the till will be served to us, the "fit" is restored. Poor environmental design can lead to poor "fit" between the setting and our behaviour, making it far more likely that we will either not know what to do or will behave inappropriately. It can sometimes be easier to learn what to do in highly structured situations, with a good "fit" between the setting and the behaviour, than in ones with a poor "fit".

Stella was used to the canteen in the college where she had a job as a cleaner. The trays were at one end of a passage, down which she had to walk, selecting her food as she went. There was someone at the end of the passage to take her luncheon voucher. The cutlery was next to the cashier, alongside the jugs of water and glasses. However, she did find the tea arrangements after the flower arranging class she attended difficult to get the hang of. Here there was a big room, three corners of which were used for different activities – painting, egg decoration and sewing – on the night she did her flower arranging. The tea was in the other corner. There seemed to be no one to pay, and she never could work out how people got sugar. The first situation was one with a good setting – behaviour fit, and the second one was not.

It is not only social situations that can have poor "fit" between behaviour and the setting. Whole neighbourhoods can be designed to make contact and prolonged interaction with others very difficult to achieve. Lack of transport routes, parking facilities, pedestrian crossings, proximity of different kinds of shops, and so on can make neighbourhoods more or less easy to use. Exercise 3.4 helps to clarify the extent to which a particular neighbourhood has a good "fit" between behaviour and environmental design.

**Exercise 3.4 Behaviour –
environment "fit"**

Sketch a map of your neighbourhood, including main transport routes and meeting places. Highlight any difficulties there might be for people in wheelchairs, those who are unsteady on their feet and people pushing shopping trolleys or baby buggies using the facilities in the neighbourhood.

To what extent do environmental features create or support different kinds of behaviours? Are some parts of the neighbourhood inaccessible to people who have any kind of difficulty walking or getting about? Does the design of the neighbourhood support different types of activities by people of different age groups? If so, in what ways?

We can often see the complex ways in which neighbourhoods have been developed physically and the ways they have developed socially. Perhaps the most dramatic example is in many of the neighbourhood developments in housing, recreation and shopping, following slum clearances. The building of high-rise flats, with little in the way of safe recreational facilities and few shops, to replace highly populated streets resulted, in some cases,

in a weakening of social networks, with fewer people knowing
their neighbours and more people living apart from their families.
These kinds of issues can be taken into account in helping people
with learning disabilities choose where it is they want to live.

Norah and Jenny both lived in a purpose-built hostel with 14 other
people with learning disabilities. This hostel was the pride of the
service in so far as it was carefully designed so that living units of
four or five people could be quite independent of each other, and
yet still be linked around a glassed courtyard in a way to provide
easy access for staff. The hostel was in lovely grounds that were
well kept, in a well-to-do suburb of a medium-sized town. Although
the hostel building was new and of high standard, both Norah and
Jenny found it very difficult to find their way around. Every corner
and corridor of the building looked the same, with red brick walls
and a window on one side looking into the courtyard and what
appeared to be the same potted plants! Unbeknown to the hostel
staff, Jenny scratched some of the paint work around the window
near to the door leading to her unit, so she could more easily
recognize it.

The hostel was about half a mile from the nearest shops, which
were reached by a road with no footpath or pavement. There was
a large pub opposite the hostel which was mostly used by people
travelling to and from it by car. It was hardly surprising that the
residents knew none of the neighbours and vice versa. They did
not go out anywhere except when accompanied by staff, and then
usually in a car. There was poor setting – behaviour "fit" both within
the hostel and between the hostel and the neighbourhood.

In this example, the physical design of the hostel made it difficult for residents to use it easily. In addition, the neighbourhood
facilities were difficult to use as a car was needed to get to them,
therefore they were difficult to penetrate.

Penetration of social settings

We cannot all take part in, or penetrate, every social situation. We
can look at situations as ranging along a continuum of those
allowing minimal penetration (where we are denied access or are
permitted merely to be "onlookers"), to those involving some
penetration (where we are actively involved in activities and have
clear roles), to those involving maximum penetration (where we
are in positions of great authority and influence).

In many situations in Britain, children cannot penetrate in an
active capacity; instead they may be excluded or only tolerated if

they "keep quiet". Pubs, and even restaurants, would be good examples of such situations. Other situations, though, may permit wide access and involvement or penetration from all sectors of the community. People with learning disabilities may not be able to penetrate some situations at all, either because physical access is difficult, or they are refused entry, or they are only allowed entry if accompanied by carers or if they join in with a group of other people with learning disabilities. Even when they are able to penetrate situations they can often only do so to a limited extent – frequently they will be onlookers rather than participants and, even when present, take only a small part in the activities. If they are able to have a role in the situation (achieve a deeper level of penetration), they benefit enormously.

Carmel was invited to join the management group of a local short-term care service. Karen helped her understand what the meetings were to be about, prior to each meeting. However, everyone talked quickly and Carmel could not think of anything to say. At this point she had some penetration of this social situation. One day she mentioned to Karen that she had an idea for helping families who needed short-term care to meet together. Karen told the Chair of the management group, who put this item on the agenda for the next meeting. Carmel went through with Karen what her ideas were: she did not want to tell the whole meeting herself, and Karen agreed to explain the ideas for her. The management group were very interested in what Carmel (via Karen) had to say, and asked Carmel if she would like to try out her ideas. It was agreed that Karen and Carmel should put the ideas to the test and that there would be support from the management group in any way they wanted. It was also agreed that there should be a standing agenda item for future meetings so that Carmel could let them know about her progress.

Carmel now had a clear role both within the committee and outside it. With Karen's help she began to give her own progress reports to the management committee. Three years later she was the only member of the original committee to be still involved with the project, and helped new members find their feet. Carmel now had a high degree of penetration into this social situation.

If a situation is penetrable by a wide cross-section of society, including people of all ages, gender, religions and class; serves a variety of different purposes, such as education, nutrition, recreation and shopping; and permits different activities, such as talking, sitting, eating, buying and so on, we can call it a **rich** setting. This particular setting will probably serve as a focal point for a wide cross-section of the community. Examples of such rich settings might be purpose-built community centres; they could just as easily be local libraries, post offices or corner shops. The richer a setting is, the more open it will be to a range of different people, and it is less likely that our behaviour will be highly ritualistic. In such a setting there is more scope for individual differences in behaviour to emerge. The penetrability of different situations is examined in Exercise 3.5.

Exercise 3.5 The penetration of social situations

Think of **five** different social situations. Choose some that are linked to buildings and some that are not. Identify different aspects of the setting that might help you decide how rich a setting it is. Use the layout below as a guide.

Situation	Physical access	Who may participate (formally or informally stated)?	What kinds of activities can people do?	What kinds of roles can people play?
1.				
2.				
3.				
4.				
5.				

Which situation is the easiest to penetrate? Which is the least easy to penetrate? Are any of these situations "rich" settings? Would any of these situations vary in how easily they could be penetrated by different parts of the community (people of different ages, from different cultures, etc.)? How is physical access linked to other ways in which situations can be penetrated? Would everyone agree with you in your assessment of the extent to which these situations can be penetrated? If not, what differences might you expect?

We can see that situations vary considerably in the extent to which they can be penetrated by different sectors of the community. If a setting is available to large numbers of different people, however, opportunities for us to play a particular role in that setting, or to take on particular responsibilities will be limited. We can say the setting is "overmanned". If, on the other hand, so few people use a particular setting or settings that we find ourselves always taking on roles and jobs with some responsibility, the setting will be "undermanned". Overmanned settings make it difficult for us all to play meaningful and contributory roles. If you have ever belonged to a club with few active members, you will have felt the strain of an undermanned setting. If you live in a community where it is the same people who are active in a number of different activities and clubs, the strains will be greater: however, so too will the opportunities for all who want to take an active part.

> Rose used to go to a 120-place social education centre. She joined in with different groups of people for different activities. There was a cafe which was run by the members and an active members' committee. The waiting-lists for people to take part in both of these things was long: the setting was "overmanned". Last year the centre devolved into four 30-place centres located around the town. The centre Rose belonged to operated a small garden centre as well as a garden, with a management committee made up of staff and centre users; there was also a user committee made up entirely of members. Apart from those with complex and multiple disabilities, every member who wanted to took a part in the running of the centre and its activities. The centre was no longer overmanned and there were not too many different settings within the centre to make it undermanned. Rose now played a responsible role, made possible by the size and number of the behaviour settings in relation to the number of people available.

We can see that the extent to which different behaviour settings are over or undermanned, and whether or not a setting is a rich one, could also be an issue of how different situations are connected.

Links between social situations

Many social situations link with others in complex ways, which is why we sometimes find it difficult to say when one starts and another one finishes. We often find that some social situations are embedded within others, which in turn are embedded in other, overarching contexts. We can look at four different levels of social contexts, each becoming more general and indirect than the others.

At the first level are those situations of which we have direct experience, often on a regular basis, such as home, work, clubs, clinics. Level two is the point at which two or more of these situations may link together: the links themselves may become separate social situations in their own right. So, for example, home and work may link in terms of how we organize ourselves to manage both. This link may become problematic when we need to stay at home to look after a sick child (a separate social situation and one that, in turn, may highlight the links between home and clinic). Level one and two situations may both be nested within those at level three, which includes situations of which we do not have direct experience but that nevertheless influence us; for instance our workplace policy on parental leave will affect our experience of the work – caring dilemma. Lastly, level four contains aspects of the situation that are of still larger scale. They include the particular cultural and ideological context of all the "lower" situations. So part of the level four context, in our example, will be employment policy in Britain, current unemployment rates, gender roles and so on. Levels three and four exert strong, if indirect, influence over our behaviour in, and experience of social situations.

It would be a mistake to see the social situations in which people with learning disabilities were involved as being limited to the immediate surroundings. We must also understand the wider context of these situations.

Hazel has just left a school for children with severe learning difficulties. Her social services department has established a supported work placement scheme, and she goes to work as a packer. Hazel enjoys going to work and likes the people there: although she is properly supervised it is very different from the closed environment of the special school. Unfortunately her wages are low, less than the combined benefits she is entitled to, and her family are having to consider whether they can afford for Hazel to continue working.

Hazel's direct (level 1) experiences are of school, the workplace and home. She has also some experience of combined situations (level 2) such as her school leaver's review, which her workplace supervisor and parents attended. Interestingly, while her local couñcil still provides special schools through its education committee, after school its social services department is trying to provide more socially integrative opportunities such as supported employment (level 3). These differences reflect the conflicting policies in the educational and social policy arena (level 4), as does experience of the "benefit trap" which creates such a dilemma for Hazel and her parents.

Social situations, then, are not discrete physical or social entities, but complex systems that are embedded in other systems, including wide social and ideological systems. We can use our knowledge of communities, social networks and social situations in order to help people with learning disabilities increase their social capability. Before we can begin to work with people, though, we must understand the nature of social skill and social competence, itself.

FURTHER READING

Our understanding of communities and networks is drawn from community, ecological and environmental psychology; anthropology and social development. We have, therefore, included readings from each of these disciplines, as well as texts that have looked specifically at the meanings of community and networks for people with learning disabilities.

Allan, G. (1983) Informal networks of care: issues raised by Barclay. *British Journal of Social Work*, **13**, 417–33.

Altman, T. (1984) *Culture and Environment*, Cambridge University Press, Cambridge.

Atkinson, R.D. (1994) *The Common Sense of Community*, DEMOS, London.

Baldwin, S. (1990) From communities to neighbourhoods II. *Architecture and Behaviour*, **6**(3), 207–86.

Barker, R. (1968) *Ecological Psychology: Concepts and Methods for Studying the Environment of Human Behavior*, Stanford University Press, Stanford.

Berger, P.L. and Neuhaus, R.J. (1977) *To Empower People: the role of mediating structures in public policy*, American Enterprise Institute for Public Policy Research, Washington, DC.

British Journal of Social Work (1986) 16, Supplement on Social Networks.

Chavis, D. and Wandersman, A. (1990) Sense of community in the urban environment: a catalyst for participation and community development. *American Journal of Community Psychology*, **18**, 55–82.

Cohen, A.P. (1982) Belonging: the experience of culture, in *Belonging: Identity and Social Organisation in British Rural Culture* (ed. A.P. Cohen), Manchester University Press, Manchester.

Cohen, A.P. (ed.) (1985) *The Symbolic Construction of Community*, Routledge, London.

Gottleib, B.H. (ed.) (1981) *Social Networks and Social Support*, Sage, London.

Johnson, T. (1985) *Belonging to the Community*, Options in Community Living, Madison, WI.

Kagan, C. (1991) *Network Development: An experiment in case management?*, North West Development Team, Whalley.

Krause, M.W., Seltzer, M.M. and Goodman, S.J. (1992) Social support networks of adults with mental retardation living at home. *American Journal on Mental Retardation*, **96**(4), 432–41 (special issue on social skills).

Maguire, L. (1983) *Understanding Social Networks*, Sage, London.

Sarason, S. (1974) *The Psychological Sense of Community: Perspectives for Community Psychology*, Jossey-Bass, San Francisco.

Suttles, G. (1972) *The Social Construction of Communities*, University Chicago Press, Chicago.

Vanier, J. (1979) *Community and Growth*, Darton, Longman and Todd, London.

Willmott, P. (1986) *Social Networks and Public Policy*, Policy Studies Institute, Research Report 655, London.

4

The nature of social skill and social competence

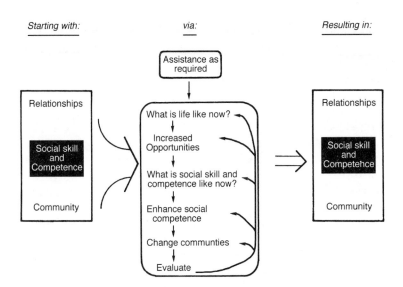

There are many different perspectives on understanding social skill and social competence. Sociological perspectives stress the importance that cultural and social factors play in our social lives; ecological perspectives highlight the importance of context and environment; social psychological perspectives focus on us as members of different groups; and within-person perspectives emphasize instincts, drives and evolutionary characteristics. We have found it useful to borrow from a number of different perspectives in order to best understand how we act in, and make sense of our social worlds.

A MODEL OF SOCIAL SKILL

We think it is useful to talk of competent social behaviour as if it were a complex skill that has been learnt, refined over time and is constantly able to adapt and change. As with other skills, such as driving a car, playing a musical instrument and so on, some of us have more natural talent than others. This does not mean that we cannot all learn to drive or play, but that some of us will learn more easily and more quickly and will be able to reach a higher standard. Most of us will be able to learn and develop perfectly adequate levels of driving or playing: so it is with social behaviour. Given the right opportunities and instruction, most of us will be able to learn adequately and be able to act appropriately in most situations, even those with which we are not familiar. However, not all of us have the opportunity to learn a wide repertoire of behaviour: furthermore, some of us may have had bad teachers and learnt inappropriate behaviour. Nevertheless, whatever our current level of skill, we can all improve and develop our competence.

People with learning disabilities may need more opportunities and time to learn the basics of social behaviour, and may not be able to acquire a wide range of different social behaviours. Nevertheless, they too can improve their level of skill and develop new skills along with the rest of us.

Once we have adopted a skills approach to social behaviour, we can begin to think about breaking the complex skill down into its component parts. Just as driving a car consists of steering, using the gears, giving appropriate signals, reading the signs around us, braking when required and so on, so social behaviour can be broken down into its constituent parts.

Figure 4.1 outlines the different component parts of skilled social behaviour.

At any point in time we can look at our social behaviour, or that of others, in terms of any or all of these linked component parts.

AWARENESS

Awareness of self and of others contributes to our effective social behaviour in a number of different ways. Our self-system is made up of our understanding of internal events (bodily sensations, moods, thoughts, values, attitudes, beliefs and emotions); knowledge about external events (how we behave, what we say, where

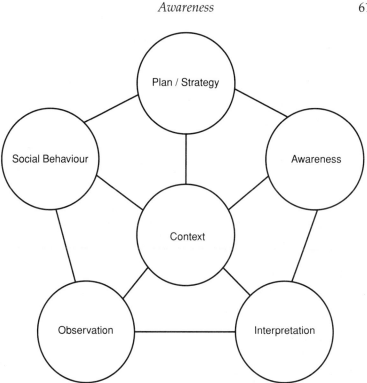

Figure 4.1 Component parts of skilled social behaviour. (Adapted from Kagan, C. (1985) Issues arising from teaching interpersonal skills in post-basic nurse training. In C. Kagan (Ed) *Interpersonal Skills in Nursing: Research and Applications*. Beckenham: Croom Helm.)

we go, etc.); personal and social identities (the roles we play, the groups to which we belong, the characteristics we like or dislike about ourselves, etc.); and the extent to which we have any sense of agency or control over the things that happen to us.

Internal events

Most of us learn about ourselves and our bodies very early on in life. We learn to recognize different sensations linked to touch, smell, sight and hearing. Not only do we recognize them but we learn to label these sensations. As children we learn to recognize and label internal bodily states, like pain, excitement, nervousness, happiness and sadness, with the help of adults who make guesses about what children are feeling at different times, basing these guesses on the context in which the feelings have arisen. The context is particularly important as the actual bodily sensations that underlie different emotions are identical – what leads us to feel different things is the context in which the changes have taken place. Thus, to have butterflies before an exam is labelled exam nerves, but to feel them before going on a roller-coaster is excitement. There is enormous scope for us to label these things inaccurately, and physical or intellectual impairment can make learning how to recognize and label internal states more difficult and sometimes impossible.

> Moira had been getting into confrontations with other people at the college she attends. It seems that sometimes other people start it but at other times she does. It seems that these scenes build up over a period of about 3 minutes. When asked about how she feels at these times Moira can't really say. However when she is taken through the steps in the last such scene in as lifelike a role-play as possible, she describes a hot feeling in her face and when her increased rate of breathing is pointed out to her she can notice this too.

Our attitudes, or the way we feel about people or things, are even more difficult to fathom. We get to know what attitudes we have by constantly comparing ourselves to other people and how they behave and think. Sometimes we may even infer our own attitudes from how we, ourselves, behave. So, when we find ourselves staying in bed on a work day, we may assume we have a negative attitude towards work. Or is it the negative attitude towards work that makes us stay in bed? The relationships between attitudes and our behaviour can be impossible to disentangle.

Just as we can have attitudes about other people (interpersonal attitudes), so we can have attitudes about ourselves. If we feel positively towards ourselves and like ourselves, we are said to have positive or high self-esteem: if we feel negative towards ourselves and dislike ourselves, we have negative or low self-esteem. As we have seen in Chapter 2, we continually compare ourselves with other people. If we compare badly, this may lead to low self-esteem: if we compare favourably it can lead to high self-esteem. The other major source of self-esteem is other people and how they relate to us. If they value our company and obviously like us and like to be with us we develop positive self-esteem. On the whole, we are happier and more confident in different social situations if we have positive or high self-esteem.

External events

Most of us are aware of what we say (even if we do not always say what we want to), but we are less aware of the non-verbal or body-language messages we convey. Nor are we always aware of the information other people pick up about our identity from how we behave.

In different situations we try to present ourselves in different ways and in different lights. It is as if we were all actors on a stage playing roles, wearing different costumes and following scripts, however informally, to different audiences. most of us have "front" and "back stage" areas. We perform for our "audience" when we are front stage, but drop our "masks" when we are backstage. Thus on our way to work on the bus we may be "backstage" and just sit quietly and unassumingly; as we walk towards the centre where we work, we can feel ourselves gathering ourselves to enter the "front stage" workplace; when we go in we are immediately in role and people relate to us in this capacity. We may play our part until home time and then flop into our seat on the bus, grateful to be "backstage" again. In this example from work, our part begins for that day when we choose appropriate clothes (costumes) to wear. We would not wear the same clothes to work that we had worn horse-riding at the weekend, nor those we had worn to work, to a night-club. Those are different parts with different costumes for different audiences.

Sometimes we get it wrong and play the wrong part for the wrong audience or wear the wrong costume for the wrong part. We have probably all been in situations where we feel under or overdressed, that is we are wearing the wrong costume. Similarly we have probably all been in a situation where things are not as we expected them to be and our behaviour does not quite fit in, that is we are playing the wrong part. Practice at analysing ordinary situations as if they were theatrical performances is given in Exercise 4.1.

Our self-presentation can influence the impressions other people receive of us and can lead to greater or lesser likelihood of meeting them again.

Exercise 4.1 Social situations as theatre

Take any ordinary situation (such as a shop, bank, workplace, leisure centre, etc.) and describe it the following theatrical terms.

What parts do people play?

What costumes do they wear?

What scripts do they follow?

How much ad libbing is permitted?

Where is the stage?

What stage props are there?

Who is the audience?

How much do they know about the performance they are watching?

How have actors learnt their parts?

What are the limitations of looking at social situations as if they were theatrical performances? What happens if all actors do not know their parts? What happens if the audience expects more from the actors than they are giving? How much improvisation is permitted in most situations? How important is the context in defining the behaviours of all those taking part?

Personal and social identity

Identity has sometimes been described as the essence of the "self" which, in turn, is the essence of a person. This view sees identity as being formed through the culmination of our experiences of significant events throughout childhood and adolescence. An alternative, but not incompatible, view is that we get our sense of identity from the ways in which other people react towards us. The first approach would suggest that our identity is formed by adulthood and is stable throughout the rest of our lives. The second approach suggests that our personal identities change as those about us change. As we move in different social circles our sense of identity changes according to the messages we get from others about what kind of a person we are. At its simplest, these messages are clear: if no one spends any time with us, or people do not talk to us when they are with us, or are constantly ordering us about or criticizing us, we begin to think badly of ourselves and feel that we are not nice and do not belong. Further encounters with people who criticize us confirm this view.

How many people with learning disabilities do we know whose experiences of other people are similar to this? If, however, other people talk to us pleasantly, ask our opinion about things, include us in things they are doing or go out of their way to be with us, we will feel and think of ourselves as likeable and have a sense of belonging. For most of us, the messages we receive from the range of people we know well and not so well are more subtle, but can have powerful influences on our sense of worth and well-being.

Identity is closely linked to role. The more a role takes over our lives, the greater its contribution is likely to be to our identity. Thus family roles will often be life-long roles and of considerable importance in determining our identity. The role of volunteer-in-the-Oxfam-shop-on-a-Saturday, however, will probably not contribute overwhelmingly to our sense of identity (unless of course it is the only role we have that enables us to **do** something for others). So, if people with learning disabilities are always cast in the role of dependent in the different walks of their lives, this will contribute greatly to their sense of self, and may be a role from which it is very difficult to break away.

Social identity arises from membership of different groups and the extent to which they are important to us. Social groups may be anything from gender groups (male, female), disability groups (learning disability, hearing impaired), work groups (the gardening group in the day centre, community health workers), to friendship groups. If group membership is important to us, we incorporate characteristics of members of that group into our sense of self and not the characteristics of other groups. This will sometimes be a deliberate process ("I am going to wear overalls like everyone in the gardening group wears, and not aprons like those in the kitchen group wear; I am responsible like other members of the gardening group and do not need watching over like the kitchen group people do), but will often happen without our having to think about it. This is partly because for every group to which we belong, there are other groups to which, by virtue of belonging to the first, we do not belong. Group membership gives us a sense of who we are and also who we are not. Exercise 4.2 explores the different ways the groups to which we belong contribute to our identities.

Most of us belong to lots of different social groups which change as we move through life. If we are excluded from particular social groups (either because we are not eligible or because something changes that means we no longer belong to that group), or cannot belong to a range of groups, our sense of identity may be threatened or fragmented. If, for example, most people we know work (belong to the social group of employed people and also to particular work groups), we may feel inadequate if we cannot get a job. These feelings of inadequacy, often accompanied with a sense of worthlessness and misery, may arise even if we have a job but are at risk of being made redundant. Similarly, if we have to leave the job, perhaps because we have a baby or are ill, we may begin to feel worthless. If, however, leaving work because of illness takes us into another group that gives us a sense of purpose again, such as joining a self-help group of people with similar health problems, the loss of identity may be overcome. On the other hand, if there is no such group to which we can belong, we may try to hide the fact that we are ill because we fear the stigma and reaction of other people knowing why we lost our job. The things that are likely to be stigmatizing will vary from one culture to another and often from one social class to another.

When we look at the lives of many people with learning disabilities, we can see the limited number of social groups to which they belong, as well as the large number of groups from which they are deliberately, or by default because of their impairments, excluded. This will have far-reaching consequences for the development of their social identities.

Vince gets up between 9.00 and 10.30 a.m. He feeds the dog, if it is in. He walks to the social services office to pick up money held

Exercise 4.2 Social groups and social identity

Think of groups to which you (a) belong, (b) have belonged and (c) hope to belong to in the future (include peer groups, class groups, race groups, interest groups, political groups, religious groups, leisure groups, friendship groups, professional groups, work groups, community groups, family groups, cultural groups, etc.). Take **two** examples of each of these categories and consider how the group has influenced how you think, how you behave and how you separate yourself from people in other groups?

Complete the chart, and then repeat the exercise for a person with learning disabilities.

(a) Groups to which you belong:

(b) Groups to which you belonged in the past:

(c) Groups to which you would like to belong in the future:

	Impact on how I think	*Impact on how I behave*	*Groups from which I differ*
(a) 1.			
2.			
(b) 1.			
2.			
(c) 1.			
2.			

Can we ever shake off the influence of social groups to which we have belonged in the past? Are there groups which define our identities more extensively than others? If so, which ones? What is the impact of long-term membership of social groups on our identities? Are there any common features of the groups which contribute to your identity? If so, what are they? How does the life experience of people with learning disabilities compare with your own in terms of group membership and social identity?

by an appointee and banters a bit with the social worker or whoever it is that deals with him that day. He may persuade someone to give him a cigarette. He walks to the "drop-in". This is a church crypt where (mainly) single men with housing and drink problems sit smoking, occasionally chatting, and where free tea and cheap cooked meals are available. He stays there until it closes at 4.30 p.m. and walks home, maybe going out later to the corner shop, to walk the dog or look in shop windows.

Vince has little to help him construct a positive identity beyond his responsibility for the dog and his acceptance by those with whom he has most dealings. While he has freedom over his use of time, his chief roles are those of client and "drop-in" user. His experience is that of dependency and marginality, and his identity and aspirations are little different from that. He cannot imagine himself doing anything very different from what he does most days.

As we can see, then, social identity is complex but important to understand as it gives us a sense of belonging and enriches our lives. One of the things that preserves our self-esteem in the light of threats to social identity is having a sense of agency, or real control, over things that matter to us.

Sense of agency

We have seen above that our feelings about ourselves are determined in part by the ways in which other people react towards us. Furthermore, we will often try to control the impression others get of us by presenting ourselves in particular ways. In order to have self-confidence and to be more effective, we must believe that we **can** control how others see us. In addition, we must believe that we can exert some control over our environments. In other words, we have to believe in ourselves as "agents" and not simply as objects to be controlled by others. If we do not experience any control, or do not **believe** that we could control things we may become ill, passive, and feel that life is futile: we may even become depressed. On the other hand, believing that we can control events to a certain extent leads to feelings of self-confidence, high self-esteem and to greater happiness, and we are able to be more effective in social situations.

Sometimes, if we perceive that we are not able to exert control and influence, we may try to fight against passivity. We try to gain some control even if it is in negative ways. So, for example, if we find ourselves in danger of losing our jobs through some rationalization process, we may begin to be active in our trade union (attempting to regain control over events that have been outside our control); or we may go home and shout at our children more or deny them things we would normally permit (gaining more control over this area of our lives when we are denied control at work). If we think we **should** be able to control events but cannot, we may "fight" against our apparent lack of control, showing what is known as reactance. Reactance can occur whenever we find ourselves unable to control events that we expect to be able to control, or when we think we are being denied freedom of choice.

Alan lived in a small hostel and attended a nearby day centre. He liked to collect things. He was particularly fond of bottle tops from soft drink bottles and would go to great lengths to pick them up when he saw them. This extended to jumping off moving buses if he saw them lying in the road, dashing across roads to pick them up and so on. Whilst most people were allowed to walk freely in and out of the day centre, Alan was not allowed out as it was considered unsafe: he would run out into the road looking for bottle tops. The front door of the hostel was kept locked for the same reason. Over time, Alan found ways of getting out from the day centre and of leaving the hostel without anyone knowing. He was fighting back against being denied his freedom.

Another resident in the hostel, Bill, was 8 stone overweight and staff were trying to get him to keep to a diet. He was often found taking food from litter bins, not because he was hungry but more probably because he was taking back some control over the getting of food that had been taken away from him by the staff who were controlling the availability of food.

The important thing for our self-esteem and self-confidence is to believe that we are able to act positively and to believe we have control in some parts of our lives. If we do not believe this we may experience stress, which in turn may lead to low self-esteem and misery. Figure 4.2 illustrates the way belief in control over events leads to positive action and high self-esteem or inaction and low self-esteem.

People with learning disabilities have often learnt to be passive through repeated experience that they are not able to exert control. Other people may make decisions for them and control nearly all aspects of their lives. Sometimes this means that it is very difficult to help people regain control over aspects of their lives, and sometimes it means that the people themselves

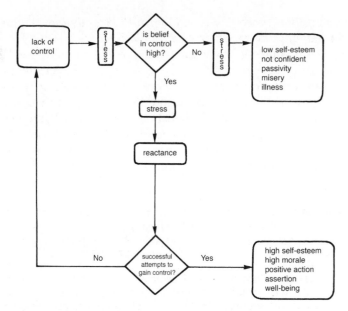

Figure 4.2 Belief in control over events and self-esteem.

may exert control in whatever ways they can, even if these ways are inappropriate. One of the things we can do is to help people gain whatever control they can over different aspects of their lives.

We have seen that several things contribute to self-awareness, including awareness of internal and external events, our personal and social identities and the extent to which we have a sense of agency. Awareness in the context of social skill, competence and capability also includes awareness of others.

Awareness of others

Social situations, by their very nature, involve more than one person. All the time we are constantly adjusting what we do and say to what other people do and say. We are aware of other people in a number of different ways, including their physical presence, the kind of people they are and their relationships with us, the roles they are playing, how they are behaving and how they are reacting to us and the situation in which they find themselves. Some of these aspects of awareness we will discuss below when we consider observation and interpretation. Here, we will concentrate on awareness of other peoples' roles, relationships with us and reactions to us.

As we move through different situations in the course of a day or a week, we are constantly aware of other people around us and how we fit in with them or not. We become self-conscious if we find ourselves with the wrong group of people or find that we stand out from the crowd in some way. This self-consciousness can lead to embarrassment. We may feel awkward, for example, if we go on a coach trip and are the only one of our age on the trip – everyone else is considerably older or younger. To feel awkward, we must be aware that the other people are different from us and the difference must be important in some way. Some of us may not mind being the youngest person on the trip but we may mind being the only woman or man.

It may not be physical difference that makes us feel awkward: take being with a group of people who talk incessantly about cycling. This is acceptable if we, too, know something about cycling or are interested in it. If not, we will feel excluded and possibly embarrassed. If we are not aware that the others are all interested in cycling, we may not be able to understand why our attempts to talk about our work or what was on television last night fall flat. If we really want to be a part of this group, we have to be aware of their interest in cycling and may have to be willing to take part in these conversations – we may even have to be willing to take up cycling ourselves to be totally accepted. Unless we are aware of the other people's interests, we cannot adapt our own behaviour in this way.

Not only are we aware of other people's characteristics and interests, but we are aware of their roles. It is through the process of interaction – what we say and do in the presence of others – that we discover other people's roles. This may be done formally, as when we are introduced to "Ms Morrison, your new line manager", or it may be done informally through the ways people talk and behave. Sometimes there are specific patterns of interaction that keep other people in a particular role relationship. We may kiss intimate friends when we say good-bye, but not people with whom we work: we may ask a colleague to brief us about what has happened on a particular shift, but not ask the postman.

Generally, we know what patterns of interaction are required depending on the role held by the other person. Sometimes, though, this can go wrong. If we visit a home for the elderly, we may mistakenly ask a relative for information rather than a member of staff: we have got the role wrong. We have probably all asked a member of the public how much something is in a shop at some time, thinking he or she is a shop assistant: we have mistaken the role.

The relationship other people have with us is sometimes negotiated even more informally. The anecdotes people tell, the amount they talk and extent to which they listen to us, all tell us how they see themselves in relation to us, in particular how superior they think they are. In order for us to know that they think themselves superior, we have to be aware of the cues they are giving.

Crucial to our social competence and effectiveness is our awareness of the perspective of other people, either of their role, their behaviour or their feelings. Being able to "take the role of the other", to empathize, is to be able to see things from their point of view. This is more than just being able to understand them, it is to be able to "stand in their shoes" and see things as if we were them. Awareness of others' perspectives is what lets us know when we have made a mistake or done something to upset someone else. It is one of the things that stops us physically attacking people even if we are boiling mad with them – we do not attack them because we know how they would feel if we did. It is what stops us standing too close to people when we are talking to them – we know how uncomfortable they would feel if we did. It is what stops us going up to strangers and telling them how much we fancy them. It is what stops us assuming we will marry people just because they have smiled at us.

Austin is a gentle man of 31, who likes to be with other people. He is 6 ft 2 in tall and overweight. Austin finds lots of things amusing: sometimes he laughs at what other people do and sometimes he laughs at things he is thinking about. For a reason that no one can fathom, Austin finds babies or children that are crying very funny indeed. When Austin laughs he suddenly makes a very loud noise which makes people jump, treat him warily and back away from him. This means that when Austin is out, say in a supermarket, waiting at the check-out, and the children in front of him begin to whinge, he will suddenly laugh. People have complained about him frightening children. He does not see what the problem is.

In this example, Austin does not understand what it is like to be other people when he suddenly laughs. He has no insight into why they may be afraid of him.

We learn to take the role of the other by getting to know lots of people in lots of different situations. Sometimes, as children, we may be taught directly about how other people feel ("If you stare like that, that woman will be cross"; "Let me show you what it feels like when you pinch me like that"; "Perhaps she's shy."). Other times we learn through trial and error, getting some things right and some things wrong along the way. Some of us do not do very well and are called insensitive or inconsiderate. Our surprise at being called these things may well be because we lack insight into our limited ability to take the role of other people and to be aware of how other people experience **us**. Sometimes this may be underpinned by a self-centredness wherein we spend more time thinking about ourselves rather than about other people.

Being aware of other people in the ways discussed above leads us to be socially effective in lots of different situations. Wide experience of different situations and different kinds of people, on the whole, make us better at being aware of others. People with learning disabilities often have a very restricted range of relationships and social experiences. They are also more likely to misunderstand or be unaware of other people's perspectives. Yet, just as we all continue to develop our awareness of, or empathy with others, so, too, can people with learning disabilities.

SOCIAL BEHAVIOUR

All social situations require us to behave in one way or another. We can look at social behaviour in terms of verbal behaviour (what is said) and non-verbal behaviour (body language and how things are said). Usually, the two types of behaviour interrelate closely. At times, though, one aspect will be more important than the other. In very noisy situations, or if people have lost their hearing or cannot talk or understand speech, non-verbal behaviour will be of most importance. If we cannot see, however, speech may be the most important, although touch, a non-verbal signal, will also play a part. Sometimes we give out ambiguous messages – we say something but our body language contradicts what we say. In these circumstances, either the speech or the non-verbal behaviour will be believed. We will explore the nature and functions of both non-verbal behaviour and speech.

Non-verbal behaviour

We can call any part of social behaviour that is not the actual words spoken, non-verbal behaviour. As we have said, non-verbal behaviour is not necessarily a separate communication system. It relates to speech in several ways: non-verbal messages may enhance, replace (as in sign language), or contradict speech. It is often non-verbal behaviours that we notice first when meeting people.

Presentation of self

On the basis of non-verbal behaviour, we form all sorts of impressions about other people's values, attitudes, personalities, interests, roles and so on. In other words, we use non-verbal behaviour to make quick judgements about the kinds of people others are. Of course, these judgements may not always be right, as we shall see later, but we make them nevertheless. As we are making judgements about other people, we are also giving away, non-verbally, a lot of information about ourselves. Indeed, we use non-verbal behaviours to create particular impressions of ourselves and to present ourselves in certain ways.

It is largely through non-verbal behaviours (including dress) that we can place people in terms of their age, gender, sometimes class or income bracket and so on. Generally, we follow conventions about what to wear, given who we are, what we are doing and where. If we get it wrong, we may be embarrassed or may lead people to believe we are "someone else". Certainly, before ever saying a word to us, other people may have decided whether or not they think they have anything in common with us or would find us interesting, based on how we have presented ourselves in a particular situation. There are times when this process becomes a conscious and deliberate one, such as when we are going for a job interview. However, it is often thought that a similar process in terms of presenting particular images to people goes on all the time – even if we do not like to admit it! Exercise 4.3 helps us see what cues we respond to when we meet people.

Exercise 4.3 Non-verbal cues and impressions of other people

Watch two people talking in any social situation or on television. If it is on television, turn the sound down. Note down all the non-verbal behaviours you can see in the chart below. Now turn the sound up, or get near enough to hear the two people without being able to make out what they are saying, and complete the chart. You can do this exercise with a friend: talk to each other and try and pay attention to the non-verbal behaviours your friend shows. Note them down in the chart below. Now, sit back to back and talk about what you did last weekend and what you felt about it, then complete the chart.

Categories of non-verbal behaviour

Facial expression (eyebrows, forehead, eye region, nose, mouth, mouth region, cheeks, eye movements, tongue)

Gesture (hand, arm, vocal, head shake, nod or toss, body, facial, leg/foot)

Proximity and touch (personal distance; self/other touching – scratching, twiddling, rubbing, hair, rings, etc.; task-related physical contact)

Eye gaze (eye contact; direction of gaze; staring; duration of gaze; avoidance of eye contact; blinking)

Posture, orientation and gait (position of limbs/head; position of body; regularity of movements; speed/regularity of walking)

Artefacts (appearance: dress, cosmetics, hair, accessories, e.g. bags, spectacles, jewellery, cleanliness, smell; emblems: badges, uniforms, possessions, e.g. cars, newspapers)

Vocal (tone and pitch; volume; speed; clarity; amount; silence; hesitations; sighs; laughs; pauses; verbal clichés; dysfluencies)

NB Combinations of non-verbal behaviours mean different things, and movement sometimes changes the meaning.

Continued

How easy was it to identify separate non-verbal behaviours? What happens to conversations and the picking up of non-verbal cues when you cannot see or hear the other person? In what ways were the non-verbal behaviours linked to the topics of conversation? How did the context in which the conversation was taking place influence the non-verbal behaviours shown? Would different non-verbal behaviours be displayed by people who are older, younger or from different cultures? If so, what sorts of differences would you expect?

What do non-verbal behaviours mean?

Exercise 4.3 will have helped you identify the different non-verbal behaviours. We usually decide what the behaviours mean according to the particular cultural and social situation in which they have occurred. The same non-verbal behaviours may mean different things in different situations. So, for example, we will interpret people waving their hands (a gesture) as they stand at their front door and other people walk away from them towards the gate as a farewell; we will interpret the same people doing the same thing as they walk towards a playground of children as a greeting. Similarly, we will interpret people speaking quickly and in a high pitch when they meet someone they know off a train as excitement, but using the same vocal cues in the doctor's consulting room as nervousness.

We may be wrong, however, in our interpretations. A particular person's non-verbal behaviour may be a habit and not mean anything.

Heather is a lively young woman who accommodates other people, is cooperative and considerate. Her mother and community support worker both say that, although she cannot tell them so, she is happy joining in with the things her brothers want to do and with whatever is on offer at the day centre. She smiles a lot, and it is this that has led people around her to think she is happy with what she does. One weekend, Heather's brother wanted to go fishing and offered to take Heather with him. At the suggestion Heather smiled. She refused to put on her coat, still smiling. She refused to go with her brother, still smiling. She went to her room, leaving her mother and brother confused. Heather seemed pleased at the prospect of going fishing on the one hand, but clearly was refusing to go. What they did not realize was that Heather's smiles were non-verbal habits that obscured what she was really trying to communicate. This led those close to her to make assumptions about how she felt and about what she enjoyed doing.

As we can see from the example of Heather, even if a person's behaviour does not mean anything, other people may assume it does. Heather had got used to smiling, and other people assumed she was pleased or happy. Another example may be of people who have got used to looking down when they talk: other people may think they are shy or anxious. They may not be, it is just that looking down has become a habit.

The thing about non-verbal habits is that they are very difficult to change. They are very well learnt, usually over long periods of time, and even if we are trying to change them we may not be able to. If we do try and change well-ingrained non-verbal habits, we may also change additional non-verbal behaviours or lose track of the conversation we are trying to hold. You can test this out by trying to change one aspect of your non-verbal behaviour that you know you do a lot and see what happens when you are talking to someone whilst trying to make your behaviour different. Even though it is hard, it may still be worth trying to change aspects of our non-verbal behaviour that seem to have a deleterious effect on the way we get on with other people.

Regulating conversations

When we meet and talk with other people we do, on the whole, manage to do this quite smoothly. It is the use of non-verbal behaviours that regulates our conversations and encounters with other people. We encourage others to speak by keeping quiet when they are talking, looking at them and smiling or making small vocalizations. Similarly, we signal our intention to begin talking by, perhaps, fidgeting a bit, looking more frequently, beginning to talk and so on. We know when people have asked us a question by the inflection in their voice, and we know when they are thinking about what they want to say next by the way they sound, any "uhmms" and other noises they make and the pattern of their gaze. In other words, we have learnt to manage conversations often without knowing it. Each of us is following subtle rules of holding conversations. If one or other of us breaks these rules the conversation temporarily breaks down – there is either silence or both of us talk at once. We do not always get it right: we may misread the non-verbal cues and begin to talk before the other person has finished. We may not have been listening sufficiently well to realize that we are now expected to answer a question or begin to talk.

The extent to which we use the range of non-verbal cues to manage conversations can be seen when we hold a telephone conversation. Here, we only have the vocal cues available, all the rest are missing. Most of us experience more breakdowns in conversations on the phone than we do in face-to-face conversations. In the telephone conversation, both parties are limited in the non-verbal behaviours available to them. Sometimes one person has more non-verbal information than the other. See what happens if you hold a conversation with a friend when one of you is blindfolded. Usually, the person that has all the non-verbal information begins to talk more and to dominate the conversation. The same thing happens if one person uses long silences – quickly the other person will begin to dominate the conversation.

This is what happens in many conversations with people with learning disabilities; certainly, those who may be visually impaired or hard of hearing will take a less active part in conversations with people who do not have such impairments. Professionals talking to people who talk slowly or indistinctly, or who do not use much eye contact, will usually dominate the conversation. Many a conversation of this sort results quickly in a distorted pattern of interaction, wherein the professional asks question after question and the person with the learning disability is reduced to one word answers and a passive part in the conversation.

We have seen how non-verbal behaviours are used to regulate conversation and often relationships. Another function of non-verbal behaviour is in the expression of emotion.

Recognition and expression of emotions

Understanding how other people are feeling and being able to show others how we, ourselves, feel enriches our social lives. The way we recognize other people's feelings is to listen to what they say and, more importantly, to watch what they do. We often decide how people feel by picking up their non-verbal cues. Similarly it is largely non-verbally that we convey how we feel.

It can be useful to think of feelings in terms of six general emotions, within which umpteen other feelings are embedded. This way of categorizing feelings is shown in Table 4.1. Different non-verbal behaviours or combinations convey different emotions, although we probably rely on the face and voice for most of our information. You might like to try and link non-verbal cues with the different feelings as suggested in Exercise 4.4.

You may have felt a bit ridiculous doing Exercise 4.4, but it does highlight the importance of non-verbal behaviours for communicating feelings. In Exercise 4.4 the verbal message was a neutral one (it had no meaning). In many circumstances the verbal messages help us gather the meaning of what it is people are communicating. However, there are also many circumstances where there is no additional verbal message accompanying the non-verbal one.

It is often not the non-verbal behaviours themselves that give us the information we need to understand how someone feels, but the **change** in behaviours. So, even if someone usually looks miserable, we can tell when they are feeling miserable because of how their expression has changed. The addition of non-verbal behaviours often tells us something about the strength of feelings people have: we know if people are angry because of how their voices and facial expressions change; we know they are getting angrier if they begin to wave their arms about or stamp their feet. The opposite is true of people who are sad: increasing stillness of their body tells us their misery is increasing. In other words, whilst face and voice tell us about the main feeling, other non-verbal behaviours modify that feeling.

Table 4.1 General and specific emotions (from Kagan, Evans and Kay, 1986). Kagan, C., Evans, J. and Kay, B. (1986) *A Manual of Interpersonal Skills for Nurses: An experiential approach*. London: Harper and Row

Angry	Happy	Sad	Afraid	Disgusted	Surprised/ interested
annoyed	pleased	sorry	anxious	shocked	curious
enraged	satisfied	hurt	alarmed	sickened	amazed
irritated	relieved	disappointed	worried	contemptuous	fascinated
frustrated	thrilled	regretful	confused		intrigued

Exercise 4.4 Expression and recognition of emotions

This exercise can be done with a friend or in front of a mirror. Choose one of the emotions from Table 4.1. Say the alphabet through, trying to express that emotion, increasing the strength of the feeling as you go through the alphabet. Note down, or get your friend to note down, the non-verbal cues that were used to express the emotion and the strength of feeling. Do the same for all the different general emotions.

Feeling	Non-verbal cues	Cues to strength of feeling	Comments
Anger			
Happiness			
Sadness			
Fear			
Disgust			
Surprise/interest			

What different cues were used to express (a) feelings and (b) strength of feeling? Were any of the feelings particularly difficult to convey? Why is this? Were any of the feelings particularly easy to convey? Why is this? What is the relative importance of non-verbal and verbal cues to feelings? Are there any particular cues that "leak" real feelings? How important is culture for the ease of expression and recognition of emotion?

Tanya has very few facial expressions, so people who do not know her well find it difficult to know what she is feeling. People who know her well, however, know that her flapping of her left hand is a clue to how she is responding to a situation. Flapping always means that she is excited, but if her hand is flapped near to her body she is usually anxious or upset, while flapping further from her body indicates a happy state.

On the whole we do not go around expressing just how we feel whenever we feel it. In Western society a great deal is made of the need to control our emotions, or at least the expression of them. We are mostly quite good at controlling our facial and vocal cues, but may give ourselves away as other non-verbal behaviours "leak" our feelings. When we wring our hands or wriggle our feet, whilst in other respects appearing calm, people may think we are "really" nervous. We may be, but these so-called "leakages" may not reveal any particular feeling, they may just be non-verbal habits we have.

If we think about it, we probably know when it is appropriate to show what feelings and to whom. We know the social rules about displaying emotions. These "display rules" are linked to culture and to different roles, and part of socialization is to learn these rules so that we know which feelings are allowed or even expected in which situation and how these feelings should be shown. At a wedding, for example, we should feel joy; we can express this joy by laughing or by crying. Even if we feel really glad that a colleague is leaving work, we also know that we should not show it. Most of these rules we pick up automatically, although some are taught to us directly ("You are too big to be cross because your younger sister has taken your toy."), and some we discover by making mistakes that cause us some embarrassment. The rules by which we know how to express what we feel are linked to the culture but also to the particular situation, and depend in part on who else is present. It is useful to consider whether there are any (a) social roles and (b) social situations in which it would be inappropriate to show anger, sadness, fear, joy, interest or disgust, and Exercise 4.5 provides this opportunity.

Exercise 4.5 demonstrates that many times we control what we feel because we do not want to look silly in front of people, our roles demand it or the situations we are in demand it and so on. Feelings that we have towards other people are also communicated non-verbally.

Recognition and expression of feelings towards people

As with the general emotions, we recognize and communicate our feelings about other people more by what we do than by what we say. In fact, in our everyday lives we do not often tell other people exactly how we feel about them, but they may well know.

Exercise 4.5 Display rules and the expression of emotion

Consider each of the general emotions in the chart below in turn, and write down (a) any social roles in which it would be inappropriate to display that feeling and (b) any social situations in which it would be inappropriate to display that feeling. Try to say why it would be inappropriate. Now repeat the exercise with a person or people with learning disabilities in mind.

Feeling	*Inappropriate role*	*Reasons for being inappropriate*
Anger		
Sadness		
Fear		
Happiness		
Disgust		
Interest/surprise		

Feeling	*Inappropriate situation*	*Reasons for being inappropriate*
Anger		
Sadness		
Fear		
Happiness		
Disgust		
Interest/surprise		

What kinds of reasons did you find for the inappropriate expression of emotions? Are the same "display rules" applied to people with learning disabilities as to the rest of us? Why or why not? What is the importance of the context for the expression of emotions? How do we learn "display rules" for the expression of emotion? What happens to (a) us and (b) people with learning disabilities if these "display rules" are broken?

We can think of our feelings towards other people as being characterized by two central dimensions, along which we can put a whole host of other feelings. These central dimensions are **friendly/warm** – **hostile/cold** and **dominant/superior** – **submissive/inferior**. In other words, we relate to other people in terms of both liking or affiliation and status. Other feelings we may have might be combinations of these two things. Interestingly, most of us are better at knowing when other people like us, than when they dislike us. This may be because, as with the general emotions, there are powerful social rules ("display rules" again) that guide what messages we give to whom and in what circumstances. There is pressure on us not to show our dislike of other people too overtly. No single non-verbal behaviour relates to a particular feeling about other people; rather it is different clusters of non-verbal behaviours that convey different amounts of liking or relative status.

Both the communication of feelings towards other people and the interpretation we make of how other people feel towards us is culturally and subculturally based. This can lead to misunderstandings and jumping to wrong conclusions about what people feel towards us. So, for example, if we did not know that a particular person had been brought up to be shy with strangers, we might think the person was being unfriendly or did not like us. Similarly, if we did not know that people in a particular part of the country always hugged people on meeting them, we might well be bemused at the over-familiarity with which we were being treated.

We have discussed the role non-verbal behaviours play in self-presentation, regulating conversations, communicating feelings in general and about other people in particular. However, as we have said, non-verbal behaviour most usually occurs alongside speech.

Speech

When we talk to other people we are also communicating non-verbally. Furthermore, we usually take a lot of social knowledge for granted, and our words only make sense within a given, well-defined social situation, group or role relationship. Conversations only make sense if we share social knowledge with the other people involved. To clarify what we mean by shared social knowledge, try Exercise 4.6.

**Exercise 4.6 The importance of
shared understanding in speech**

Record (transcribe) a short conversation from a television programme, real life or from a book. Look at the conversation sentence by sentence and ask yourself:

What does the listener already need to know in order to make sense of this sentence?

What does the speaker assume on the part of the listener when she or he speaks?

What kinds of prior knowledge are assumed in the conversation (knowledge about each other, about tasks or activities, about social attitudes, etc.)? How would you know the conversation has taken place (a) between these two people; (b) in this country at this time; (c) in this situation?

You will probably find the list of things known outside the conversation itself is long. Each sentence alone conveys only a very small part of the total knowledge required in the conversation. In using language to communicate, not only do we take for granted a wealth of shared social understanding, we also know what to say to whom, when, where and how. We could look at speech in terms of its order and structure (grammar), in terms of the ways patterns of sounds are put together, or in terms of the meanings of words and phrases. It is, however, probably more useful for us, in the context of social skills, competence and capability, to look at the ways speech is used in social situations.

Speech arises out of and develops in the context of social interaction. Long before we can actually speak, we have learnt to communicate our wishes and feelings to others and to interact. Not only does language enable us to communicate to other people, it also provides the means whereby we think.

Language, thought and experience

With speech we can convey our internal private worlds externally to other people. This enables us to share experiences and to be a part of the cultures in which we live. Language and culture are closely linked: the way we name and categorize things reflects our way of seeing the world; the labels we have for things influence how we see them and, thereby, how we think. Thus it is difficult for us to disentangle inner speech (thoughts) from external speech (social communication). The two are mutually dependent.

The situation is further complicated by our experiences, many of which will be cultural. So, for example, it used to be uncommon in Britain for anyone other than close family members to call each other by their first names. Most people called each other Mr this or Mrs that – they addressed each other formally, however long they had known each other. One result of this was that most social encounters were conducted far more formally than nowadays, and people described themselves as having fewer friends than we might now. Not only do people talking at different points in history think differently about their worlds, but so do people who speak different languages. Since we understand things largely in terms of the labels we have for them, people who speak different languages (and thereby have different labels available to them) may well experience their worlds differently.

This issue is at the heart of the debates about how to refer to people with learning disabilities. The argument goes in part like this: if we continue to use terms like "the mentally handicapped", we come to see people in terms of their handicap. In our culture "handicap" means unable to do things and "mental" means stupid or mad. This will frame how we think of people as not only different from ourselves but also negatively, in terms of how society at large values them. Implicit in the debate is the understanding that language and thought are intertwined, and also that language reflects cultural priorities. The assumption is that if we change the labels we use to describe different groups of people we change how we think, and eventually we may alter the cultural importance of the differences themselves.

Addressing people we meet

Cultural and historical factors help define status differences between people as well as levels of intimacy, so we generally address people of higher status more formally than those equal or inferior in status to us. (Nearly everyone we have referred to in this book has been referred to by their first names only – what messages does this give you about them and the authors' relationships with them?) Similarly, we address people we know well more informally. If we get it wrong and address people of higher status too informally we may be looked on as presumptuous or "too big for our boots". On the other hand, we may be thought of as snooty or cold and unfriendly if we address people we know well formally.

To see how complicated these issues are, think about the parents of your spouse, boyfriend or girlfriend. When you first get to know them you may call them Mr and Mrs as a mark of respect. As you get to know their son or daughter more intimately, at what point do you acknowledge the change in relationship with their parents? Many of us go for years avoiding calling our parents-in-law anything at all, in case we are thought too forward or too rude. It can be quite unnerving if, after 20 years of marriage and avoiding calling them anything, we suddenly have to write to them – how do we start the letter? This type of situation is made much easier if the parents-in-law would tell us what they want us to call them. Even this, though, is not without its problems. If they tell us to call them by their first names as soon as we start dating their son or daughter, we may feel they are trying to push us into a closer relationship. If they insist we call them Mr and Mrs we may feel offended and kept at a distance. The point about forms of address is that they help define the nature of our relationships as well as our interactions with each other.

Elizabeth Williams is in her seventies. She has recently been resettled from the long stay hospital in which she has lived for the past 40 years to a small-group home near her niece in a nearby village. Staff in the house have great difficulty managing Lizzie: contrary to all the reports from the hospital which described her as easygoing and tolerant, Lizzie flies off the handle whenever she is spoken to and keeps ordering the staff to "show some respect".

At Lizzie's programme planning meeting, which her niece attended, house staff, the district development manager and the community nurse were discussing how they might work differently and more constructively with Lizzie. Lizzie sat grumpily throughout the meeting. At one point, Lizzie's niece asked why they were calling her "Lizzie", as she had never been called this in her life. Close family and friends called her "Elizabeth" and everyone else has always called her "Miss Williams". It emerged that a hospital social worker had introduced Elizabeth as Lizzie, and no one had thought to question it. Most of the so-called management difficulties turned out to be because Miss Williams was annoyed at the nickname she had been given.

We also find that staff often get the names of members of minority communities wrong, in writing or in pronunciation. What does this suggest?

Just as there can be strict social rules that we follow when deciding on forms of address in certain situations, so there are rules to conversations more generally.

Rules of conversation

A great deal of what we say is in accordance with rules. These rules, which may be explicit (clearly stated) or implicit (assumed), determine the level of detail we go into, the content of what we actually say, the style in which we speak and the order of different bits of speech. Some rules govern different types of conversations, whereas others are specific to particular situations and roles. Think about any informal conversation; how do we know how to manage it? What are the rules we are following? General rules that govern most conversations include the following:

- each person has the chance to talk;
- only one person talks at a time;
- gaps between utterances are brief;
- the order of speaking is not fixed in advance;
- utterances follow other rules of relevance, such as
  - question – answer;
  - statement – acknowledgement;
  - offer – acceptance or refusal;
  - apology – acknowledgement or rejection.

If either of us breaks these rules, the conversation will break down even if only temporarily, as illustrated in Exercise 4.7.

Are some conversations more likely than others to break down because rules are broken? Are some types of relationships more prone to conversations breaking down than others? How did age difference affect the conversation rules? Are the rules of conversation the same for both partners in the above examples? If not, how do they differ? What difference might the context in which the conversations took place make to the rules underlying them?

Exercise 4.7 Rules of conversation

Choose a conversation from the list below and write the rules underlying it on a piece of paper. Repeat this for all the conversations. Now look at the conversations again and consider if the rules are the same if one person is 20 years older than the other.

Conversations:

- ☐ asking a person with learning disabilities what it is she or he would like to do at the weekend;

- ☐ talking to a colleague who has been assaulted at work;

- ☐ comforting someone you know well who has been bereaved;

- ☐ suggesting to a client where he or she might buy some elastic;

- ☐ explaining to a client why she or he should not kiss a waitress good-bye;

- ☐ talking to parents about their surprise and happiness at the different things their son or daughter has been able to do recently.

Sometimes, just listening to what is said may lead us to think the conversation has broken down and rules have been broken. So, if a person with a learning disability says to her care assistant "Can I put my coat on?" and the carer replies "Today is Friday", it would appear that a rule of relevance has been broken. However, if we know, as both of them know, that on Fridays they do not go out but instead do housework, the conversation makes more sense. This is because both of these people have a shared understanding about the context in which the question was asked that we, as outsiders, do not have. This highlights the importance of the context in which conversations take place in order to fully understand them.

Role, social groups and speech

Factors determining what we say and how we say it, then, depend in large part on the situation, the roles of the people talking and the rules associated with them. The more formal the situation, the greater the constraints on who says what to whom. Weddings, committees and so on are examples of formal situations with predetermined roles and rules of speech. One way of thinking about these regular patterns of speech, that are the same whoever is actually taking part in the conversation, is to see them as rituals.

The type of speech we adopt is linked, too, to the roles we play in a particular situation and the extent of shared understanding between ourselves and those to whom we are talking. We can distinguish between different language codes that we use in different situations and in different roles. The more shared understanding there is between us and the people we are talking to, the more likely it is that we will converse in a restricted code, making it difficult for anyone who does not share our knowledge to understand what we are talking about. If, however, we are talking to people with whom we assume little in the way of shared prior knowledge or understanding, we may use an elaborated code. With an elaborated code we explain terms more fully and do not use short cuts, such as "take it over there". We explain what we would like to be taken where. The more we share experiences and understanding with people, the more we are likely to talk in restricted codes (restricted to those who share this understanding or knowledge).

Restricted codes help us define different social groups. We can ensure people are welcomed as members of our group or excluded from it by the way we talk. Those who are familiar with the language being used are "in" and those who are not are "out". Language, therefore, can be used to define and reinforce the separate identity of a social group to which we belong. Jargon is a good example of a restricted code. We can happily discuss "packages of care", for example, with colleagues from the health and social care fields without the risk that they will think we are talking about a parcel to post. We can discuss "case assessment" with the same colleagues whilst being pretty sure they will not think we are talking about how a suitcase will stand up to air travel. In the same vein, when we use language like this in an individual review (**not** a one-woman stage show), to which we invite people with learning disabilities and their families, we are in danger of excluding them from meaningful participation from the start. By the same token, if we **want** to avoid any meaningful participation, then an effective strategy might be to talk in professional jargon throughout!

The use of restricted codes – even jargon – is not always bad. As we have seen, they build on shared understanding between people, and can therefore economize on what is said. They can also help strengthen a sense of social identity. Restricted codes do not always use specialist terms or phrases, and they can also assume a great deal of understanding. Take this example of a conversation between a mother and her son who has learning disabilities.

MOTHER: I see it's there again?
SON: Yes, she told me it would be, even if I carried on doing it.
MOTHER: We should start again and this time do it as it says.
SON: Yes. He will be pleased if it goes.

This is an "insider" conversation or one that is using a restricted code. For all we know they could be talking about weeds in the garden, frogs in the pond, decorating the hall – anything in fact. Furthermore, they could be referring to any number of different people. What do you think they are talking about? Why do you think this?

Clearly, if we do not understand a restricted code (and restricted codes do not have to be expressed through language, they can also be non-verbal), we can be confused and feel excluded. Another way in which we can be confused in a conversation is when people talk in ways that could mean more than one thing.

Meaning

In any conversation there can be a mismatch between what we meant when we said a certain thing and what other people take to be our meaning. In just about any thing we say there are surface (manifest) and hidden (latent) meanings. The total message picked up by other people is often the hidden meaning. The situation is made even more complicated because we often **want** other people to pick up the hidden meaning and not the surface one. The way we use language in social encounters depends on this. When we ask someone "Do you want beans or fish for tea?" we may want to know which of the two things is wanted. We also want to convey that there is only either beans or fish for tea, and probably also that we are getting the tea, but we say none of these things. The hidden meaning is acknowledged if the reply is "Fish. Thanks". If, however, we had said "There is beans or fish for tea", we may have been meaning "Please will you cook tea tonight". If the answer is "Fish", that is essentially saying "I am not cooking". Even if the intention was not to give the message that the person is not cooking, we might take it as such and say, in reply to "Fish", "Why is it I'm always the one to cook" (probably meaning "You never cook"), and so it goes on.

Steve used to get very upset at his Social Education Centre. At these times he would lash out, bite, throw things and scream. The staff used to restrain him by forcing him to the floor and then immobilizing his limbs until he was still. Over the months they found that at these times they could simply ask him to lie on the floor, and so long as he had not become too upset he would comply.

Later, a physiotherapist was running a relaxation class for Steve and three others. To help Steve become more fully relaxed he was asked to lie on the floor. Steve became extremely tense and the session was abandoned. Steve knew that he was not in a disturbed state and understood the physiotherapist's request in terms of the restricted code he had learned before. He was upset by what he took to be an unjust suggestion about his behaviour. The physiotherapist did not know about the special meaning that "lie on the floor" had for Steve.

With all this potential for misunderstanding, it is a wonder we can ever get on with other people at all! Certainly, to get on with other people means that as far as possible we have to relate to each other on the same level of meaning. The only way we will really know how what we have said has been taken is to see how other people react to us. Just to know we have made a joke tells us nothing unless people laugh.

We have seen that the use of particular styles and codes of language can both reflect relationships between us and others and create particular kinds of relationships. Also that regular patterns of speech can be seen as rituals. The more ritualistic speech is, the less meaning it has – after all it is just part of the ritual. Meaning, however, is complicated and a source of great misunderstanding. Despite this, there are some rituals whose meanings are important because they set the tone of the encounter to follow. These are greetings and farewells.

Greetings and farewells

We have called greetings and farewells rituals because in one form or another they occur over and over again in different situations and with different people. We set the tone of our relationships and particular interactions by the way we open a conversation. When we greet or open a conversation with other people we create certain expectations about what is to follow. This may be due to how we speak, for example whether we are cheery or miserable, or it may be something about how we have arranged the room or the situation – a quiet room with comfortable chairs and no telephone may give a particular message to the person who has come for a supervision session, whereas inviting them in to a crowded office with lots of other people present will give a very different message if the purpose is still ostensibly supervision.

When we open an encounter we may be doing any of a number of things, including attracting and gaining other people's attention; making some kind of statement about our relationship with them; establishing rapport; arousing motivation or interest in others; finding out what the others expect from the situation; making links with previous conversations; finding out how much the others know about something; setting out the purpose of the meeting; or explaining our own reasons for being there. If we get the opening ritual wrong, the whole encounter might proceed badly.

In order to see how we use different types of opening ritual or greetings for different purposes, complete Exercise 4.8.

Similar issues arise when we consider parting or closure rituals. They can be just as varied as openings and can set the tone for the next meeting or conversation we have with people. You might like to think how you might close the conversations you opened in Exercise 4.8. What functions would you hope your closures would serve?

Both opening and closing rituals, as well as conversations in which different meanings can be taken, involve non-verbal behaviour as well as speech. In part, how we interpret conversations depends on the **way** things are said, and the different non-verbal behaviours we use. Nevertheless, we have seen that the context, including cultural and role contexts, as well as the situations we find ourselves in also determines what we say and how it is interpreted. Before we go on to look at aspects of observation and

---

Exercise 4.8 Greeting rituals

Describe as fully as you can appropriate greetings and openings for the following interactions:

☐ welcoming a person with learning disabilities to your day centre for the first time;

☐ meeting a parent who wants to lodge a complaint about some aspect of your work;

☐ a pre-arranged meeting with a friend who is upset about something that has happened at home;

☐ being asked to go to see your manager but not knowing why;

☐ opening a training workshop involving experienced professionals;

☐ passing a person with learning disabilities who is weeping silently.

It is likely that you have identified different kinds of openings for these different situations. What would you be trying to do in the different situations? In other words, what function would you hope your opening would serve? What is the relative importance of physical setting, non-verbal behaviour and speech for effective interaction openings? How easy is it to recover from misunderstood interaction openings?

---

interpretation in social situations, we would like to briefly consider one particular form of speech that can help or mar social situations, namely questions.

Questions

We use questions in lots of different ways and for different purposes. The proverbial "Do you come here often?" is a question being used as a conversation opening (also a chat-up line!). We use questions to find out about people and to get to know them better. Questions used in this way can demonstrate our interest in other people and help us show them they are interesting people. We use questions to find out what people know, and this can be experienced as threatening and challenging. We also use questions to order people about and to get them to do certain things. In one sense questions are always a form of control (think back to the section on rules of conversations; questions require answers), but this control can vary in its intensity. If we use questions inappropriately, we may be thought of as nosy, rude and demanding.

We use questions for different purposes in different situations. The reasons we question our teenage daughter about her whereabouts when she comes in will be different from the reasons we question a colleague's whereabouts when coming back from a union meeting or a manager returning from a budget meeting and so on. In all these situations we may want to know who else was there, what they said and did, what the person did and so on, but the purpose and hidden meanings will be different.

We use different kinds of questions, too, to get different kinds of information. Factual information is best obtained by using closed questions ("What time did you finish?" "Was Jane there?"). Closed questions do not encourage a great deal of talk from the other person – they usually imply short, factual replies. Open questions will usually generate more information, but can put pressure on people to say things they would prefer not to ("Tell me about it?" "What happened then?"). Nevertheless, open questions are particularly good if we want to get the other person's own version of events.

We often use multiple questions that cause a great deal of confusion. Multiple questions are those asked in quick succession, which may or may not be closely related and do not give people a chance to reply ("Did you go straight there or did Jane take you or did a crowd of you go?"). The main problem with multiple questions is that the other people do not know to which one they should reply and they may feel bombarded, as if they are being interrogated. If we want to make people feel uncomfortable and inferior, a good way of doing this is by asking a lot of questions, particularly multiple questions.

Once again, the use of questions and the meaning they have depends on the situation we are in and the role we have. The way other people respond to our questioning will give us some clue as to how they have interpreted it. If we are to be sensitive to the impact of any aspect of our social behaviour, we must be able to observe and make sense of or interpret other people's responses and social behaviour.

OBSERVATION AND INTERPRETATION

In order to be socially skilled, we must be able to observe, interpret, and understand correctly the situations we are in and the people we are with. More than this, we have to be able to predict other people's likely behaviour in particular situations. The perception of situations and of people is one of the most complex tasks we are faced with and yet one that is often overlooked in efforts to help people with learning disabilities become more socially competent. Whilst observation and interpretation can sometimes be usefully separated, we usually make interpretations as we observe and base further observations on what we interpret. We will illustrate this in a number of ways throughout the section. Before we go on, you might like to try Exercise 4.9 and distinguish between observation and interpretation for yourself.

The perception of situations helps us know what should be going on in a particular situation, how we should be behaving and how others are likely to behave. So, for instance, different behaviours are expected of people in a cafe from those in a theatre, in a shopping street from in our sitting-room and so on. We must first perceive other people before we can relate meaningfully to them – if we mistake the person delivering the post for the person who delivers the milk, we may try and pay the wrong person for the milk; if we confuse our boss for our friend we may try to be too intimate and get rebuffed. Furthermore, in any interaction with other people, we are constantly monitoring their reactions and adjusting our thoughts and feelings about them. If we did not do this we would not be able to pick up that our friend wanted to go, or that the shopkeeper was waiting for a reply to her question, or that a particular relationship was becoming more intimate. We have talked above about how non-verbal behaviours lead us to form impressions about people when we first meet them; this impression formation is a part of the observation and interpretation of others.

Exercise 4.9 Observation of social behaviour

Watch people in different social situations and make notes about what you see and hear according to the chart.

	The setting	What you saw and heard (i.e. what you observed)	What this meant (i.e. how you interpreted what you saw and heard)	How the setting influenced behaviour	How you felt as an observer
A person alone					
Two people in the same place but not together					
Two people talking to each other					
A group of people interacting together					
A group of people which includes yourself					

Was it easier to observe non-verbal behaviour than speech? Did you have any difficulty separating observation from interpretation? If so, why might this be? What differences in observation were there between the different scenarios? How easy is it to observe when you are part of the group? How might some of these difficulties be overcome?

When we observe and interpret objects in the physical world, such as a table, house, bowl of spaghetti or a tree, we are generally paying attention to surface characteristics like size, colour, texture and smell. If we are unsure of what we have seen or heard, we can go back and check – it is unlikely to have changed in the interim. Some aspects of perceiving people are similar. We use height and size or sound of voice, in part, to determine someone's age or sex. Beyond this, we are mainly concerned with characteristics that cannot be directly seen, touched, heard or smelt. Characteristics like personality, likeability, attitudes, interests and role cannot be directly observed. Instead they must be inferred. This is what makes perception of people so much harder than perception of things, and why we make more mistakes in making judgements about people. It is also why observation and interpretation are so closely linked. When we make judgements about people we are rarely, if ever, unbiased observers: we have pre-existing feelings, attitudes and ways of understanding the social world that influence our observations and judgements from the start. Things are made more complex because any two people are likely to think differently about the same other people, to perceive them differently. Even so, there will be some aspects of observing and interpreting other people that we do share, and that form a sound basis for further judgements about them and for knowing what is expected of us and of them in any situation.

It is similar with the perception of situations. Whilst there are some physical aspects of the situation that are relatively easy to identify, such as size of room, furnishings, numbers of people present, heat and so on, there are also social aspects of situations that have to be understood and that are open to many different interpretations. Judging the purpose of a particular situation requires us to make inferences about what the situation means to us and to others: a medium-sized room with four chairs round a table may be for the purpose of eating (a dining room) or holding a meeting (a committee room) – the physical layout may be the same but the social purpose is different. We will look at the perception of situations in more detail when we consider the importance of context, below. Here we will concentrate on the perception of people.

Noticing and attending

Before we can make any judgements about who people are, why they are here and doing what they do, we must notice them and pay attention to particular characteristics.

Lucy is 53 and she lives quite independently, doing her own shopping, including that for clothes. She likes modern fashions and is currently wearing what 18-year olds are wearing. Only when asked to notice what people of different ages wear does she realize that she might stand out as strange.

Brian is quiet although he would love to talk more with some of his colleagues at the supermarket where he works. In fact they would like to talk more with him, but when they create opportunities for him to speak he seems to miss them.

Gary goes to football matches with a friend. When he was buying a battery at an electrical shop he saw part of a match on TV and cheered when a goal was scored.

Lucy had not noticed how her peers dressed or the age of the people who wear the clothes she admired. Brian does not notice the signs people give when it is his turn to speak, nor does he notice when they are more directly showing an interest in him as a person. Gary's cheering was appropriate to a football match but he had not realized that people do not behave that way in shops. In each case the person failed to observe the social behaviour of others.

As you go about your daily business, try to think about what it is that you notice about people you pass or meet for the first time. Some of the first things we notice about people are usually their sex and their approximate age group. We then know immediately whether they are similar or dissimilar to ourselves in important ways. Even at this stage we may assume things that are incorrect about them. Having observed that a person is male and middle-aged, and we know ourselves to be male and young, we may assume we share some things and cannot share others. We may or may not be correct in our assumptions. Nevertheless, age and sex gives us a way of locating people in the social world. We can see how disturbing it is not to be able to tell someone's sex when we overhear people saying, with indignation "Is that a girl or a boy. It's impossible to tell nowadays". Implicit in this statement is the knowledge that it is socially important to be able to tell. If the first thing we noticed about people was the colour of their shoes, we would be able to assume very little else about them. For most of us, colour of shoes is not useful social information.

If we do not observe and pay attention to people in the first place, we cannot go on to understand them or relate to them in meaningful ways. However, the sense we make of our observations may be quite idiosyncratic.

Implicit personality theories

We all bring pre-existing ideas about people and experiences of other people to bear on new social encounters. These ideas include our understanding about which characteristics go with which other characteristics: we might think that people who are tall and thin are intelligent, witty, understanding and helpful, therefore as soon as we meet a tall thin person we assume they are as we know tall thin people to be. However, others of us may think that tall thin people are bad tempered, boring, sarcastic and critical, so when we meet the same tall thin people we make different judgements about them. We may even notice different things: those of us that have the first implicit personality theory about tall thin people will have noticed how intelligent, witty, helpful and understanding the person was; those of us with the second will on the contrary, have picked up the bad temper, boredom, sarcasm and criticism. Different things will have been noticed and different interpretations made, even though both groups saw and heard the same person doing the same things.

Sometimes our implicit personality theories include characteristics that we think we, ourselves, possess, at other times they include opposite characteristics to those we hold ourselves. Generally, we form implicit personality theories from characteristics that have relevance for us. So, for example, some of us may think social class is important and make quick judgements about people's class when we meet them, while others will think friendliness important and make judgements about this and so on. If people remind us of other people we know or have known, we may assume they are like this other person in terms of their characteristics. We each have our own preferences, likes and dislikes in other people, and these contribute to the development of our implicit personality theories. We may have adopted certain beliefs about others from, for example, our parents or teachers, and these may also be incorporated into our implicit personality theories.

Exercise 4.10 provides you with the opportunity to explore your implicit personality theories.

What we are doing when we use implicit personality theories is two-fold. Firstly, we are cutting down on the enormous amount of social information that we could pick up when meeting people, and secondly we are categorizing them in some way, again in

Exercise 4.10 Implicit personality theories

You can explore your own implicit personality theories in two ways. You could discuss with someone you know well how you think you usually make judgements about people, then have your friend tell you how she or he thinks you form judgements about people. The other way (and perhaps more fun) is to think about someone you know a little at work, perhaps someone who works in another team, in the canteen, or is a tutor on a course. With a friend, if possible (so you can see the amount of overlap or otherwise in what you think of the person), try to estimate the following about that person:

age

background

personality

beliefs, values and attitudes

interests

lifestyle (type of house, diet, marital status, children, etc.).

Talk with your friend about how you arrived at your judgements, and discuss the amount of overlap and difference between your perceptions.

How much of what you judged about the person was based on fact or prior knowledge? How much did you and your friend agree on things you did not know, as facts? Why did you or did you not agree on these things? Can you identify any implicit personality theories you or your friend used in doing this exercise? What were the origins of your implicit personality theories?

order to economize on the amount of information that could be available. If we did not do this, we could not cope with the vast amount of information that is available as we meet so many people in so many situations on a daily basis. When people say "I treat everyone as an individual – I don't make any assumptions about them before I know them properly", treat this with some suspicion. We could not suspend all previous knowledge and understanding and still manage to form relationships with people as there would be just too much information for us to interpret.

Implicit personality theories are, then, one way in which we categorize information about other people. Stereotypes are another.

Stereotypes

Stereotypes are generalized statements about things. We all use stereotypes to help us organize and understand our social worlds. This process of stereotyping requires us to categorize things, attribute characteristics to the category, and then infer that all members of the category share the characteristics by virtue of belonging to that category. We can hold stereotypes about situations (meetings are boring; this is a meeting therefore it will be boring), things (detached houses are clean and tidy inside; this is a detached house so it will be clean and tidy), people (middle-aged women are considerate; this is a middle aged woman so she will be considerate), roles (greengrocers are funny; this is a greengrocer so she or he will be funny) – about anything in fact.

It is unlikely we could do without stereotypes, but it is important to realize that they are not necessarily true in any sense. Some stereotypes may be widely held and are culturally based (British people are unemotional; football supporters are violent; women are caring). Others are more personally held (people who drive wearing hats are unpredictable), and then are very similar to implicit personality theories. Stereotypes are not necessarily a bad thing as they can give a good starting point for understanding other people. However, because they could be wrong, they may lead to distortions in how we see others. If we are aware of our own stereotypes or the extent to which we succumb to cultural stereotypes, we can then test them out and modify our judgements as necessary.

Stereotypes that are linked to roles can lead to the process of labelling.

Labelling

When we hold expectations about other people's behaviour, attitudes, beliefs, character, etc. by virtue of the role they play, labelling may occur. The labelling process is as follows: a role is identified and given a label in terms of personal characteristics; people are identified who occupy that role; they are then assumed to possess the characteristics. We expect the **person** to possess the characteristics of the **role**. If these expectations of role are widespread, the person may become labelled and may begin to behave according to the expectations and adopt the characteristics assigned to the role. It can be difficult to break away from the label.

Any role can be labelled, whether is it a formal or an informal one. Take for example the care assistant who has always been willing to swap rotas at short notice and therefore gets many requests for last minute changes. The more this care assistant is labelled **willing colleague**, the more difficult it will be to break away from this role. Labelling not only leads us to make inferences about what people will or will not do, it can lead to a self-fulfilling prophecy whereby we expect people to behave in particular ways and they end up doing so. You can see for yourself the power of labelling linked to role when you consider how you knew what to do when you started your present job. Do you behave differently at work from at home – if so, why is this?

One of the things that links implicit personality theories, stereotypes and labelling is expectation. When we meet people we expect them to be like this or do that. The other thing that links the three processes is a tendency for us to look for consistency in our judgements about other people.

Consistency

In many different spheres of our social lives we seem to try to maintain consistency. This is particularly so when we make social judgements. Having once thought of a person as easy to get on with, it would take a lot of contradictory instances to make us change our minds. This is why, although we like to think of ourselves as open-minded when we meet people, first impressions tend to stick. What seems to happen is that when we pick up information that contradicts what we first thought, we explain it away. So the person we thought was easy to get on with could be obstinate and unfriendly the next few times we meet. We may well assume the person has had a bad day, is preoccupied with something or is not feeling well. We come up with all sorts of things so that our initial judgements can stand and we still see the person as easy to get on with.

It has been suggested that we tend to group other people's characteristics around either "warm" or "cold". Once we have judged people to be "warm" (or something positive that is associated with warmth), we tend not to change our minds and to reconsider them to be "cold", The converse also holds true: once we have judged someone to be "cold", we do not change our minds easily to think of them as "warm".

Once we have made some preliminary judgements about people in terms of their "warmth" or "coldness", our subsequent perceptions of them may become distorted as we strive to be consistent in our judgements. We operate what can be called a "halo effect". We generalize our perceptions of other people from our first impressions. A danger here, again, is that we may be incorrect in our generalizations but not see this. We can develop strong expectations about what other people will be like and this can result in a self-fulfilling prophecy that they will be like this. Some of the ways we generalize around key characteristics when we form judgements about other people is again due to the personal relevance of these characteristics.

Personal relevance

We are extremely selective in what we notice about other people. Some of this selection may be due to the categories we use to understand other people or our urge to be consistent in judgements. We will also perceive those characteristics that have personal significance, especially those characteristics with which we can identify and judge to be similar to our own. Thus when we meet people who share our values, attitudes, beliefs or are similar in some other important way, we may well judge them more positively than we might do otherwise. This is, in effect, another version of the "halo effect" in operation. When we meet other people for the first time, we often try to find something in common. So if we find people come from our home town we may feel more positively disposed towards them – unless of course we hated our home town and then we may feel more negatively disposed towards them.

Our selective perceptions of other people are often, then, due to the personal relevance of particular characteristics, and can lead to halo effects or other forms of categorization. It is as if we had a framework or schema into which we put our observations and interpretations in order to be able to make sense of them.

Schema

As we grow up and gain experience of other people, we develop our own ways of organizing, interpreting and remembering the plethora of social information to which we are exposed. These frameworks are known as **schema**. We form schema from what we know about ourselves, other people and from our general experience with life. The narrower our experiences, the simpler our schema will be; the more extensive our social experiences, the more complex our schema will be. Once formed, our schema determine both the ease with which new social information is picked up and processed, and the ease with which it is brought to mind.

It is our schema that help us select information about other people in particular social situations. Because all of us have had different social experiences and have developed different schema, we will all notice different things about the same social situation: any five people who visit the same part of a day centre on the same occasion will pick up different things about the people there and about what they were doing and why. Our schema lead us to attend to only some things and not to others; they lead us to categorize what we see or hear differently; they lead us to generalize differently from what we have noticed and so on.

> Wayne has just moved into a flat. The young woman whose flat is opposite his came out at the same time the other day, and as they walked to the bus stop they chatted about the weather and a disaster reported on the TV news. When Wayne got to the drop-in centre he told everyone about his girlfriend in the flat opposite.
>
> Dorothy has just started a work experience placement in a kitchen. Yesterday her supervisor suggested a better way of hold-

ing a knife when cutting up vegetables. Dorothy told her mother that evening that she had been told off at work.

Wayne and Dorothy made misinterpretations that could affect their future interactions with the people concerned. Wayne's misinterpretation might have been due to a lack of knowledge or understanding about the development of relationships or about norms of interaction with neighbours. Dorothy's misinterpretation might have been based on lack of knowledge about the role of a supervisor. Both Wayne and Dorothy may have misinterpreted the other people's intentions because of their experiences (or their lack), expectations, stereotypes, or because of strong personal motives they had.

Not only might we categorize our observations and interpretations differently from other people because of our differing schema, sometimes we can even construct what we see or hear. Our schema lead us to make generalizations that may or may not be correct. We have seen how this can happen in terms of people's characteristics. It can also happen in relation to their behaviour.

Five people visited the day centre. One person was easily frightened by noise, and he noticed that one member of staff was shouting particularly loudly at a group of people with learning disabilities. No one else in the visiting party noticed this. When they discussed their visit afterwards, they were surprised that the first person said he saw several of the people with learning disabilities hitting each other. No one else noticed this. What was going on? There are several alternatives. Firstly, perhaps having noticed the shouting he also picked up the fighting. No one else saw any of this because it was not relevant to them – they would have been concentrating on something else. Secondly, perhaps the visitor noticed the shouting because of the personal relevance noise had for him. Having perceived the member of staff shouting, he interpreted this as due to general affray within the group and this led him to believe he saw some people with learning disabilities fighting, although no such event had occurred. He had constructed this event, not maliciously with an intent to tell lies, but in good faith believing it had happened. What was really happening was that he was generalizing from one thing that he had seen to another that he had not. His schema led him to expect the two things to happen together.

This kind of distortion in perceiving what people do and why, if it happens some time after the actual event can lead to the **reconstruction** of events as if they had happened. This is why eye-witness testimony to accidents or other events is notoriously unreliable – people are convinced they saw things that were not there. Think back to a recent outing with a friend. Talk with each other about what other people were doing, who had been where you were but to whom you had not been particularly paying attention. How similar are your accounts?

What all this shows is that the perception of other people, their characteristics and their behaviours is complicated and open to considerable biases of interpretation. This makes accuracy of observation and interpretation very difficult to achieve. However, it is possible for us to discuss with each other the most likely interpretations of people and their behaviour and to come to some kinds of agreement. If we could not do this, social relationships would be impossible. We can also become more aware of our own biases in observation and interpretation. Lastly, but not least, we can extend the possibilities of observation and interpretation, via expansion of our schema, by gaining more and more experience in a variety of different social situations, by meeting a wide range of different people and getting to understand which of our observations and interpretations are useful to the development of our relationships.

PLAN AND STRATEGY

We have seen that picking up cues from people and situations helps us understand them and leads to more effective relationships. We also need these cues in order to make decisions about how we will respond to others or what we will do in particular situations. In other words, we pick up cues from others, make sense of them and then act in some way. The simplest example of this is during a conversation. If we are talking to friends we look out for cues that tell us they are interested in what we are saying. If we observe them to be looking out of the window or yawning, we may interpret this as boredom. We then have a dilemma. What do we do? Do we carry on talking regardless; stop talking; change the subject; ask them a question in order to get them to start talking; burst into tears or what? In such circumstances we will rapidly go through a problem-solving process whereby we:

- recognize that there is a problem (they do not seem to be interested in what we are saying);

- identify a goal (what we want out of the immediate and per-haps the more long-term situation: this may be in the long term to ensure our friends continue to like us and in the short term to keep them interested);
- think up a number of alternative strategies that may help us achieve our goal (all the things that we could do in the circum-stances);
- ·assess the likely impact of each of the viable alternatives for achieving what we are aiming for;
- decide which one we will try (for example introduce a joke into what we are saying);
- put our strategy into action by saying or doing something (telling the joke in an animated way);
- assess whether or not it had the desired effect (look out for signs that their interest was caught again) and, depending on this, maybe trying a different strategy and so on.

Clearly, in the example we have used this process is very rapid. In other situations, though, we may deliberate more fully on each of the different stages, although we are usually placed in the position of having to make quick decisions once we have worked out what alternatives are available to us. Let us consider each stage in more detail.

Problem recognition

We experience different kinds of problems in different social situ-ations. In the example above we have used a problem within an interaction as illustration. This kind of problem is the stuff of interpersonal relationships. We go through a continual process of picking up cues from other people that lead us to adjust our own behaviour in some way or another. Because we perceive other people inaccurately a lot of the time, we may wrongly define the problem. In the above example, for instance, we may interpret the signals given off by our friends as being that they disagree with what we are saying, or even that they do not like us. Within interactions, the definition of the problem is based on the observa-tion and interpretation of social cues which, as we have seen, is prone to a number of distortions and biases.

More generally, though, we may be faced with other types of social problems. We may not, for example, know what to do in a particular situation: we may go to a new pub for lunch and not be able to work out how food is ordered. In this kind of a situation we will probably more deliberately go through the problem-solving process. However, we may have defined the problem incorrectly: we will never get our lunch if we define the problem as one where, for some reason unknown to us, the bar staff are ignoring us; if we had thought it was table service, we will feel embarrassed to discover we had judged the situation wrongly. Redefining the problem will open up a much wider range of alternative strategies we could use to get our lunch. Part of the way we define the problem in this situation is to watch what other people are doing and then apply this to our own predicament. Once more, our ability to do this depends on our observation skills and the way we interpret what we see happening around us.

Other types of social problems arise even before we get to wherever it is we are going. We may have to try to anticipate how to behave in advance. So, for example, on our first day in a new job we do not know what to wear. We do not know what sort of clothes other people wear. We have to make a best guess at what to wear, bringing to mind all our previous knowledge about types of work situations and suitable clothing.

In order to identify social problems we must be able to distinguish different features of the situation we are in or intending to be in, and match this up with our current knowledge and experience. We must also have a sense of purpose in the situation itself.

Social goals

A sense of purpose implies that we have goals of one sort or another that we are trying to achieve in any social situation. We may have personal goals (what we want out of an immediate situation); interpersonal goals (what we want others to do in a situation); or social goals (what we want in the long term). Not only do we have to have insight into our own motivations and goals, we also need to be able to judge other people's intentions and interests in the situation.

All these goals are closely linked to particular situations. We would be somewhat amiss if we went to the library expecting to be able to buy our vegetables. Similarly we would be off course if we expected a proposal of marriage immediately following our first meeting with someone. Goals have to be appropriate for the situation. They also have to be realistic: it is no good going to buy the television we want if we do not have the money to pay for it. Similarly, we may be ill-advised to expect to strike up an initial friendship with someone with whom we had absolutely nothing in common. Making plans and identifying goals helps us make our time and social relationships more fulfilling.

> Kamal went out. After a walk through the city centre, he caught a bus to the airport. He watched the planes taking off and landing as he had several times before. By now it was dark. He went into the terminal and had a sandwich and coffee. He watched people coming and going, especially the women. He looked around the airport shops and watched people arriving. He went up to watch the planes again and then again wandered around the terminal. He tried to chat to some young women. By now it was late and he had missed his last bus. He lay down on a row of seats. The police picked him up and he had to walk the 8 miles home.

Kamal had time to fill but had no plan for filling it.

Being able to identify a goal or goals does not necessarily mean we know how to achieve them.

Generation of alternative strategies

Those of us that are comfortable in different social situations and can cope with different circumstances as they arise probably have a wide repertoire of strategies we can employ for achieving particular goals. Being able to think of alternative ways of doing things means that we can then choose the one that is likely to be the most effective. Unless we know what could be possible, we will not be able to respond flexibly and do something else if one thing did not work. For example, suppose we have met some people briefly but would like to get to know them better. If we go up to them and say "I would like to get to know you better" and they cold-shoulder us, we will be stumped, unless we know of alternative things to do. Had we known about alternative things to do in the first place, we may not have been so unsubtle in our approach!

We can see some of the difficulties involved in identifying the goals of social situations in Exercise 4.11.

If you do this exercise, you may notice a number of things. Firstly, it is very difficult to identify social goals (including our own) without knowing something about the people involved and

Exercise 4.11 Identification of goals and alternative strategies

Look at some clips from television programmes – films, drama series, soap operas, etc. Take any one character in any scene and see if you can identify her or his goals. What is he or she trying to achieve in the situation? When you have identified the main goal or goals, see if you can identify any subsidiary goals. Then look at how this character has tried to achieve the goals. What other things could have been said or done to achieve the same thing?. Set out in a chart like the one below.

Character

Main goal(s)	*Alternative strategies to achieve these goals*
1.	
2.	
3.	
etc.	
Sub-goal(s)	
1.	
2.	
3.	
etc.	

Were there any things that could have been done that would have had more impact? Would there have been more or fewer alternatives if the character had been older, younger or from a different culture? If so, why? How easy was it to identify the character's goals? How important was the context in helping you decide what the character's goals were?

their previous encounters. Secondly, the context helps us define our goals. Thirdly, any social role helps define the goals people have. Lastly, social goals and strategies may vary according to age, sex and culture. Nevertheless, if we are unable to generate alternative ways of doing something, we may well get "stuck" in our dealings with people.

> Denise wanted very much to be liked by anyone who visited the hostel in which she lived. When anyone came to visit she would quickly approach them and take them by the arm, asking them what they thought about the football match. Denise did this even during the summer when very little football was being played. Most people she greeted in this way drew back from her, unable to talk to her as they did not know to which football match she was referring, and often as they had no interest in football. Denise did not know any other ways of opening a conversation with strangers. Nor did she have any insight into how they might feel being approached in this manner.

Knowledge about social alternatives comes largely with experience of different social situations and people. This experience also helps us estimate the likely consequences of any particular course of action.

Impact of different alternatives

When looking at alternative ways of handling a problem, we may well build into our thinking some estimates of the likely effects each of them may have. These effects could be in terms of the extent to which a particular strategy will help us meet our goal. On the other hand, the effects may be on ourselves – will some alternatives be too embarrassing or humiliating? We also anticipate the likely effects different alternatives will have on other people: what possible reactions will they have to our strategy. If we had thought in advance that other people would cold-shoulder us if we approached them, as in the above example, it might be preferable not to try to get to know them better. In other words, we may redefine our goal. Assessing the likely impact on ourselves, our goals, other people and the situation itself helps us narrow down our alternatives and make a decision about which alternative we will try.

Try assessing the impact of the different alternatives you thought up for the television character in Exercise 4.11 above. You might find it useful to make a chart, setting the different alternatives against impact on the character, different people she or he is involved with, other people who may be affected, the overall situation, the achievement of the character's goals and so on. There may be some people not in the scene who will be affected by some of the alternatives. List them as well. You could then give them a score, depending on the impact you think they will make. Does this make it any easier to decide which alternative would have been the best? Of course we can rarely (if ever) draw up such a chart for ourselves in the course of our everyday interactions, but we may be going through something similar in our heads, especially for particularly complicated situations.

Social decision making

Once we have some possible alternatives we need some way of deciding which one to follow. If the decision is not an important one and the consequences of making mistakes slight, we can try any of our alternatives. It will not matter if we get it wrong or make a mistake. However, if the social problem we are faced with is of significance to us, we are generally more careful about which alternative we will choose.

We use different decision rules for different circumstances. One of the things we do is to assess each alternative in terms of its likely benefits to us. If there are likely to be a mixture of different benefits, or of benefits and disadvantages, we work out the probability that the different benefits will be as expected. Then we may choose the alternative that is likely to give us the greatest overall benefit. Or we decide that some benefits can compensate for lack of others, or for disadvantages. Another thing we may do is to identify a particular benefit that must result from any alternative we choose, and thereby reject all those alternatives that do not lead to this outcome.

Of course, just as there are biases in identifying the problem at the start, so there are biases in the process of actually making a decision about what to do. We may expect something to happen as a result of what we do, but it may not. We may have misread the situation or the other people involved. We may have chosen an option not because it is likely to be successful in our estimation, but because we think other people will expect us to behave in particular ways. In other words, we conform to pressure from other people and do not rely on our own judgement. This pressure may be real or perceived. Certainly, if we are members of groups, the decisions we make in the context of social problem solving in groups can be affected by a number of things.

Group decision making

When we are in a group we are subject to a number of influences that do not exist to the same extent when we are not. Pressures to conform to what everyone else is saying or doing, even if this is contrary to what we would want to say or do ourselves, can be very strong. Part of this may be because we want to be accepted or liked by others in the group; part of it might be to do with consistency, again. Just as we like to be consistent within our thoughts and perceptions about other people, so we like to be consistent with other people.

If there are people we like or admire in the group, their opinions or suggestions can be particularly influential. We are more likely to agree with them than disagree with them; again perhaps this is because we do not want to risk their disapproval. If there are people in the group who know more about a particular thing or situation, we will tend to defer to their views, just as we will if there is a designated leader to our group.

Recently a self-advocacy group had begun in the day centre. George and Elise were pleased to be part of the group and that Angela, the member of staff in charge of their work group, was leading the group, as they liked her a lot. After some time Angela noticed that the group always agreed with anything she said (although individual people, such as George and Elise, did not always agree with her outside the group). She did not think she was actively influencing the group members. When she talked this through in her supervision session, she learnt about some of the features of group decision making. It looked as if the dynamics of the group were leading to particular decisions rather than others. It was decided that an independent chair should be sought who may be less likely to create the same effect, as the group members would not know, like and esteem an independent chair from the outset. When this was done, members began making their own decisions.

Something interesting happens when a group of us, who all start out with different opinions about something, get together to come to a joint decision. The group as a whole will tend not to come to a conservative decision as is often thought to be the case, but will tend towards those with the most extreme views. Whether or not this is just a different form of conformity we do not know, although it is strange that the group decision ends up more extreme than some kind of average position.

In groups, just as in other social situations, we often take account of the opinions of other people who are particularly significant to us. Even if they are not actually present and exerting influence on us to conform, we may be influenced by what we think they would say or want us to do, if they were present. Sometimes even people who are dead can have this kind of influence on us.

On the whole, whether in groups or not, we do not decide to put one of our alternatives into practice unless we think we can see it through. So, for example, we will not offer ourselves to stand in as managers in order to solve the problem of our manager leaving unless we think we will be able to do the job. We try to avoid failure experiences, though of course we may be wrong about what we will or will not be able to do.

Action

Once we have decided on a course of action, we have to put it into practice. This takes us back to the social behaviour – non-verbal behaviour and speech – that we discussed earlier. Clearly, our ability to succeed in our strategy depends in part on our ability to say and do things appropriately and in part to our self-confidence.

Most of us will at times, though, do things that do not have the desired effect. We make people cross when we had intended to make them laugh; we bore them when we intended to make them interested; we come over as cross when we had not intended to and so on. We only know whether we have got it right by being open to the effect of our actions on others.

Evaluation

Evaluation of the efficacy of our strategy involves looking out for cues from the other person that tell us something about how they have reacted. We also need to judge for ourselves whether our strategy had been a good one and whether it achieved the goals we had hoped for. If not, were there other unintended outcomes that were just as beneficial to us, to them and to the social situation, or not? This is, of course, where we came in. If everything is satisfactory (remembering that picking up cues from other people can lead to lots of distortions) we can just get on with our conversation or whatever it is we are doing. If not, the problem-solving process begins again.

One way of thinking about effective social behaviour is not to think that we have to get all things right all the time, and not to assume that we even need to know what to do in all situations. Instead, it may be that those of us that are most effective are those who can judge the effect of whatever it is we have done and make adjustments as necessary. The more extensive our range of alternative strategies for doing different things in different situations and the more responsive we are to feedback about the effects of our behaviour, the more socially skilled we will be. Three things are needed:

- we must know about different interpersonal actions and how they fit into different kinds of social situations;
- we must be able to convert knowledge of social convention, role requirements and so on into action in different social situations; and
- we must be able to evaluate our behaviour as accurately as possible and adjust it as necessary.

In Exercise 4.12 the full social problem-solving process is explored.

In one sense, all interactions with other people can be looked at in terms of social problem solving, and this can certainly be useful if we want to extend our social knowledge and repertoires of ways of interacting. More complex interactions, such as those that attempt to change people's opinions, handle conflict, be assertive, deliver bad news and so on, are more obvious situations wherein we make the social problem-solving process explicit. However, to use the full process described above would often mean slowing down or even halting the interaction sequence, so we cannot always apply it at the time we might want to: we "think on our feet", perhaps using some elements of the approach.

More generally, the nature of the problems, the viable alternatives for handling them and the factors entering the decision-making process are all affected by the social context.

Exercise 4.12 Social problem solving

With reference to the different stages of the social problem-solving process, i.e.

☐   problem recognition;

☐   identification of a goal;

☐   alternative strategies;

☐   assessment of likely impact;

☐   social decision making;

☐   action;

☐   evaluation;

consider how the following situations might be handled using a social problem-solving approach.

1. Relatives of a young man in your care want him moved to a more secure living situation. They are angry about an incident that occurred when he was no holiday and returned with a gash on his ankle. The young man does not want to move.

2. Two women share a house with a third woman. One of them likes to sit in the same chair every day while they watch television. This frustrates the other two considerably. There is a row when one of the others sits in the chair one evening.

3. Think of an incident that occurred involving people with learning disabilities recently. Outline the problem and how it might be handled using a problem solving approach.

Are any stages of the problem-solving process more difficult to handle than others? How might you handle these situations differently from the ways in which people with learning disabilities might handle them? What barriers to effective problem solving do you think there are?

CONTEXT

Our understanding of the contexts in which we meet and relate to other people is an essential component of social skill, competence and capability. We can look at social contexts in terms of their physical features, social features, rules, roles and patterns of sequences of interaction required. Before we go on to do this, let us explore what different situations mean to different people.

The meaning of social situations

We all view situations differently from each other. Whilst there will probably be some areas of overlapping understanding of different situations, there will also be areas of difference. To explore this, try Exercise 4.13.

If you do this, you may be surprised at the different ways you each saw the same situation. Let us illustrate the types of differences in perception that might arise. Consider two friends, Amy and Anna, going to a gym together. Amy calls for Anna and they drive to the gym, get changed and spend an hour doing a range of different exercises alongside about 20 other people, before changing again and driving home. They discuss their visit to the gym. Amy describes it as follows.

(i) It was a workout with my friend; (ii) it began when I called at Anna's house and picked her up in the car; (iii) we go because we like to spend time with each other and we are both very busy; (iv) some of the other people are strangers to us, but we know some of them quite well and we usually share equipment with a couple of people we know better than others; (v) there was an incident in which a bloke got cross with us because we were taking too long on one of the pieces of equipment; (vi) we share information about what we have been doing since we last met: we do not interrupt each other when we are exercising, but wait until the exercise has stopped before resuming our chat; (vii) going to the gym is just one occasion when we get to meet up.

Anna's account is rather different.

(i) It is a physical workout; (ii) it starts when we enter the gym after changing and ends when we have finished our exercises; (iii) the purpose is to get fit; (iv) there are two instructors and

Exercise 4.13 The meaning of social situations

Next time you go somewhere with someone else (this could be shopping, to a meeting, to an evening class, to the gym – anywhere in fact), take some time to discuss how each of you understood the situation. Consider:

☐ how you understood the situation;

☐ the boundaries of the situation (i.e. when you entered and left it; any physical features that helped define the purpose of the situation);

☐ the purpose of the situation;

☐ the roles of other people there and the channels of communication that existed;

☐ any discrete episodes that occurred that had particular significance for you;

☐ the rules governing your behaviour and the behaviour of others in the situation;

☐ how that situation links with other areas of your life.

In what different ways did you see the situation? Had you had a different partner, would your perceptions of the situation have been different again? If so, how? Would different situations have led to greater or lesser differences between you? If you had been sharing the situation with a person from a different culture of a different generation, how do you think the situation would have been perceived?

about 20 people working out – some of these are experts; (v) there was an incident where one of the really fit men was understandably frustrated because he had to wait for some of the equipment; (vi) warm up: follow your exercise routine: do not strain; (vii) it is part of an overall fitness programme that includes walking and aerobics.

Amy and Anna describe the same situation differently. Not only are different aspects of the situation important to them but they notice different things and interpret the same episodes differently. So, whilst there may be some objective features of the situation that are identical, we may all interpret situations differently. How we interpret the situation will determine, in part, how we behave and how we feel. We come to know about the meanings of social situations as we gain experience of lots of different situations. Sometimes people with learning disabilities make mistakes in their interpretations of the situations they are in, or do not pick up the cues the rest of us do in order to distinguish between them.

Andrew had a friend, Derek. They used to go to football matches together. They would sit in the stand, cheering their team on and talking to each other. Andrew liked classical music but had never been to a concert. When Derek managed to get tickets to hear the local orchestra, he was confident that Andrew would enjoy the performance. He certainly did enjoy the concert but, much to everyone else's annoyance, Andrew would not stop talking to Derek, despite Derek's pleas to him to keep quiet. When they talked about it on the way home and Derek asked Andrew why he did not stop talking, Andrew pointed out that he had never had to stop talking to Derek at football matches. What he was doing was seeing and stressing the similarities between what Derek thought of as quite different situations. Both were opportunities to go and watch something with Derek. Andrew, therefore, behaved in the one situation as he had in the other.

We cannot separate social situations from the people using them. Not only are our behaviours and experiences influenced by the settings in which we find ourselves, but we also shape and create social situations. If no one used Amy and Anna's gym, it would be a warehouse of equipment rather than a place where people came to work out; if there was no equipment, people's exercise routines would be limited. We can see how people can change the meaning of the situation if we look at how a church hall is transformed into a gym when it is used by the yoga class, or how the conference room is turned into a dance hall when a New Years Eve party is held in it. Our actions and the contexts in which they take place are inseparably bound up together.

In order to know what is expected of us in a particular situation we need to understand something about the complexity of situations. We can look at a number of different aspects of situations.

Physical aspects of situations

Physical features of any situation can make it easier or more difficult for us to be there at all; they can make it easier or more difficult to talk to, and get to know people once we are there; and they can affect our moods, which in turn may affect how we do whatever we are there to do. One way in which we can distinguish different physical aspects of settings is to look at "boundaries", "props", "modifiers", and "spaces".

Boundaries

Boundaries are the physical enclosures of the situation we are in, and the ways in which these can vary are clarified in Exercise 4.14.

Exercise 4.14 Boundaries of social situations

Think of at least **four** different social situations. Describe the boundaries of these situations.

Situation	Boundary
1.	1.
2.	2.
3.	3.
4.	4.

Do these situations have a physical boundary? What is it? Do you think everyone who shares the situation would agree on what is the physical boundary to the situation? What other kinds of boundary did you identify? What are the most common boundaries to social situations?

Hedges may surround the field in which we are having a picnic; walls may surround our bedroom; walls with a much bigger expanse of window may surround our kitchen; a fence may surround our house; partitions may surround different sections of a department store; road signs may surround our village and so on. It is partly by noting and understanding the boundary markers that we understand the purpose of the setting: so, if we do not pick up the signs around the room in the library that say "Silence", we will not know that this room differs from the room we have just come from where people were meeting to discuss an art exhibition. It is the setting boundaries that tell us what to do.

It is often the physical boundaries of a setting that help us feel we belong in some way: when we get inside our house, we know we are "home". Even this, though, is not that simple. If we have travelled from afar, we may feel at "home" when we get back to our country, village, town or suburb. We identify the boundaries of particular situations with reference to our experience – they do not have any absolute meaning of their own.

Props

Props are those features of a setting that are contained within a boundary. Within the boundary of our house we have furnishings, decorations and various objects. The props help us know the meaning of a situation, link a situation with our sense of identity, and they also guide our behaviour. It is the props in a house that tell us which room is the dining room and which is the bathroom. The props, and the purpose we understand the room to have, help us know where we should eat and where we should bathe. They also determine how many people we relate to and where. It would be unusual for most of us to talk to as many people in the bathroom as we do in the dining room.

The way we furnish and decorate our houses gives us a sense of ownership and also makes statements to others about the kinds of people we are: decorating a dining room with black paint and egg boxes on the walls may signal a different kind of person from the room with pastel pink walls and flowery curtains. Similarly, a bare room signals something different from a room cluttered with knick-knacks; a room cluttered with family mementoes signals something different from one cluttered with war memorabilia and so on. Exercise 4.15 explores this.

The way different props are arranged can limit opportunities for contact with others. Evening classes that take place in a school, for example, may have the desks and chairs arranged in rows. The further towards the front we sit, the more we might never know

---

**Exercise 4.15 Props for social
situations**

Look around the room you are in at the moment. Note down
all those features that might affect how you talk to different
people – indeed, whether there are some people you would
not allow to join you here. What do the things in this room
tell you about the people who use it? If the contents of the
room were changed completely, would its purpose change?

---

who else is in the class. We are likely to talk to those next to us or
near us, if to anyone at all. Contrast this with the coffee room
where breaks from the same evening class are spent. If there are
no tables and chairs we can move around and talk to different
people; we can certainly see who else is there. If there are small
tables and chairs we may get talking to a small group of people
for longer or in more depth – if we get a chair of course: if we do
not, we will probably talk to no one. If the floor is very highly
polished and we are a little unsteady on our feet, we will not even
go for coffee.

In all these situations it is not our personalities or social skills
that is determining who we talk to and in what way; it is the
physical features of the setting. People may think of us as friendly
or unfriendly, based on whether or not we talk to them – in other
words, they may attribute our behaviour to us, as people, and not
to the setting, even though it is this that has encouraged us to talk
or not. The polished floor in the above example may be thought of
as a prop; it could also be thought of as a modifier.

Modifiers

Modifiers are those physical features that affect the quality of the
situation – they modify it. The common kinds of modifiers include heat, light, noise and smell. If our home is too noisy, it may
be difficult to talk to others and they may not enjoy visiting us. If
our home is too hot, people may get fidgety and easily distracted;
they may think visiting us is unpleasant. If our home is too
brightly lit, people may get headaches, leave before they have to
and not want to come again. Similarly, if our home smells un-

pleasant, people may not enjoy their stay. In other situations, modifiers may make it more or less likely we will visit and, therefore, limit the opportunities there are for contact between people: a noisy, crowded pub might not only be unpleasant to sit in, but we may not be able to hear what our companion is saying and we might not notice other friends who are also there.

Whilst these modifiers can strongly affect how we experience different situations and how we are able to act in them, we will all experience them differently. So what will be hot and crowded for one person, may not be hot and crowded for another. Similarly, the number of people there would have to be, say at a party, before we say it is too hot and crowded might be different from the number of people there would have to be in the butcher's. Whilst some of us may find musak irritating in some places, we may not in others. You may like to think for yourself what aspects of situations make you frustrated, annoyed, impatient and so on? What effect does this have on how long you stay in the situation and how you act towards others when you are there. Although the physical features are important and may make some forms of behaviour impossible, our perception of them is probably more important to us.

Spaces

Spaces refer to the distances there are between people and/or objects within the boundary and the meanings that are attached to them. If we have to share a bunk-bed with someone in our bedroom, we will either think it an invasion of our privacy (if we do not particularly like the other person) or we will get to like the other person, because, in general, close distance in a bedroom signals some form of intimacy. The same distance between ourselves and other people at a meeting will signal nothing to do with liking, intimacy or the encroachment of our personal space. It will simply mean we are two people at a meeting.

As before, though, the kinds of meanings we attach to different kinds of spaces will differ. Sometimes spaces between people and objects can limit or enable contact. Suppose, for example, we go for a meal to a Chinese restaurant and are sitting around a large circular table. There may be much less chat if there are four of us round the table (relatively large spaces between us) than if there are eight of us (relatively small spaces between us). Similarly, if we use a wheelchair and have lots of books, papers and bits and pieces around us, we may have created a barrier between us and other people that keeps them at a distance and limits the chances of more intimate conversations. If we talk to strangers on a bus, we are more likely to talk to the person sitting next to us than a person sitting several seats away. We, too, will not consider it so strange to be asked something by someone sitting next to us than by someone who is not. The spaces, themselves, have some kind of meaning for us that guide our behaviour.

> Jean lives in a small house with her family in a seaside town. The bungalow is on a sharp corner of the road, facing a tall concrete sea wall. Just round the corner, the road straightens out and young people like to use it as a "rat-run", seeing who can accelerate their cars in the shortest distance. This means that people do not often walk along the pavement as it is considered unsafe. The nearest shops are about half a mile away and most people travel there by car, including Jean and her family. Jean uses a wheelchair. One of the downstairs rooms has been adapted to be a bedroom with an *en suite* sitting shower. The other room is used by all the family as a sitting room. Jean does not like to have friends round as she feels uncomfortable taking them to her bedroom (because of the shower), and the sitting room is always crowded. Furthermore, Jean has to ask someone to make a cup of coffee as the surfaces in the kitchen are too high for her to use.
>
> When Jean's social worker visits, Jean sits glumly in the sitting room and says very little. She agrees she does not know anyone who lives nearby and rarely has anyone visit her at home. Jean's social worker thinks Jean has a problem getting on with people and has recommended she attend a social skills group at the local college. Her social worker has never visited Jean at the college where she would have seen her mixing freely with her friends. We can understand Jean's so-called lack of social skills as being due to physical features of the environment she lives in.

Physical features of situations can deny us access to particular events or activities, influence our behaviour, ease interactions with others, contribute to a sense of well-being, which in turn may influence our relationships with others and both contribute to and reflect our personal identities. Those aspects of our environment we can call the portable environment can also limit the ways other people relate to us, and influence the thoughts and attitudes they may hold towards us.

Portable environment

Social situations, as we have seen, are not static things: they vary over time and as a result of our activities within them. The environment we experience depends, in part, on the way we present ourselves within it. We often present ourselves in ways that do not encourage other people to accept us readily, or in ways that encourage others to categorize or label us. The kinds of cars we drive, for instance, tell people something about us (which may or may not be true). As we drive up to them, they form different impressions if we arrive in a sparkling clean, new Rover, than if we arrive in a beaten up 2-CV. Our car is our portable environment. Other people will get different ideas about how they might relate to us if we arrive in a van that has AMBULANCE written on it or the name of the local authority on the side.

The clothes we wear are another aspect of our portable environment – they are situation props we carry around with us. So, too, are the things we carry. You can see the importance of these personal trappings if you think about getting on a train which is quite crowded. Think about what you think or do if you see a vacant seat next to one whose occupant has obviously left to go to the buffet or toilet and has left a marker on the seat. Is there any difference if the thing that is left is a cardigan, a Walkman, a Chinese newspaper or four cans of lager? It is the person's portable environment that you are using in making judgements about her or him.

Other types of portable environment that can set the scene for different types of encounters with others include moveable features of our houses, such as signs like "Beware the Dog", burglar alarms, poorly kept front gardens, the nature of rubbish waiting to be collected, reinforced glass in the windows, signs in the neighbourhood like "Children playing", "Danger, Elderly People" and so on. Think some more about the importance of portable environments by completing Exercise 4.16.

Joanne has Down's syndrome, is considerably overweight and her tongue is visible. She lives at home with her father. They both like to be outdoors. When they go out, Joanne wears a coat that used to be her grandmother's. Joanne has always worn and continues to wear short white socks. She takes her teddy bear with her, under her arm and she and her father walk arm in arm. Her neighbours were most surprised to discover that Joanne's next birthday was her fortieth.

Exercise 4.16 Portable environments

Next time you are walking around your neighbourhood, look out for any information that tells you something about the people who live there.

Feature of the portable environment	Messages about the people
e.g. unkempt front hedge	e.g. these people may be lazy, disorganized, busy, etc.

Can you tell what kinds of people might use different situations? Can you tell with whom you might have something in common? Are there some people with whom you think you would have nothing in common? What makes you think this?

We have seen that whilst physical aspects can be identified, they derive their meaning for us in part by the cultures in which they exist and in part from the purpose for which they are used. The social purposes of situations depend in largely on who is there, what they are doing and why.

Social aspects

People, themselves, are an important part of any social situation. Sometimes the situation changes as more people enter it; sometimes it changes according to the role of the people using it; and sometimes it can change as a result of what the people are doing in it. In practice, it is difficult for us to disentangle these aspects.

Take for example the chemist's shop. We may be the only person in it and be waiting for a prescription. Gradually more people come into the shop and one person strikes up a conversation with the counter assistant about young people's attitudes to work, then appeals to someone else to support a point of view. Before long, four or five customers, the pharmacist and the assistant are all debating the pros and cons of government employment policies. If we interrupt and ask "Is my prescription ready?" we may be seen as an outsider: we will not have realized that, at least temporarily, the situation within the setting has changed from customers-in-a-chemist's-shop to local-political-debating meeting. Different behaviours are expected of us in the latter situation than in the former. In this example we can see that there was a complex mix of numbers of people in the shop, the roles they adopted and their behaviour.

Roles

In order to know how to behave in any situation, we have to know something about the different roles we and other people are playing. In our chemist's shop, the pharmacist, while dispensing prescriptions, may not be the person who takes our money: this may have to be explained to us since chemists' shops differ in their internal organization. Our role relationships often dictate the nature of our interactions with others, and our behaviour can best be understood, not by knowing anything about our personalities or social skills, but rather by knowing our roles. The more formal the role, the less individual interpretation of the role we are able to make.

In our everyday lives we relate to many of our acquaintances in terms of our roles. As customers, for example, we behave in certain ways towards shopkeepers, and these interactions are similar to those of other customers. Our role of neighbour, on the other hand, is open to a wider range of appropriate behaviours. Even though this may be so, there are some behaviours that are not appropriate: it would be unusual for us to offer to pay our neighbour for our television licence, or to ask our neighbour to do something for us that we may ask a work colleague. In order to begin to see the ways in which roles define social situations complete Exercise 4.17.

The more socially skilled and socially competent we are, the more reliably we can interpret our different roles and relate meaningfully to our different role partners. The roles we play in a particular setting may put some limits on who we can talk to and what we can do. Changing roles can open up new opportunities.

Alex is a young man who lives in a busy part of town. He is easily distracted and it is not safe for him to be out on the streets by himself. However, he likes walking around the streets. Every day one of his carers goes walking with him. John, one of his carers, walks close by him and hardly says a word to him. Danny, another carer, also walks close by but talks to him, telling him stories and

---

Exercise 4.17 Roles and social situations

Identify different social roles you play. Consider who your role partners are and in which settings you meet. What behaviours are appropriate and inappropriate in this role and in this setting? An example is given in the chart below.

What is your role?	*Who is/are your role partner(s)?*	*In which settings do you meet?*	*What behaviours are expected?*	*What behaviours are inappropriate?*	*Other comments*
Badminton player	Other badminton players; recreation worker	Sports centre entrance lobby; changing rooms; sports hall; cafe	Playing badminton; talking about the game; other friendly chat	Asking her/him to remove your rubbish; not following the rules of the game; etc.	Badminton players may know each other in other capacities – they may be work colleagues, friends, relatives

How much appropriate and inappropriate behaviour was determined by the role? How much appropriate and inappropriate behaviour was determined by the particular setting in which the role was played? How important are role partners in determining appropriate and inappropriate behaviours?

---

things about what he has done since his last shift. Although Alex does not talk, he looks at Danny when he is talking to him. Other people round about see Alex in a different role on the different occasions. With Danny, Alex is seen as a "friend", someone worth talking to; with John, Alex is seen as a "person who is being taken out for a walk". More people say hello to them when Alex is out with Danny. When Danny takes Alex to the pub and Alex goes up to the bar for the drinks, he is in the role of "customer". As such, he communicates with the bar staff and other men at the bar smile at him and nod their heads.

Alex's role is determining the amount he mixes. Imagine what would happen if Alex began to take one of the neighbour's dogs out with him for a walk. His roles would now expand to include "dog lover/walker", "helpful neighbour", and this may open up possibilities for contact with other dog walkers and so on.

Role–rule contexts

As we have seen, many roles are closely linked to rules about what is or is not appropriate or acceptable behaviour. Role–rule contexts also guide our behaviour and understanding them helps us become more socially skilled. Some role–rule contexts are explicit (clearly stated): "staff only" rooms in a day centre tell us that we may enter only if we are staff; regulations like "only children under 12 may use this playground" tell us what we may or may not do in the park at different ages. Others are implicit (or assumed): at home, it may be custom and practice for one person to do the gardening and another to put away the washing – we may even have arrived at this division of labour without realizing it; at work, certain things may be done by some people rather than others for no other reason than "that's how it has always been done". The force of roles and role–rule contexts can determine our behaviour. You can look at this for yourself in Exercise 4.18.

Kirklea is a hostel for 26 people who live in 8 units, each described by a different colour. People in blue unit plan and organize the summer open day. They have all shown they can contact the necessary people, sort out who will do what, arrange the timetable, send out the invitations and so on. People living in the other units cannot do these things. Or can they? We do not know, because it has always been Blue unit that runs the open day. Why? Because that is how it has always been – no one there now knows why it started that way, just that that is how it has always been. Custom and practice has determined social opportunities for, and the social capabilities demonstrated by the residents of Kirklea.

Social rituals

By social rituals we mean relatively predictable patterns of behaviour that take place in a particular physical setting. Many situations contain rituals, which may be defined by the physical features of the setting, and/or the social purpose of the setting and/or the roles we play in the situation. For example, when we go to the theatre we sit in rows of seats all facing one direction. We

---

Exercise 4.18 Role–rules contexts

Think of any situation with which you are familiar. What explicit and implicit rules or regulations govern your behaviour or the behaviour of other people? How do you know what these rules are? Complete a chart like the one below.

Situation	Implicit rules	Explicit rules	How did you learn about these rules?

How many of these rules are linked to custom and practice, social conventions or other social attitudes, such as what is expected of people of different sex, age and so on? What different ways of learning the rules did you identify?

---

have not particularly chosen to do this, but this is how the auditorium is arranged. Of course we sit in the seats partly because our purpose is to watch the play and so we need to be able to see the stage, but it is also because of our roles as members of the audience. Our behaviour here is best understood by knowing the situation and not by knowing anything about us, as people: we are replaceable – tomorrow night another set of people will come and behave in the same way. We have relatively little choice in our behaviour and it is likely that other people will put us right if we do not do what is required.

Other settings are similar. Most shops, for example, clearly define the physical spaces that we, as customers, can use from those used by the shopkeepers and assistants. Once more, our behaviour is best understood by the requirements of the setting and our roles within it, rather than by knowing about people, their interests and characters.

It is very easy to make mistakes in understanding what is going on in a particular situation if we do not understand the ways in which situations and roles give meaning to behaviour.

Tanzillah is friendly towards everyone she meets. She smiles at and likes to shake hands with people. She does her clothes shopping in a large department store but does not like the assistants there because, as she says, "They are all unfriendly". What Tanzillah does not understand is how the particular arrangements for paying for goods in this store make it impossible for staff to act in what she would call friendly manners. The counters are high up and the staff are separated from the customers by wide tables. They are attached to their tills by the keys which are on chains and have to be inserted in the till when it is being used. Tanzillah would like to get round the other side of the counter to shake hands with the assistants, but she has been told she cannot.

The situation controls the space that people with different roles can use and this in turn defines their behaviour. As it is, Tanzillah really cannot tell whether or not they are friendly (in her terms), and mistakenly attributes their behaviour to their characters.

Behaviour settings are not static, instead they change as the people using them, and the purposes for which they are used, change. So, if our shop gets more and more used by people who spend large amounts of time chatting to their friends, the shopkeeper may decide to turn one section into a coffee-house. Similarly, over time, Amy and Anna's gym may turn into more of a social club than a gym as people using it want to socialize more. People in these examples are adapting and changing their roles and thereby making different demands of the settings.

Social rituals can also be linked more closely to roles. If a couple using the gym wanted to have their wedding in there, the registrar and all those involved could still interact with each other coherently, even though the setting was not designed for this purpose. The behaviour of all involved will be patterned in just the same way as if it were occurring in a registry office. However, the gym may be closed that day to Amy and Anna if they had not been invited to the wedding. They are not able to penetrate this **situation**, although they have been and will be able to use the **setting** frequently. We will consider the penetration of situations further in Chapter 6.

We have seen, then, that different aspects of situations can affect how we behave in particular settings and also the meanings we give to other people's behaviour in those settings. Unless we understand some of these issues we will not be able to adapt our behaviour appropriately, nor will we be able to make sense of other people's behaviour. In other words, we will not be socially skilled or competent. Social situations, themselves, can contribute towards greater opportunities and social capability or they can act as obstacles to both opportunities and social capability.

From this discussion of components of social skill and social competence, we can see how the different aspects of social skill contribute to people's social capability. Taken with our understanding of relationships and of communities, we are now in a position to work with people with learning disabilities in order to enhance their social capability. In doing this we must be able to describe:

- what a person's life is like now;
- how social opportunities might be increased;
- what social skills and social competence is like now;
- how social skill and social competence might change;
- how communities might be strengthened to include disadvantaged people more fully; and then
- evaluate change.

The first step is to describe what a person's life is like now.

FURTHER READING

The nature of social skill and social competence is discussed in most introductory social psychology books. Few texts, however, stress the cognitive aspects of social skill or the understanding of social situations in their discussions of social competence, so we have chosen a selection of readings that will address all of the issues raised in the chapter in greater detail.

Argyle, M. (1984) *The Psychology of Interpersonal Behaviour*, 4th edn, Penguin, Harmondsworth.

Argyle, M., Furnham, A. and Graham, J.A. (1981) *Social Situations*, Cambridge University Press, Cambridge.

Birkitt, I. (1991) *Social Selves*, Sage, London.

Edgerton, R. (1967) *The Cloak of Competence: Stigma in the lives of the mentally retarded*, University of California Press, Berkeley, CA.

Fiske, S.T. and Taylor, S.E. (1984) *Social Cognition*, 2nd edn, Random House, New York.

Forgas, J.P. (1985) *Interpersonal Behaviour: The Psychology of Social Interaction*, Pergamon, Rushcutters Bay.

Goffman, E. (1959) *Presentation of Self in Everyday Life*, Anchor Books, New York.

Hahney, H. (1986) *Problem Solving: A cognitive approach*, Open University Press, Milton Keynes.

Hargie, O. (1980) *Handbook of Communication Skills*, Croom Helm, London.

Harré, R. (1993) *Social Being*, 2nd edn, Blackwell, Oxford.

Hollin, C.R. and Trower, P. (eds) (1986) *Handbook of Social Skills Training, Vol. 1: Applications across the lifespan*, Pergamon, Oxford.

Kagan, C. and Evans, J. (1995) *Professional Interpersonal Skills for Nurses*, Chapman & Hall, London.

Orford, J. (1992) *Community Psychology: Theory and practice*, Wiley, Chichester.

Trower, P. (ed.) (1984) *Radical Perspectives in Social Skills Training*, Croom Helm, Beckenham.

What is life like now?

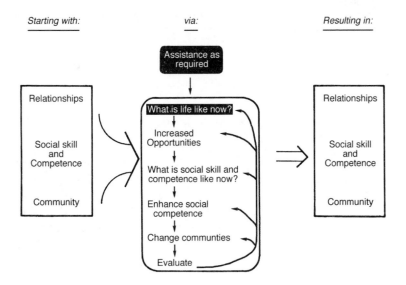

This chapter describes a process (and the thinking behind it) for getting acquainted with people with learning disabilities with a view to identifying relevant ways of improving their patterns of social opportunity. This is another way of thinking about "needs assessment" (see Chapter 1). We offer a framework for getting to know people with learning disabilities sufficiently well to begin introducing relevant opportunities. The ideas here are drawn from our own experience as researchers and practitioners and from those of other practitioner colleagues. This work in turn has drawn upon the ideas in Brost and Johnson's (1982) pamphlet, *Getting to Know You,* and the work of O'Brien and Lyle (1985/6)

on the *Framework for Accomplishment*. The general analysis offered by Doyal and Gough (1991) also forms a foundation for our thinking. A number of assumptions underpin this approach.

PRINCIPLES AND ASSUMPTIONS

All people have basic needs in their lives

An example list of such basic needs is as follows:

- autonomy (control over what happens to you)
- health
- individuality
- respect
- belonging
- meaning and purpose
- growth and development
- protection from threats to body or mind
- stability and continuity
- security of income.

Some services can help meet some of these needs, but needs are for things more basic than services. By and large, different kinds of people do not have different basic needs, although they may have very different ways of having these needs satisfied, and some people may have more specific needs that are linked to these general needs. People who are highly dependent, such as those with learning disabilities, are likely to experience many of these needs very intensely, since they are not being satisfied.

Many people with learning disabilities need help to have their needs met

People with learning disabilities have their lives complicated in two ways: by their impairments and by the way society, services and individual people respond to them, disabling and handicapping them. These complications are difficult to overcome without help. So this assistance, which can take many forms, is an extra need for people with impairments.

In the initial stages of our work we are trying to discover the particular combination, at this time, of those basic human needs and this extra need for assistance for the person with whom we are working. Doing this requires careful description of the person, the situation and the way learning disabilities affect fulfilment of needs and interests.

Extra needs for assistance are not needs for services

Extra needs for assistance are not simply needs for formally organized **services**, although, of course, some of the things that services (among other things) might produce can meet some of these needs.

> Sue has some difficulties expressing herself and in speaking clearly. This means that she is often ignored or talked down to, and she finds it difficult to get people to respond to her wishes. We could say, "Sue needs speech therapy", but in terms of what she needs to do or get, we would be more accurate in saying:
>
> Sue needs to be able to communicate more effectively, in order to express her needs and preferences and to socialize. Speech therapy is one form of assistance that might help her to meet her ordinary needs for communication. Other means to this end might include assertiveness training, so people are forced to give her more time and attention; training in the use of gestures to assist and underline what she is saying; physical remediation of dental problems; or recruiting people who are good listeners to be around her and model respectful interaction to others she meets.

If we jump straight to the means by which the needs could be met, we risk forgetting what needs the services are meant to help address (especially where professional groups have their own interests). Instead, we want to understand the person as a whole rather than as depersonalized sets of technical problems. Furthermore, we want to find or design ways of meeting needs that imaginatively combine non-service resources (friends, neighbours, community facilities and organizations) with one another **and** with the more formal human service supports (professional and non-professional paid staff).

Learning about needs is a collaborative process

To learn about someone's situation and needs we have to be able to "stand in their shoes" – to understand what their situation is like **for them**. This cannot be done from a distance: the work of getting to know people should be highly participative, with an emphasis on sharing experiences with them, rather than trying to find out primarily by proxy methods, such as interviews with carers or the administration of checklists. If we want to find out about people, then we must go with them into the situations in which they spend time. This is not the only source of information, as we will see later, but it is one that we emphasize strongly, given what most professionals tend to have learned to think and do. Whilst we should avoid keeping too distant, we should also be careful not to confuse our role, for example denying that we are primarily a person helping others to greater social capability, but are, instead, their friends. We will pursue this further, below.

The task, then, is to work in collaboration with a person who has a learning disability in order to build up a picture that describes her identity in relation to pattern of life, and to plan, organize or deliver the various forms of assistance that will be required if individual needs are to be met and her interests addressed.

General ideas about needs generate specific ideas about specific needs for individual people

We use general ideas about what people need in order to generate some specific ideas about what a particular person needs at this point in time. We suggested above one possible list of needs that all people share. However, we all differ from one another in the detail of what we need, and this varies over time, too. In our task of getting acquainted with a person with learning disabilities, we use these basic notions about what all people need as a kind of baseline for assessing what her or his experiences might mean in terms of needs.

Bill Griffin lives in his own flat and is supported by a visiting staff member who not only helps with the practical things but also gives Bill useful advice and listens to what concerns him. This staff member calls three times a week and stays for two hours at a time according to a rota. Bill also meets people at the College course that he is attending and sometimes chats with other men of his age at the allotment that he has recently taken on.

Bill thinks life is much better than it was in the mental handicap hospital where he spent 25 years, but he complains of being lonely. Nobody calls to see Bill, and while he mentions friends, it turns out that they are people with whom he might interact for around 15 minutes per week.

> We come to the conclusion that Bill needs someone to take
> a particular interest in him, not as part of their job, but because
> they share interests with him and they like his company and
> because they have a personal commitment to him. Bill needs
> to be "special" to someone: we also suspect that he might
> benefit from developing stronger ties with the locality where he now
> lives.

In coming to these conclusions we are making comparisons
between what we believe is desirable for all people and what we
see happening to Bill, through our observations and from what he
tells us. The general human needs of "respect" and "belonging"
become translated in Bill's case into "someone to take an interest
in him" and "ties to his locality". Our first attempt to meet these
needs is to introduce him to a recently retired relative of a staff
member who is also keen on gardening and who introduces him
to the local bowls club. If we had gone in with the checklists or a
similar distancing approach we might have ended up making a
very different intervention, such as "Bill needs a place in the day
centre" or "Bill needs to develop home-care skills", engaging in
sophisticated coercion to keep his flat tidy or eat three square
meals a day!

Having clarified the major underlying assumptions of our approach, we will move on to look at methods of finding out about
what life is like now for a person.

ORIENTATION

The first part of helping people with learning disabilities develop
their social skills, social competence and social capability, then, is
to get to know something about them and their life circumstances
and opportunities. Let us look at how we might do this. How do
you come to know a person – any person? Before you read on,
give some thought to Exercise 5.1.

When you completed this exercise, did you mention any of the
following:

- spending time with the person: sharing particular activities;
  talking; seeing how the person gets on with other people;
  finding out about way of life, interests, beliefs and the influences on his or her life; getting close to the person's own
  experiences;

- making your own sense out of what you see, hear, experience: making inferences and interpretations; drawing conclusions and making judgements about the person's nature;
- sharing particular situations: spending time with the person in different contexts; playing different roles?

These three aspects usually fit well together in our experiences of getting to know people, but sometimes one or other aspect will assume greater importance than others. Some of us, for example, may be happy getting close to people and finding out a lot about them. However we meet, we like to find out as much as possible as quickly as possible: it is our personal style. Others of us may be more comfortable keeping more of a distance, making our own judgements and forming our own interpretations: we prefer to think rather than ask. Others again may place great store on the context in which we meet and the roles we play.

Exercise 5.1 Getting to know other people: personal styles and preferences

Think about someone you have got to know recently and jot down a few ideas about how you got to know her or him.

Is this how you usually get to know people? Do you get to know men in different ways from how you get to know women? Are there different issues involved if you are getting to know someone at work from out of work? How do you get to know people who are much older or younger than yourself? How easy is it to get to know people from other cultures?

To find out the important things about another person we have to combine these styles, or at least switch from one to the other frequently. We cannot begin to work with people with learning disabilities unless we get to know them first. This is especially true if we are working with them on any aspect of social skills, competence and capability. If we do not get to know them we will not be able to make sensible suggestions about how their social opportunities may be increased, their relationships extended or their personal skills improved.

INTRODUCTIONS

We want to be introduced to our focal person in a way that respects that person's dignity, while setting the occasion for communication and a productive collaborative relationship. If we do not take some steps to shape our introductions and first contacts, then other circumstances will do the shaping.

In working with someone, we cannot help but give a message about what we are doing: we cannot expect that assumptions will not be made about who we are, what it is we are doing and why. If we do not explain, the situation may be misunderstood and the person appear uncooperative or unwilling to enhance social capability. We need to explain both the purpose of what we are doing and how we will be working, including what the person may do which will be different from usual. We also have to try and explain what might come out of this piece of work (which of course assumes we have some outcome in mind!). Sometimes we will be in the position of pointing out that we may not be able to do anything very much to improve the overall situation. Until we get some way into the work, we will not know what is and is not possible. The essential thing here is that we are clear, ourselves, and willing to be open and honest, with respect to the person we are working with, about our aims and intentions and how we anticipate some enhancement of life experiences. If we do not expect this, we must ask ourselves why we are beginning this work.

We might have some doubts about the ability of the person to understand our explanations. This presents us with a challenge from the start. Verbal explanations are not the only ways in which we can help people understand what it is we are trying to do. For instance, this might be the message we want to get across:

At the moment we don't really know you. We would like to learn more about you and help you to learn more about both yourself and us. In doing so we want to know everything that is relevant to improving matters for you, including those things that you and those around you are not very proud of. It is not our job to judge you, but rather to respect you as an individual human being with the same worth as any other.

Perhaps you can help us to see what might help you to lead a richer life. We might make mistakes and we cannot guarantee to be able to change everything, but we will try to consult you and, at the least, to minimize the damage to you.

Exercise 5.2 Meaningful introductions

You may like to discuss this exercise with a colleague or friend. How might you introduce yourself to the following people.

☐ Lilly is a middle-aged woman who has used disability services for many years and obviously has many abilities, such as being able to express herself well and to read. However, you are told that she tends to say yes to any suggestion that a person in authority makes. What would you do when visiting her for the first time at her home?

☐ Ged is a young man living with his family. He has begun to wreck things around him, but he is not aggressive towards people. He has been labelled "autistic" and, indeed, he speaks little and has difficulty following what people are saying. He seems to find it difficult to feel comfortable with people he has not known for a long period of time. How might you try to arrange your first contact with him?

☐ Balbinder is a woman of 27 who has no speech and limited voluntary movement. She is living in a local authority hostel and attends a day centre. There seems to have been a failure to provide her with access to aids for communication, although she can indicate yes and no. How would you suggest that you are introduced to her?

Whom else might you involve in your introductions? To whom else might you introduce yourself and outline the possible work that could be done? How does your role influence how you make your introductions?

Of course we would not actually say this in these words, but this message would need to be embodied in everything we say and do. Exercise 5.2 helps us look at how this might be done.

As we continue to work with the person it will be possible and desirable to remind her or him of what it is we are doing. There is a balance here, of course, between the social and task oriented aspects of our work. Whenever we work with people in the area of social skills, we have to do this from a position of having, ourselves, developed good, constructive and friendly relationships with the people with whom we are working.

However, being friendly (a style) is not the same as being friends (a role). As we have seen, an integral part of our approach to social skills is helping people with learning disabilities develop relationships, including friendships. It is not usually helpful to confuse both ourselves and the people with whom we are working by insisting that we are their friends. Where relationships are limited in their number and quality, we may impair people's opportunities and ability to understand the nature of friendship by promoting pseudo-friendships where the boundaries are unclear to all of us. Look back at Chapter 2 on relationships, which may help disentangle some of the issues here.

This does not mean that we have to make our interactions unduly artificial through constant reminders of the task-orientated and possibly time-limited nature of what we are doing. We just need to be sure we do not pretend the relationship is something it is not. Perhaps the best advice is to act as if it is a working partnership. Just as in other walks of life working partnerships we have with people may develop into friendships, so they might with people with learning disabilities. However, this is not automatic, and these friendships will have other features that distinguish them from other working partnerships we have. Go back to Chapter 2 to remind yourself of the issues and complete Exercise 5.3 to help clarify the boundaries to working partnerships.

SPENDING TIME WITH THE PERSON

Spending time with the person who has a learning disability is the most important part of the process of getting to know that person: there can be no substitute, no proxy, no shortcut to this, as we all know well from our ordinary experiences of getting to under-

---

Exercise 5.3 Boundaries around relationships at work

Think of examples of the following relationships: colleague; person with learning disabilities with whom you work; friend. For each of them, list the task activities you help the person with and those you do not; also list the social (non-work related) activities you share and those you do not.

		Boundary	
		Within relationship	Outside relationship
Colleague	task activities social activities		
Person with learning disabilities	task activities social activities		
Friend	task activities social activities		

What differences are there between the different kinds of relationships? Have you had to strike a balance between friendliness and task orientation before? How did you deal with it? Was that satisfactory to you and to the other person? What happens if the boundary moves in one direction or the other?

---

stand another person. This cannot be stressed too strongly. It is all too easy for us to fall into the trap of "doing an assessment" from whatever perspective our professions provide. Assessments are usually limited to some particular aspect of functioning. When we are helping people in the area of social skills, we are concerned with every aspect of their social lives.

Professionals learn a variety of means and excuses for maintaining a distance between themselves and people they are supposedly serving. We can begin to unlearn some of this by making ourselves spend time alongside the person.

We have to try to put ourselves in the place of the person. We do not need to have long conversations (although if these develop, that is fine). Instead, we have to try to both observe and, as much as we can, experience what happens to the person. This means being very accurate, in a common-sense way, about what is happening. For example we can describe Julie's experiences in different ways. We could say, "Julie attends the ATC". On the other hand, we could say:

> Julie spends weekdays in a room with 28 other people with various disabilities and one staff member. About half of the day she spends sitting doing nothing, otherwise she is either doing copy-writing or assembling paper hats. She enjoys some of the work but she tells us through speech and through her behaviour that she gets bored by the monotony and the general lack of activity: she is embarrassed by being grouped with some of the others in her section.

In other words we need to open our eyes to what is **actually** happening to the person, getting beyond the jargon that often disguises a rather distasteful reality. Ask "what would this be like if it was me, or my mum, or my cousin or someone else close to me?" Not surprisingly, it is difficult to do this when you are directly involved in caring for, supervising or teaching the person.

We should spend time with the person on several occasions in several different settings. All of us act differently and experience different things in different situations: this is a big part of what we want to discover about the person on whom we are focusing. We are also the same in different situations! We want to find out about these similarities and differences. Where and when to try might include:

- sizeable chunks of morning and afternoon;
- sharing a meal with the person;
- a leisure activity;
- a place or activity that the person is not used to;
- a meeting concerning the person (even if the person does not attend);
- a therapy or treatment session;
- unstructured time;
- typical evening activity.

These should take us into a variety of different places at different times. They should cover the range of different activities the person does and the different people she or he meets. They should cover different times of day as well as different times of the week.

At this stage we need to keep separate the WHAT from the WHY. The task here is to understand what it is like for the person. Later we will try to change things, and then we will need to take account of the factors that create the present state of affairs.

Exercise 5.4 contains a record form that asks some key questions and may help you to organize the information you collect. Try to get into the habit of making a record of this sort for, but not during, every visit.

Exercise 5.4 Summarizing information

After meeting a person with learning disabilities, complete the following form. Make any changes to the form you want as a result of this experience and try out your new form. Aim to ensure as much information as possible is included on the form.

RECORD SHEET   *Observation/Contact across settings*

Use a separate record sheet for each setting
Situation   Activities

People present

Why was your focal person there?

Where else could this take place? (Where would you go for this activity or purpose?)

Observations: What did you see happening?
   What was the person doing?
    With whom?
   What was going on around them?
   Who came up to the person?
    What was said and done?
   Other observations

Continued

Impressions: How did it seem and feel to you?

How comfortable did you feel in this setting, physically and emotionally?
How would you feel if you were in this person's place?

Interpretations:

How would you rate the person's experience here, in terms of:

community presence
respect
capability
power
participation

What might be the likely effect on the person:

	today?	next year?	in five years?
positive			
negative			

What have you learned about the person from this?

In what other situations would it be useful to see the person?

Review: How did this activity go?

Do you think your presence changed the situation or the way the person acted? How might you tackle things differently another time?

What have you learned from doing this (other than things about this person)?

How easy was it to collect this information? What changes did you need to make to the form? Was some of the information easier to collect than others? How easy was it to put into words your thoughts about what it must be like to be the person?

TALKING TO OTHERS

While nothing can replace spending time with the person, it is important to talk to all the "significant others" – i.e. the people who influence, care about or have lives entwined with that of your focal person. The list of important people in your person's life is likely to be a short one. It is likely to include family members, others who depend on services and key service providers, but perhaps few other people. Significant others can provide information:

- about the person;
- about how others see and know the person; and
- about their influence on the person's life.

When other people tell us something about a person, we can easily be trapped into believing what they say. It is only when we talk to the next person that we get a different story and realize we have to be cautious in how we use the information we receive from others. Remind yourself of the issues involved in perceiving others that we discussed in Chapter 4. Some possible pitfalls you may meet in asking others about a person include:

- believing explanations at face value that blame the person for the situation;
- your own "halo effects": "I don't like this fellow – I won't accept what he says"; "She seems nice / sensitive / observant – her view is likely to be correct" – we may be unaware of how our impressions of the informant are affecting our observations and interpretations;
- "false contradictions": "If he is right, she has to be wrong" – try to build up your own understanding of how two people can come to say very different things about a person and why this might be.

Exercise 5.5 contains a record form that summarizes information from others about a person. As before, try to get into the habit of filling in this kind of form after every visit or whenever you have discovered something you did not know about someone.

IN THE ARCHIVES: INFORMATION FROM RECORDS

Our services often show their worst tendencies in their official records about those they are meant to serve. Files and casenotes

**Exercise 5.5 Summarizing
information given by other people**

Ask at least three other people about your focal person with
learning disabilities. If possible try to involve people who
know her or him in different capacities (family member, care
assistant, day services officer). Summarize the information
you have gained and make any changes to the form you
think appropriate.

RECORD SHEET   *Accounts of the person by others*

Use a separate record sheet for each informant
Informant   Involvement with person

Main messages about the person

New information

Information corroborating other accounts/findings

Likely bias of informant

Your conclusions about this person's impact on the life of your
target person

Review: How would you do this differently next time?

What have you learned from this activity?

How easy was it to collect this information? How easy was
it to decide to whom you should speak? What differences
were there in the stories you were given? Why was this?

can be very misleading, recording people's difficulties, often out of context, to the exclusion of their successes. They may also be written very subjectively, from the biased point of view of the staff member writing them. Records may also be large, poorly organized and illegible. If records are so often unwieldy, inaccurate and incomplete, you might like to think about how we can make best use of them in our task of finding out about the person. It is a good idea to clarify your purpose in using case records as a means of finding out about someone every time you are tempted to do so.

We suggest that you use casefiles like this:

- At the beginning, draw on them in making a list of people you will want to talk to.

- Later on, after you have spent time with the person and other key people, use the records, together with what you have been told, in constructing a history of the person.

- The records are also likely to contain factual information about the person's impairments, interventions used before, drugs prescribed, etc., and in context this may be important.

- Records are a useful further source of information about how the person is and has been seen by others, particularly by service providers, and this can give insights into what the person has had to contend with in the past.

- Finally, there may be thoughtful and accurate contributions that validate, extend or suggest caution for your own findings.

Your work will of course add to the person's casefiles. Can you avoid some of the mistakes you have seen made to date? It might be useful to prepare a summary to go into the casefiles that gives a respectful yet accurate account, and the main life events, of the person.

In Exercise 5.6 we suggest a way of summarizing the vast or paltry information gained from case records.

MAKING PATTERNS: INTERPRETING OBSERVATIONS

Once we have collected information by spending time with a person, talking to others or looking through case records, we will probably have a great deal of information. Our next task is to interpret the observations we have made in order to pick out the most important issues for that particular person. To do this we need to look for patterns in the "stories" we have collected. In

Exercise 5.6 Summarizing information from archives

Look through the casenotes of the person you are getting to know and summarize the information you find, using the framework below. If more than one agency is involved, make sure you go through all casenotes (if you are allowed access). If family members have told you they have a diary, photographic or other account of the person's earlier life, you may ask if they would let you see it (but do not forget whose diary or photo album this is – make sure you treat it respectfully). Make any necessary adjustments to the form, but keep the summary brief.

RECORD SHEET   *Information from archives*

Records used

"Hard information" (dates, places, interventions, etc.)

"Soft information" (opinions expressed, images of the person, myths)

Things to follow up as a result of studying archives

Review: How did this activity go? How might you tackle things differently another time?

What have you learned from doing this (other than things about this person)?

What information did you find most useful from the files? Do you think this was a good way to spend time finding out about a person. How could it be made more useful?

Exercise 5.7 Organizing information

Look at all the information you have collected and summarize the important issues under the following headings.

Basic information
age, sex, family, living arrangements, services used, how described (briefly)

Main points about history

Life now

Typical weekly/daily timetable of where, what and with whom

Places map

Important personal ties (frequency? intensity?)

Control over environment

Health status

Recent achievements: learning, breakthroughs, new interests, increasing autonomy

Image: reputation – how people see the person (positive/ negative)

What works for this person?
(What seems to produce good results? What does not?)

How do services impinge on this person?
(How would you describe their overall effect? Focus on the outcome for the person.)

Where is this person going in life?
(What would you predict for the future if nothing changes? What sense of purpose is there in what this person spends time doing?)

Continued

Who is committed to this person?
(How far are they likely to take things on behalf of the person? What is their commitment and how do they see a positive future for the person?)

Additional information

How easy was it to identify the important issues under each heading? Is there any more information that you now see should be collected? Are there any gaps?

Exercise 5.7 we suggest some headings that have proved useful in organizing complex information about a person.

Once we have a collection of key issues for a particular person we need to consider how we can best organize them so we can see their relative importance and how they bear on one another. Here are two suggestions: the first involves making a picture depicting the issues that you have identified. Within the picture you can show how each issue influences other issues, resulting in the actual pattern of experiences. Figure 5.1 gives a relatively simple example of such patterns – see how much you think you understand about Theresa's life from this picture.

The second way is to write an account of how the important issues for a particular person connect, trying to indicate their relative weight. It is a good idea to use metaphors freely in order to express what you think is going on. Again, see how much you think you understand about Theresa's life by reading the following account.

Theresa is 27 years old. Theresa wears typical clothes for a woman her age and shows some interest in her appearance. She can help in dressing herself and seems more comfortable in casual wear. She is somewhat overweight but has managed to diet, even though food has always been a big motivator. Of late, Theresa has lost interest in food, which staff said she used to really enjoy.

Some time ago, Theresa accidentally lost her two front teeth. Unfortunately she is unable to tolerate a plate and as a result is not as pretty as she used to be. Physically, Theresa finds stairs difficult and walking any distance tiring. When calm she has control over her balance, but when she does not wish to do what is expected of

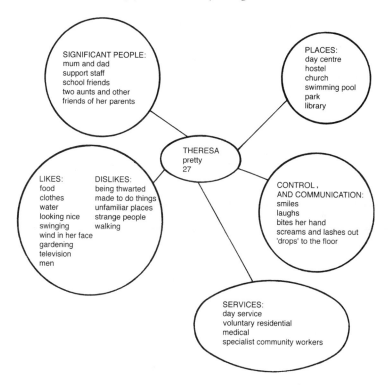

Figure 5.1 Visual summary of Theresa's pattern of experiences.

her she will drop to the floor, bite her hand and refuse to move. Sometimes it is difficult for people to understand the reason for her "dropping". No one really knows how she expresses pain or discomfort.

The description of Theresa and her life circumstances goes on for another four pages.

For the past eight years she has lived in a local authority hostel for people with severe learning disabilities. Five years ago Theresa's parents moved to another part of the country and attempts are being made to transfer Theresa to a suitable place nearby. A few months ago, Theresa spent six weeks at a hostel near her parents with a view to her living there permanently. The hostel is a multi-purpose residential and day-care centre for adults run by an independent organization. Although Theresa seemed to have settled initially, the staff experienced considerable behaviour difficulties which they could not cope with and which they felt put others at risk. Thus, Theresa returned to her original home and, although she was pleased to be back, she has been less cooperative and more unpredictable than before.

The description of what works and what does not work for Theresa in terms of different kinds of supports goes on for another two pages.

Of the two methods, our preference is for the first, visual method, as we are able to summarize a great deal more information more easily and can tell, at a glance, something about how the issues link together. However, you may not be a "visual" person and may find report writing easier, in which case the second method will be more useful. Try one or other method of summarizing patterns of experience in Exercise 5.8.

We now have an overall account of what a person's life is like now. This is a form of knowledge about the person, not the "last word" or "scientific truth" but a model of a life, a summary of themes and issues, a starting point, which you will develop as you learn with the person.

Exercise 5.8 Patterns of experience

Draw a picture or write an account of the important issues relating to the person you have got to know, highlighting how these issues interrelate. Find some way of emphasizing the relative importance of different issues or connections.

What difficulties arose for you in identifying the patterns within the person's life experiences? Did any of these patterns surprise you? If so, in what ways? How much of "you" is there in the patterns you have drawn – your priorities, professional assessments and so on? Would the patterns have been the same if a lay person or a relative of the person you were describing had identified them? What are the advantages and disadvantages of your way of seeing? How many alternative ways could this picture have been drawn? Why did you opt for this solution?

FURTHER READING

Each of the following texts will help in describing the life of a person with learning disability in positive ways, taking account of different dimensions of quality of life.

Brechin, A. and Swain, J. (1987) *Changing Relationships: Shared action planning with people with a mental handicap*, Harper and Row, London.

Brost, M.M. and Johnson, T.Z. (1982) *Getting to Know You*, Wisconsin Coalition for Advocacy and New Concepts for the Handicapped Foundation. (W.C.A., 2 West St, Madison, Wisconsin, 53702), Madison.

Doyal, L. and Gough, I. (1991) *A Theory of Human Need*, Macmillan, Basingstoke.

Kagan, C. (1991) *What Do We Know About Care Management?*, North Western Development Team, Whalley.

Kinsella, P. (1993) *Supported Living – the new paradigm?*, National Development Team, Manchester.

Mount, B. and Zwernik, K. (1988) *It's Never Too Early, It's Never Too Late: A booklet about personal futures planning*, Minnesota Metropolitan Council, St Paul, MN.

O'Brien J. (1987) A guide to personal futures planning, in *The Activities Catalogue: A community programming guide for youths and adults with severe disabilities*, (eds G.T. Bellamy and B. Wilcox), Brookes-Cole, Baltimore.

O'Brien, J. and Lyle, C. (1986) *Framework for Accomplishment*, Responsive Systems Associates, Decatur, Georgia.

Pearpoint, J., O'Brien, J. and Forest, M. (1993) *PATH: Planning Alternative Tomorrows with Hope. A workbook for planning possible futures*, Inclusion Press: Toronto.

Schalock, R.L. (ed.) (1990) *Quality of Life: Perspectives and Issues*, American Association on Mental Retardation, Washington DC.

6

Increasing social opportunities

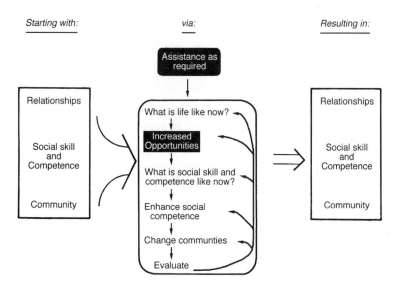

Starting with: via: Resulting in:

By the end of the last chapter, in which we described what life is
like now for a particular person with learning disabilities, we had
summarized a wealth of information about a particular person.
What do we do next?

DEFINING PRIORITIES

We have to work out where to begin. In doing this, we can take a
number of different approaches, but the essence is to do three
things.

- Construct a vision of what a more desirable state of affairs
  might be.

- Form an idea of what kinds of change will most clearly and strongly help move the person and the community in that direction.
- Define clearly some practical and feasible first steps to take.

In so doing, we will also have to question **ourselves** closely. We should ask ourselves these questions.

- Why do this?
- What assumptions am I making about
  the person and her interests
  the community
  services
  the interconnectedness of things?
- What are my motives in making these kinds of changes in the person's life?

These questions will help us clarify our own motives, and also help us ensure that the interests of the person with the disability are kept at the forefront of our minds. However experienced we are, we should never cease to question ourselves and our practice.

We begin be trying to imagine what a better future might look like for the person. We might not be able to reach this future straightaway, but it will help give us a sense of the direction in which we could be helping the person move. In this way we are less likely to fall into the trap of making superficial, cosmetic changes which are easily achieved. Similarly, if we can keep a desirable future in mind, we may be less likely to make the kinds of changes that are inspired simply by wanting to move away from a negative situation in order to create one that is the lesser of two evils. An example of the latter kinds of changes would be all those efforts professionals made in the 1960s and 1970s in response to the horrors of large-scale traditional institutions, which led them to create mini-institutions in their place.

THINKING ABOUT DESIRABLE FUTURES

We discussed earlier how, in our society, having a seriously disabling condition increases the risk of having material, social and developmental needs unmet or seriously compromised, for example through segregation and isolation, exploitation, poverty, or discrimination leading to a lack of identity, conferring or learning experiences and opportunities. We now want to look at what things might look like if these risks could be removed and the constraining experiences undone. A chance to describe such a future for someone you know is given in Exercise 6.1.

**Exercise 6.1 A desirable future:
the outsider's view**

Think about someone with a learning disability you know well (this could, perhaps, be the person you got to know and explored important aspects of life with in the previous chapter). Imagine you could be transported forward in time, say by ten years. Describe, either in words or in a picture, what the person's life could be like. Do not restrict the possibilities you come up with by saying to yourself, "this would not be possible or realistic", or "this is too idealistic". At this stage, do not pretend there is likely to be a miracle that will change the person in some way, but do not be afraid to dream. Where would the person be? With whom? What would be happening? What would have changed? Given this, in what ways might the person have changed?

How does this account compare with what you want for your own future? Would you have described the same desirable future for people who are older, younger or from a different culture? If not, how might it differ? What values and beliefs are reflected in your picture of a desirable future? Does the person see these things as desirable? How do you know?

What you have done in Exercise 6.1 is to bring to bear on your description of a desirable future for someone with learning disabilities all your knowledge about what is or is not possible for different kinds of people in terms of their life opportunities, achievements, acceptance in society and so on. Your selection of things will have been underpinned by your own values and assumptions about what is good in life. How do you think this compares with the future that the person sees for herself or himself? In Exercise 6.2 we ask you to discover the image of the future held by a person with a learning disability. Try to find this out from the person you had in mind for Exercise 6.1.

Exercise 6.2 A desirable future: the insider's view

How does a person with learning disabilities you know well describe a desirable future? You may be able to find out by asking him or her to draw a picture of how the future might look; to choose some pictures from a book that show what the future could be like; or to sit with you while you try to imagine the world as the person sees it and how it could change in the future. You may need to ask those near to the person how they see the possible future, or perhaps you may find out by listening to discussion between the person and other people or by watching them play together. In other words, you may need to be creative in how you find out about a person's dreams. Summarize their dreams below.

How easy was it to get this information? What restricted the person's ideas about a desirable future? How might you go about finding out this information with people who are younger, older or from a different culture? How might you do this exercise in the future?

It is likely that the two pictures you have drawn or written about in Exercises 6.1 and 6.2 differ somewhat. How can they be combined? In Exercise 6.3 we ask you to combine the two pictures in order to make a fuller picture, and then to consider how this future might be reached.

At this stage it is useful to look again at the context in which the person is living and life experiences to date, in order to identify what might present an obstacle to being able to move towards or achieve such a desirable future. Exercise 6.4 gives a framework in which we can identify those aspects of people's lives and the

---

Exercise 6.3 Towards a desirable future

Combine the pictures you have got from your ideas of a desirable future for a person with learning disabilities and their own ideas about a desirable future.

Now list the things that might help the person to get there, with your help and the assistance of others.

Were there any aspects of your visions and the person's visions of desirable futures that were difficult to combine? Why might this be? What kinds of things have you listed as aids to reach this future? Have you resorted, to the "possible"? If so, why is this?

---

overall context in which they are living that will help us move towards this desirable future **and** those aspects that may present obstacles to more desirable futures. This framework is called a force-field analysis. In it we are asked to identify those forces in a person's "life-field" that help or hinder progress towards a desired goal.

IDENTIFYING RELEVANT CHANGES

Having obtained some idea of what might be desirable for the person, we need to know what kinds of changes in circumstances are most relevant, at this stage, to that future. We have to identify which changes will make a real difference to moving forward towards the desirable future. We can use O'Brien and Lyle's list of five accomplishments to help organize our thinking about what changes could be made. Our restatement of the Five Accomplishments is as follows.

**Exercise 6.4 Force-field analysis:
desirable futures**

Describe the forces or aspects of the person's life experiences
and the context in which the person lives that will help
move nearer to and further from the desirable future you
described.

The desirable future for   is:

     Nearer to   Further from

In the person and those around the person

In the community
(i.e. in the rest of life outside the formal services)

In the service(s)

Were you able to identify more helping or hindering forces?
Why is this? Did you involve the person with learning disabilities and those close to her or him in this exercise? How
might you get more involvement from them in thinking
these things through? Can you see which forces are relatively weak and which are relatively strong? Can you see
any ways of strengthening helping forces and weakening
hindering forces? What will it take to be able to do this?

---

1. Presence in the community – means sharing places and activities with ordinary members of the community.
2. Participation – means having a variety of relationships of various types with other people, including some who are not paid

for the relationships, who are personally committed and who are socially valued, i.e. not solely staff, family or other clients.

3. Power – means having real control over what happens to you, including protection of rights and involvement in making decisions.

4. Respect – means being seen and treated as a valued human being; having a positive identity and self image; and being enabled to make a positive contribution to social life.

5. Capability – means having the resources to get things done that are important to you including the maintenance of bodily and mental health and integrity: a variety of possible means, including becoming personally competent (and not just in terms of specific skills) and being able to get assistance.

This list is not the only way of defining important things for people (we might want to include something on having a purpose in life, on the importance of continuity, on the importance of being the most important person to at least one other person, on spirituality, for example) but a framework of this sort can be used as a way of organizing our ideas about important things to aim for, and it can help us to ensure that we do not miss areas of importance.

Different things are important for different people at different times: for someone stuck in an institution, it may be that all of the accomplishments are compromised by the lack of community presence. **Presence** is, then, the key thing to work on. The other things will not happen automatically once the person is living in the community (that is, has some degree of community presence) as some early resettlement programmes assumed, but it will be difficult to do anything profound about any of the other areas within the institutional setting. The setting itself sets limits to participation, power, respect and capability. Can you think of situations where other accomplishments might be of particularly great importance?

It is useful, at this point, to return to the information you have already collected about What Life is Like Now (see Chapter 5). Try organizing this information in terms of the five accomplishments, as shown in Exercise 6.5.

Not only can this framework be used to organize information about what someone's life is like now, it can be useful for deciding which areas of life are the most impoverished. Knowing this helps

---

Exercise 6.5 The five accomplishments as a framework for understanding

Organize the information you have collected about a person with learning disability according to the five accomplishments. Only include information about what the person's life is like now – do not include things from the past.

Presence

Participation

Power

Respect

Capability

Are there some areas in which greater achievements have been made than others? Why is this? Were any of the categories difficult to complete? Are there some areas of the person's life now that have been included in this summary? Are any adjustments to the categories required?

---

us identify in which areas change may make the most impact and help the person move towards a more desirable future. Exercise 6.6 invites you to explore changes that could be made in each of the areas and their likely impact on the person's total pattern of experiences.

Exercise 6.6 The five accomplishments as a framework for identifying relevant changes

With a particular person in mind, think about each accomplishment in turn (move along the top of the chart). Imagine you could help make an impact on this aspect of the person's life. Make a guess about the likely spin-off for each of the other accomplishments (down the side of the chart). Complete the chart by filling in each of the top boxes and writing in the likely impact on each of the other accomplishments in the column below. We have also given an example.

Worked example: Alan Jenkins has a mild learning disability and is currently living in hostel accommodation with people with mental health problems.

| | *work on:* | | | | |
	Presence	*Power*	*Respect*	*Participation*	*Capability*
via:	Move to own flat in ordinary housing development. Supported by worker who supports 5 people in this complex	Service allocates 5 hours support per week. Housing rights advice available	Given age-appropriate clothing. Always introduced as Mr Jenkins	Joins local fishing club, with service worker also joining for first month	Training in community and social skills
for impact on:					
Presence	[–]	Possibility of deciding to live in own flat	Seen as having right to live among us	Uses club house, tackle shop and takes part in matches	Has skills for moving around the community and asking for help if lost
Power	Can choose meals, company (within limits)	[–]	Little change	More options for leisure time	Reduced dependence on paid staff
Respect	Tenant. Not confused with people with mental health problems	Seen as having right to both special and ordinary services	[–]	Seen as having own (appropriate) interests. Some risk of being patronized	Seen as competent to do these things
Participation	Neighbours available but likely to remain mere acquaintances. Potential isolation?	Not dependent on service for main social contact	Less likely to be stigmatized but no direct impact	[–]	More opportunity and skills for engaging with people

continued

	Presence	Power	Respect	Participation	Capability
Capability	Would have opportunity to learn a variety of householder skills. Availability of advice and help to accomplish things he wants to do	Pressure to learn more skills since level of support only sufficient for some "doing for"	Indirect effect – others more likely to offer assistance because less obviously marginalized	Learns angling skills, including manual dexterity and how to behave as part of a group	[–]

work on:

	Presence	Autonomy	Respect	Participation	Capability
via:					
impact on:					
Presence	–				
Power		–			
Respect			–		
Participation				–	
Capability					–

How easy was it to identify the impact that changes in any one area might make in the other areas? Are some areas of life more influenced by changes in other areas? Were there any examples where changes in one area would have no impact in any of the others? Why is this?

OPTIONS FOR CHANGE

We may now be in a position to see which changes in which areas of life will have the greatest impact for change across the person's whole life experience. Having got an idea of the key areas to work on, it is now time to spell out, clearly, with the person, how relevant changes in her or his pattern of experiences may be made. We now have to think about alternative things that could be achieved in this area. Whenever we are thinking about change, there are always choices we can make about precisely what changes could be made, how and by whom. Try identifying options for change in the area of life experience you have identified that will make a difference to the person with whom you are working, as in Exercise 6.7.

Exercise 6.7 Generating options

Think about the area in which changes might be desirable. Write down as many different ways in which these changes could come about as possible. Do not reject any possibilities as being impossible at this stage, and try not to think about "what has been possible in the past". Be as imaginative as you can.

What should change (in the area of which accomplishment)?

How might change be brought about? (Generate as many alternatives as possible.)

Could you generate many alternatives? What would help you generate more? What would help you be more imaginative about the alternatives you were able to generate? Did you involve the person with learning disabilities and those close to them in this task? What would make it possible to get more involvement from them in thinking about what could change?

SETTING OBJECTIVES

Some of the options that have been identified, if you have been successful in using your imagination, will be improbable and difficult to achieve in the context of your work and the person's life. However, others may be turned into specific objectives for change. Objective setting begins to turn general ideas and dreams into practical realities.

If they are to be helpful in guiding what we do, how and when, objectives should be all of the following.

- Clear: You will know when you have achieved them. Try to describe what you want to achieve in terms of what someone else would see happening, rather than in vague general terms.
- Relevant: Achieving the objective will make a difference for the person you are assisting. It will not be a cosmetic change that makes little real difference to the person's situation, and it will be (or will become) important to the person, rather than merely fulfilling expectations of what looks good.
- Practical: However ambitious the objective is, it should be something you stand a chance of achieving. You might have ideas for longer term change, but what is the first step on the way to that?
- Measurable: You will want to be able to tell that the objective has been achieved. This may mean you will need a way of gauging it, measuring it or demonstrating the achievement in some way.

Another way of thinking about objectives is by means of the SPIRO mnemonic. This is a mnemonic that helps us remember to take the following into account when setting and choosing between objectives.

Specificity: exactly what you are trying to accomplish
Performance: exactly what behaviour is implied
Involvement: precisely who is going to do what
Realism: proper consideration as to whether it can be done
Observability: the extent to which other people can see a difference, or whether the difference can be assessed

This way of thinking clearly and precisely about objectives helps us avoid some of the pitfalls of setting distant goals. The more distant the goals set, the more general they are likely to be and the less achievable, with relatively little demonstrable impact on a person's life. Furthermore, as Figure 6.1 shows, we are less likely to retain a personal involvement with and commitment to distant goals. Lastly, distant goals take a long time to realize, and this can mean that people with learning disabilities, and those close to them as well as you, the worker, can become demoralized and begin to feel that change is impossible.

Look now at your options for change. Take some of those and turn them into objectives, meeting the criteria discussed above. Choose four or five different objectives and check their relevance

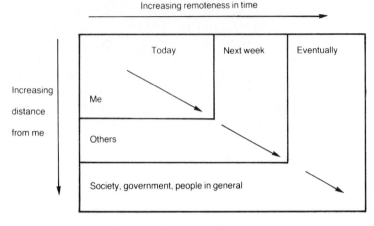

Figure 6.1 Dangers of setting distant goals.

in rather the same way as we checked the relevance of the area of life experience to work on. In other words, try to anticipate the likely impact on areas of the person's life experience, as well as their likely impact on different people. This will help ensure that the people to benefit most from any changes that are made are people with learning disabilities. Again, you can use a matrix technique to make some comparative estimates of the likely effects, as illustrated in Exercise 6.8.

Exercise 6.8 Setting objectives and assessing their impact

Write each objective for change in a box at the top of the chart (do not forget to make sure they are stated in clear, relevant, practical and measurable ways). Then take each objective in turn and assess its impact on each of the areas of life experience listed at the side. You can do this by ticking the box if you think there will be any impact; writing a note of what the impact will be; or by rating the impact according to a rating scale from 1–5 where 1 = little or no impact and 5 = substantial impact. You may want to add a +/− sign to indicate whether the impact is likely to be positive or negative.

continued

	Suggested objectives				
	1	2	3	4	5
Presence					
Power					
Respect					
Participation					
Capability					

A further check for relevance for the person is to assess for whom the intervention you are contemplating is likely to produce benefits. Repeat the exercise, by assessing the likely impact each objective will have on the different people who may be affected.

Objective:

Person	Likely benefits	Likely costs
Person with learning disability		
Family member		
Staff member		
Management		
etc. (List as many people as you want – do not forget to include yourself.)		

You might also find it helpful to try both these tasks for different points in the future, e.g. next month, next year, five years' time.

How easy is it to find objectives that create maximum benefit to the person with learning disabilities? What difficulties arose during this exercise? Will the impact of the different objectives change over time? If so, in what ways?

METHODS OF ACHIEVING OBJECTIVES

The objectives that you have identified above are most probably those that define some kind of outcome for a person, such as "use two different community resources"; "get to know someone who is not paid to be with the person"; "go to a keep fit class"; "buy an age-appropriate outfit"; "sample a new meal at B's restaurant" and so on. Each one of these objectives has a number of ways in which it could be achieved. Just how do we decide which keep fit class, with whom and so on? Checking out the objective with its impact on other areas of life may be one way to prioritize method as well as outcome.

> So, if we are pursuing the objective of "buying Joe an outfit that is appropriate for a man of 32", one way of maximizing the impact of this on other areas of his life is to go to a busy shopping street at a normal shopping time to buy it; encourage Joe to choose some or all of his outfit; ensure the outfit is of good quality; try to enable him to be accompanied by a non-paid person when going shopping and so on.

However, we should also bear in mind a number of things about social opportunities and social situations in general when we try to decide how objectives could be pursued. In particular, we should consider the sustainability and accountability of the opportunities we create; the independence our options have from formal services; and the invisibility of formal supports.

Sustainability   Wherever possible, we should choose options that are based on relatively permanent social arrangements rather than transient short-term ones. What is the track record of the arrangement you are considering connecting with? Often the most robust arrangements serve multiple functions (e.g. social–recreational, economic, cultural, political), and are based on more than one reason for people to come together. This suggests that, for example, local church organizations are often a viable basis for socially integrative opportunities, while free-standing volunteer recruitment, on the other hand, may have few sources of social and community support.

> In our example, staff had made contact with the local volunteer bureau, and a student in his final year in B . . . town had been befriending Joe. Dave, the student, was asked to go shopping with Joe. Had the staff thought of asking one of the men at the local

working men's club, such as Walter, who knew Joe a bit, they would have hit on a potentially more sustainable solution. But none of the staff lived locally and none of them really knew what the working men's club was anyway, nor did they know any of the members of the club.

Accountability Given the vulnerability of people with learning disabilities to being let down by others, as well as to more severe threats, it is important to establish safeguards for the arrangements that you make. This begins by being clear about who has taken responsibility for the welfare of the person concerned and what the nature of that agreement actually is. You will also need to be clear about the means to be used to monitor and review what is happening. Since, in our example, we are now outside the world of formal services, this has to be done sensitively. Remember also that people are no safer in the care of paid staff and families than with those who have made a personal commitment, so it is important that the person's welfare is checked on with the humility that this implies, consistent with actually finding out what is going on. If a proper assessment of risk has been made at the outset the task will be easier.

Walter met Joe and his key worker when he gave them a lift in his taxi to the observation lounge at the airport. Walter got on very well with Joe who is difficult to understand as he does not speak clearly, especially when he is excited (as he was on the day he went to the airport). Walter offered to return to collect Joe and the worker when they had finished at the airport. When they were parting, Walter asked if he could have the privilege of driving Joe again. He did so on a number of occasions. He and Joe clearly got on well together. However, the staff looking after Joe did not encourage Walter in any way. After all, he was not experienced in working with people with learning disabilities as they were, and Joe could be very difficult. Now, why should Walter's commitment to Joe be any less than that of the staff – indeed, as he was not paid to be with Joe daily, we could argue his commitment may be more than that of the staff. If the staff had asked Walter to go with Joe to buy his outfit, they may have been able to foster and support a growing relationship that would have other spin-off advantages for Joe.

Independence from formal services If people are to take part in ordinary community living, that should be based as much as possible on the ordinary structures of the community (where such exist!), rather than on special human service arrangements. You will have to maintain a balance between keeping contact with community contexts and dominating them so much that they lose their non-service identity.

> Walter belonged to the local community "structures" whereas Dave, the student, did not – at least not on a long-term basis. The naturalness of the contact between Walter and Joe was made even more difficult as the agency which supported Joe insisted that volunteers were registered and vetted. While there were good reasons and real concerns behind this, the outcome was that volunteers were being "professionalized" and this process itself distorts naturally occurring community structures.

Invisibility of special supports   Many people require additional special supports. Their needs for these will have to be identified accurately, and this is where effective formal services are vital. However, once such special needs are identified it is important to arrange to satisfy them as invisibly as possible.

> Joe, for example, has communication difficulties, as we have seen. He can become agitated at times, particularly when he wants something and cannot make others understand what he needs. The manager of the support staff initially suggested that Joe always be accompanied by a member of staff when he went out with Walter, "in case Joe has an outburst and needs restraining". However, Joe's speech therapist was able to demonstrate that Joe only had these outbursts when he could not make himself understood, and that there was a limited number of things Joe actually wanted to ask for when he was out. A pocket booklet was constructed which Joe was taught to take out and point to the appropriate symbol for drink, food, go home now, toilet, etc. As a result Joe received expert help, but after four training sessions he was in a position to communicate his main wants to Walter without having to create a disturbance, and there was no need to use the support staff, who, in any case, had other demands on their time.

So, now that you are in a position to prioritize objectives by which you might try and increase the person's social opportunities, thereby maximizing their experience of presence and participation in the community, their autonomy and capability and the respect accorded to them, you need to think how these objectives might be met.

When you have decided **how** you will meet the objectives you prioritized, you might like to work through Exercise 6.9 in order to check the extent to which you are able to address issues of sustainability, accountability, independence from formal services and the invisibility of supports.

Exercise 6.9 Making the most of opportunities

Take each objective you are aiming to meet and consider how you will meet it. Comment on the extent to which your plans could do more to enhance sustainability, accountability, independence from formal services and the invisibility of special supports.

	Sustainability	Accountability	Independence from services	Invisibility of supports
Objective 1				
Objective 2				
Objective 3				
Objective 4				

To what extent were you able to think of ways of maximizing sustainability, accountability, independence from formal services and the invisibility of special supports? Were any of them easy to address? Would they have been different if you had been considering them in relation to a person with more or less complex disabilities? Would they have been different if you had been considering them in relation to a person who is older, younger or from a different culture? In what ways?

ASSESSMENT AND MANAGEMENT OF RISK

Here we are concerned with two kinds of risk: risk to the person with a learning disability and risk to others. We must not forget that people with learning disabilities are vulnerable, both to things like traffic and to the exploitation or abuse of others. This arises from the combination of the process of social devaluation, whereby they come to be seen as of less worth than others; their disabilities, which can make it difficult for them to identify the problem and do something about it; and the social stresses in our society that produce people willing to abuse or exploit others. We have also seen that services are not immune from exploitation or abuse, and indeed both have been part of the culture of service provision in the recent past. However, a responsible service has a primary function of protecting the interests of its users, both in direct contact with the service and outside the boundaries of the formal service itself. Under-protection (which includes neglect) is as serious a problem as over-protection.

> Fergus used to live in a hostel. A very diverse group of people lived there, including those with profound learning disability and extreme physical impairments, and people like Fergus who lived fairly independent lives, using the hostel as a base that provided some degree of security. Others used the hostel for respite care, which added to the demands on the small staff team. When the hostel was being closed, everyone was assessed for the amount and type of support that they would need in more ordinary living situations. Because Fergus can find his way from place to place, go shopping and cook simple meals, it was decided that he could live in a flat on his own, with 35 hours per week support from a residential social worker.
>
> Things seemed to be working very well for the first 18 months, but then the worker was replaced with 5 hours per week from a different worker. Fergus resented this and his behaviour began to deteriorate. Eventually he left his flat and turned up the next day at the social services office in a very distressed and disturbed state. It later transpired that during the two months since his support worker was changed his neighbours had been systematically stealing from him and had made serious threats to prevent him telling anyone. He had also been subject to a consistent torrent of verbal abuse and ridicule.

A second kind of risk involves the possible risk to others from a small minority of people with learning disabilities, at certain times and in certain situations.

> Ada lives at home with her mother. A community nurse has been working with her on personal hygiene and road safety. As her mother gets more frail, Ada has begun to take more responsibility for household tasks. One of these is making light meals such as beans on toast. Ada has no problem in actually accomplishing this, but in conversation she mentioned how much she likes lighting the stove: it transpired that she has become fascinated with flames and

she often lights matches for the fun of it. There is concern that she might start experimenting with lighting other materials, with obvious consequences not only for herself but also for her mother and the young family in the upstairs flat.

Managing risk involves:

- identifying the risk factors (behaviour/actions of others, other environmental dangers);
- assessing the severity of the risk (likelihood of encountering it; potential consequences);
- identifying possible methods for
  - reducing the likelihood of encountering the risk, or
  - reducing the severity of its consequences, or
  - responding when the risk is encountered despite steps to prevent it;
- evaluating each potential method in terms of: practicality, appropriateness for service provision identified above (for instance in terms of the four criteria: sustainability, accountability, independence from services and invisibility of supports) and likely effectiveness;
- choosing a method or methods and drawing up a clear action plan (see Chapter 4, section on goal setting page 108) for implementation;
- monitoring and evaluating the risk management strategy.

Risk management is best agreed by the various people who are involved so that a way forward can be agreed by all parties, as many minds can be brought to bear on the problem solving as possible and so that responsibility can also be shared. It is important to be able to demonstrate (e.g. through documentation) that you are acting in good faith and have followed a structured process for assessing and managing risk: employing authorities will generally accept "vicarious liability" for their staff if these conditions are met. Exercise 6.10 will take you through the above framework for assessing and managing risks.

Exercise 6.10 Assessing and managing risk

For one of the actions you identified in the above exercise (Exercise 6.9: Making the most of opportunities) identify a

Continued

possible risk, its likely severity and potential means of reducing the likelihood of encountering the risk or experiencing severe negative consequences from it. Evaluate the pros and cons of each method and make a decision on the approach to use and how you will implement it.

Throughout, bear in mind the general philosophy of increasing the person's social capability (social competence + community competence) and implementation in ways that maximize sustainability, accountability, independence from formal services and invisibility of special supports.

Method	Feasibility	Appropriateness	Likely effectiveness	Conclusion and action

Form for risk management planning   Risk:

OPPORTUNITIES IN COMMUNITIES

Choosing outcomes and methods of working that maximize sustainability and make best use of community resources relies on us **knowing** what resources there are locally (and more widely, particularly regarding different communities of interest) that we might be able to use, foster or create. It also relies on **being able** to make use of them. We must not lose sight of the different kinds of communities we may want to use and contribute to at different times and for different purposes (see Chapter 3).

Whatever the kind of community, we need to know about, be able to use and make contributions to facilities, people and organizations. The local swimming pool is the facility; the centre manager or the swimming coach are some of the people; the swimming clubs are the organizations. In order to use or help people with learning disabilities contribute to communities, we must know about them. Exercise 6.11 gives a framework for discovering and noting information about relevant communities.

Exercise 6.11 Discovering communities

To know about the communities into which we are trying to help people with learning disabilities be included and to which we are trying to help them contribute, we will need to know a number of different things, including physical features, facilities, access, networks of people and organizations.

Physical features	*Immediate locality*	*Further afield*
Weather patterns		
Geographical and design features (hills, pavements, kerbs, crossings, access to public buildings)		
Transport routes, facilities, times		
Telephones, bus shelters, toilets, etc.		

Facilities	*Immediate locality*	*Further afield*
Shops		

Leisure activities
    formal
    informal		

Continued

Facilities	*Immediate locality*	*Further afield*
Employment		
Education		
Health		
Financial		
Domestic services		
Council services		
Eating and drinking		
Places of worship		

NB For each of the above you will need to know who uses the facilities and how penetrable the settings are.

Organizations	*Immediate locality*	*Further afield*
Work		
Leisure		
Hobby/interest		
Religious		
Political		
Charity		
Voluntary		
Cultural		

NB For each of the above you will need to know who is involved in the organizations and how penetrable the organizations are – are they "closed" to established cliques, etc.

People
You need to know who is involved in what and who knows whom in the locality and further afield. You may like to keep a list of:

Continued

☐ chairs, organizers, directors of local organizations and community groups

☐ people with particular roles (church minister, postmaster/postmistress, doctor's receptionist)

☐ people with a lot of local knowledge (manager of the stationer's shop, postwoman/postman, community police officer)

☐ popular community figures (athletics star, actors, councillors)

☐ people with particular opinions (who write to or are featured by the local papers about particular issues, campaign leaders).

You can find out this information from the local library, looking at local notices and in local papers and talking to local people. Not only will you need to know who individual people are, but – often more importantly – who they know. Keep a directory of people you know, or know of, like the one below (and make sure you keep it up to date).

Name	Activity of interest	Role	Address and Phone No.	Details of contact made (if any)
Jean Barker	Community transport	Organiser (also member CHC)	c/o Midplace Library, Softman St 796 4421	Met informally in chip shop – does not know I work with people with learning disabilities
Fred Presser	Football supporters	County secretary	Woodville, Marcham, Nr Northplace 8812157	No. Regular letters to Midplace Reporter

Whenever you can, draw a relationships map as in Figure 6.2.

What gaps are there in your knowledge about the immediate locality and relevant communities further afield? How

Continued

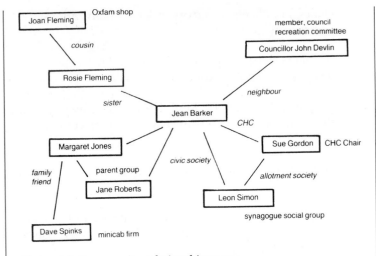

Figure 6.2 Community relationships map.

might you fill these gaps? What sources of information did you use to find out some of the information? Are there any other sources of information that would be helpful? How much of this information did you get from the person with learning disabilities and their families and friends? Is there further information you might need for people who are older, younger or from different cultures? How will you get this information?

WORKING WITH COMMUNITIES

You will have seen from Exercise 6.11 that knowing about local and relevant communities is complex. It is extremely time-consuming collecting the information. Whilst some if it may be available from local authority planning departments or local libraries, it is well worth trying to obtain as much of it as possible directly. The advantage of this is that you will not only be making contact with people as you find out about the community, but you will also be able to gauge the possibilities and potential limitations of the locality, facilities, people and so on. Better still, find out about the community together with a person with learning disabilities. One thing should be apparent: this information is very much easier to obtain if you live in the locality. Whether you do or not, the sooner you get in touch with people who have a lot of inside information and contacts in the neighbourhood and wider community, the quicker your task will be.

It is one thing to know about the locality and the community at large, it is another to be able to use the resources that are available. Making contact with formal organizations is not usually difficult for professionals, nor is it difficult to make contact with people who have a formal role in a community group, organization or facility. Much harder is making informal contact with people who may or may not have a formal role (you may not know when you first meet them). Many people who are not used to this kind of work find this part of it a source of great pressure and sometimes distress. We have heard workers say on many occasions something like: "Oh yes, I can see what's needed – but I couldn't do it; I'm not the sort of person who can just strike up a conversation with anyone".

We have found it useful to think of working in and with communities as rather like private detective work. You have to be able to find things out and remember details about what appears to be a most unpromising lead, but first and foremost you have to be orderly and structured in how you go about your work. Some of the stress for workers arises from an almost total lack of structure to their work and the purpose of their work. You already have some structure: you know the direction you are helping a person move in and have identified priorities for making changes that help move in that direction. Now you have to find ways of helping to maximize the development of relationships with other people who might share places, interests or activities. Thus we are not suggesting we should all be getting to know everyone we could possibly know in the community and turn ourselves into charismatic extroverts. Instead, we are suggesting you find out about relevant people, activities and so on, in line with the objectives you have set with the person with learning disabilities. This helps direct your activities. Exercise 6.12 gives you the chance to clarify the differences between making purposeful contacts in the community and making ad hoc contacts with people.

Making contacts for a purpose, then, is a far more organized and thoughtful process than happening on chance encounters. This means, though, that it is necessary to be prepared whenever you meet people you hope can help make changes in the lives of

Exercise 6.12 Making contacts

1. Describe a recent instance when you got to know something about someone you had not met before in your neighbourhood. Describe the event in the relevant sections below.

What were your intentions on that day?

What led up to meeting the person?

How did you find out whatever it is you found out?

Was anyone else involved in this encounter? If so, what role did that person play?

What did you do with the information you discovered?

2. Think about why you might want to make contact with someone you have not met before or find out something you did not know about people in the neighbourhood in relation to any of the objectives you are pursuing with a person with learning disabilities. Answer the following questions.

Why do you want to establish contact with **this** person?

In what way(s) might this person help you achieve your objective?

What is it you would like to come out of the contact?

Has a meeting been requested? If so, by whom?

Continued

How will you achieve your goals for this contact?

How will you present yourself and the person with whom you work to this person?

How will you establish that you are a genuine and reliable person?

How will you generate interest or enthusiasm for whatever you want to discuss or discover?

How do you intend to leave this meeting?

Any other consideration?

What differences were there between these two encounters? How might you think differently about utilizing chance encounters in the street? How might you think differently about asking people you already know to various degrees for information or practical help of some kind? Are there some kinds of assistance that it is easier to ask other people for, with or on behalf of people with learning disabilities than others? If so, what kinds of things? What backup would you want from your manager or organization if you are establishing contact with non-professional people in the community?

people with learning disabilities, whether you already know them or not.

It is important to build on any encounters whether these happen by chance or not. Here are some examples of such interactions with people in the community:

- receiving visitors;
- shopping;

- dealing with trades people;
- accompanying people with learning disabilities in a variety of community activities;
- relationships with immediate neighbours;
- involvement in community organizations as a service and as an individual with an interest;
- involvement with other services and service-type organizations (police, schools, youth organizations).

Some communities will have obvious events and structures that can form the basis for additional transactions with the service – carnivals, church fétes, harvest festivals, etc.

These contacts are an opportunity for service users to interact with people from the "real world" outside the service. It is worth considering how people with learning disabilities can be presented in the most positive light possible: carrying out some kind of role or responsibility; having something appropriate to talk about; doing as much of the liaison as possible, with staff acting as scarcely visible support – and how these interactions can become a possible basis for something more: inviting the decorator to share a birthday cake; answering questions about people in ways that give an accurate and respectful representation; seizing opportunities offered by both service users and others (Would he like to help me carry the ladder? Would she like to meet my daughter? Can I see inside your van?). We will pick up on different methods of working with resources in communities throughout the next chapters. What we have done here is to look at how we can get to know about resources in our communities and at some of the issues to do with making contact with ordinary people in neighbourhoods and communities.

In this chapter, then, we have explored what it means to set objectives for change, and how we can best ensure that those objectives not only make a relevant and substantial difference to a person with learning disabilities, but that the process of achieving the objective, itself also enhances other life opportunities.

Just as we could undertake a force-field analysis of things that may help or obstruct progress towards desirable futures for a person (Exercise 6.4), so we can undertake the same analysis for each objective. Try to anticipate likely barriers you will encounter in attempting to make these changes: use your chart of the forces taking the person towards/away from the desirable future to give you some clues here. You can also refer back to your picture/ account of the issues confronting the person (see Chapter 5 on finding out about the person).

Identifying the potential obstructions to achievement as well as the potential facilitators will help us choose which objective we should start with, or help us see that there are other objectives (in weakening hindering forces or strengthening helping forces) that must be achieved before we can begin on those we have already identified. If we do not do this, the obstacles to progress may be so strong that our attempts to enable change are doomed to failure from the start. Exercise 6.13 is a force-field analysis of each objective.

Exercise 6.13 Force-field analysis: objectives for change

Describe the forces or aspects of the person's life experiences and the context in which the person lives that will help you enable progress towards achieving each objective for change that has been identified.

Objective ————————————————————————

Nearer to	Further from

In the person and those around

|

In the community
(i.e. in the rest of life outside the formal services)

|

In the service(s) (including your own skills)

|

Were you able to identify more helping or hindering forces? Why is this? Did you involve the person with learning disabilities and those close to the person in this exercise? How might you get more involvement from them in thinking

Continued

---

these things through? Can you see which forces are relatively weak and which are relatively strong? Can you see
any ways of strengthening helping forces and weakening
hindering forces? What will it take to be able to do this? Are
there other objectives that must be met before you can begin
to work on your original one?

FURTHER READING

Some of the following readings may give ideas about how opportunities
might be increased: others draw on work in social development to explore the boundaries of participation by local people in developing opportunities for all. The advent of case management augurs well for
approaches that look for increased opportunities and we have included
some of the more interesting accounts of case management.

Atkinson, D. and Ward, L. (1986) *Talking Points 3: A part of community:
    Social integration and neighbourhood networks,* Campaign for People with
    Mental Handicaps (CMH), London.
Burton, M. (1992) *Roads to Quality,* North Western Regional Advisory
    Group for Learning Disability Services, Manchester.
Cragg, R. and Garvey, K. (1990) *What's On? A comprehensive menu of
    ordinary living activities for adults,* R. Cragg, Kidderminster.
Firth, H. and Rapley, M. (1990) *From Acquaintance to Friendship,* British
    Institute of Mental Handicap (BIMH) Publications, Kidderminster.
Gottleib, B.H. (1983) *Social Support Strategies: Guidelines for mental health
    practice,* Sage, London.
Hawtin, M., Hughes, G. and Percy-Smith, J. (1994) *Community Profiling:
    Auditing social needs,* Open University Press, Milton Keynes.
Higgins, P.C. (1985) *The Rehabilitation Detectives: Doing human service
    work,* Sage, Beverley Hills, CA.
Lakin, K.C. and Bruininks, R.H. (eds) (1985) *Strategies for Achieving Com-
    munity Integration of Developmentally Disabled Citizens,* Paul H. Brookes,
    Baltimore.
Lippert, T. (1987) *The Case Management Team: Building Community Connec-
    tions,* Minnesota Metropolitan Council, St Paul, MN.
Midgley, J., Hall, A., Hardiman, M. and Narine, D. (1986) *Community
    Participation, Social Development and the State,* Methuen, London.
Moxley, D.P. (1989) *The Practice of Case Management,* Sage, London.
Pearpoint, J., O'Brien, J. and Forest, M. (1993) *PATH: Planning Alternative
    Tomorrows with Hope. A workbook for planning possible futures,* Inclusion
    Press, Toronto.
Peck, C.A., Odom, S.L. and Bricker, D.D. (1993) *Integrating Young Children
    with Disabilities into Community Programmes: Ecological perspectives on
    research and implementation,* Paul Brookes, London.
Shearer, A. (1986) *Building Community,* Kings Fund Centre/CMH,
    London.

Swain, J., Finkelstein, V., French, S. and Oliver, M. (1993) *Disabling Barriers, Enabling Environments*, Sage/Open University Press, London.
Tyne, A. with others (1988) *Ties and Connections*, Kings Fund Centre, London.

7

What are social skill and social competence like now?

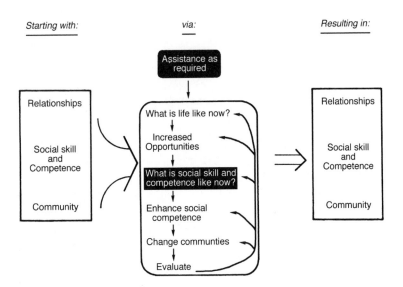

So far we have looked at one side of social capability: the way in which we can work to increase opportunities for people with learning disabilities to become part of the real world, sharing in the kinds of activities, places, relationships and decisions that the rest of us take for granted. The focus, therefore, has been on the opportunities people have, but if we restrict our attention to increasing opportunities we only partly understand capability. To be a capable person also means being able to do things, and "being able" in social situations is what we mean by social competence. Exercise 7.1 is an exploration into what we mean by "being able".

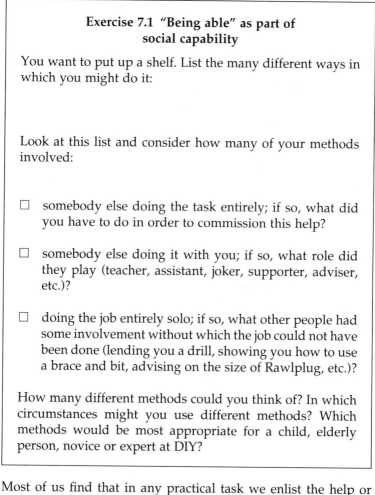

Exercise 7.1 "Being able" as part of social capability

You want to put up a shelf. List the many different ways in which you might do it:

Look at this list and consider how many of your methods involved:

☐ somebody else doing the task entirely; if so, what did you have to do in order to commission this help?

☐ somebody else doing it with you; if so, what role did they play (teacher, assistant, joker, supporter, adviser, etc.)?

☐ doing the job entirely solo; if so, what other people had some involvement without which the job could not have been done (lending you a drill, showing you how to use a brace and bit, advising on the size of Rawlplug, etc.)?

How many different methods could you think of? In which circumstances might you use different methods? Which methods would be most appropriate for a child, elderly person, novice or expert at DIY?

Most of us find that in any practical task we enlist the help or assistance of others in various ways. This may not be direct assistance – we may consult an instruction book, for example. Rarely are we able to undertake a practical activity without some kind of assistance. This illustrates that personal competence, coupled with the competence of those around us, leads us to be capable of doing things. It is the same in social situations. Here, though, we are not talking about manual skills like putting up a shelf and practical assistance from those around us, instead we are talking about social skills and practical assistance from those around us leading to our social capability. We can put this as follows.

$$\begin{array}{ccccc} \text{Social} & = & \text{Social} & + & \text{Competence} \\ \text{capability} & & \text{competence} & & \text{of the} \\ & & & & \text{community} \end{array}$$

UNDERSTANDING SOCIAL SKILL AND
SOCIAL COMPETENCE

We are interested in helping people be able to do more things, and to do them better. The more a person can do, the more self-respect he or she is likely to have and the more others will value that person, who will also be able to exert more control over what happens. Thus, enhanced social competence may increase social opportunities.

Those of us who do not have learning disabilities and have always lived in the community, sharing our lives with others in different communities (including neighbourhoods and communities of interest), are able to do many things for ourselves. Our communities and the people in them have been our teachers. In Exercise 7.2 we look at ways we have been helped to become more socially competent by the competence of our communities.

As we can see, we have been helped to become socially competent in a variety of ways, but mostly informally, incidentally and accidentally. Increasing social opportunities may be enough to help people with a learning disability (particularly those with only moderate disabilities) become more personally effective, through any of the kinds of learning listed above; however, most are going to need some extra help in learning to function more capably. If we are to help people with learning disabilities enhance their social skill and social competence, we have to be clear about what must be learned.

WHAT IS RELEVANT?

Our time and resources are limited. Likewise, the person with whom we are working has probably had much time wasted in the past: it is important that we are constantly questioning what we focus upon and then what we do is likely to be relevant. It is not always easy to know what is relevant for a particular person, but some help should be gained from our understanding of what her or his life is like now and the ways we have found for increasing

Exercise 7.2 Community competence as an aid to social competence

Look at the list of ways you may have been helped to become more socially competent. Try to think of an example for each of them, from your own experience. Then consider what difficulties people with learning disabilities might have in making use of these forms of help.

Type of assistance you have had in learning	Example of this type of assistance	Difficulty people with learning disabilities may experience in using this type of assistance
Others modelling or demonstrating what is required (you observing)		
Direct instruction		
Indirect instruction (writing, TV, etc.)		
Trial and error (being allowed to experiment and try a different way)		
Shown the consequences of our actions		

Were any of these forms of assistance difficult to identify? Have they changed as you have got older? Are there any other forms of assistance that you have experienced?

opportunities. Understanding what people's lives are like now encourages us to get to know them in the context of different experiences and situations and gives us some information about what they want to do. It also helps us understand the limitations that situations impose and the difficulties they face in different situations. Finding ways of increasing opportunities helps us know what kinds of opportunities might be possible.

We can get further information about what might be relevant, especially in terms of people's social skill and social competence, if we refer back to Figure 4.1 in Chapter 4. Figure 4.1 presented a model of different components of social competence. When we use this model to identify what could change to make things better for people with learning disabilities, we can ask a number of questions, as shown in Figure 7.1.

Now we will show how this model can be useful for deciding what it is important to work on. You may find it useful to review the related material in Chapter 4 in conjunction with the following sections; it provides more detailed explanations of the concepts used here.

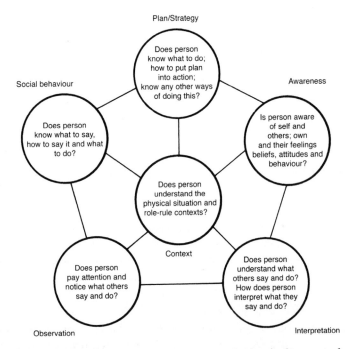

Figure 7.1 Model of social competence: agenda for finding out about social competence. Adapted from Kagan, C. (1985) Issues arising from teaching interpersonal skills in post-basic nurse training. In C. Kagan (Ed) *Interpersonal Skills in Nursing: Research and Applications.* Beckenham: Croom Helm.

AWARENESS

Awareness of ourselves and others is an essential component of social competence. If we are not aware of ourselves, we may have no idea of how close or distant we are, how loudly we are shouting, whether we look pleased and so on. If we are not aware of others, we cannot judge how they are feeling, either within themselves or towards us. We cannot estimate what they think of us and we are not, then, able to adjust our own behaviour as necessary. In the following example, Les may well pick up that people avoid him or try to get away from him. They may even talk patronizingly to him so as not to get him worked up.

Les likes people. He refers to anyone who spends any time with him as "my mate". He shows this by thumping them very hard on the shoulder when they are talking to him and when he next sees them. He has no idea that people find this "friendly pat" painful and even frightening. He cannot judge how hard he is hitting nor what it is like to be the person he hits.

Les has a problem with awareness. He thought he was being nice to people whereas in fact he was building up an image of an unpredictably aggressive man. People who are unaware of others' interests or needs, or their own interests, needs or behaviour are unlikely to function in a way judged as competent. Their perceptions of others will be shallow and frequently mistaken: there can be little room for empathy if the perspective of the other person cannot be taken. Similarly it is important to be aware of what we want, feel, think and do in order to plan, adjust and troubleshoot our actions. Social behaviour without self-awareness is like driving a vehicle without knowing whether it is a mini, an articulated lorry or a sports car.

Exercise 7.3 Provides a framework in which you can think about the extent to which a person is socially aware.

It is often not enough to rely on only one source of information or incidence wherein you think people have demonstrated the extent of their awareness. Always test out their awareness in a different situation.

Alf had been confused about gender identity. He always saw himself as more similar to the women he knew at the training centre rather than the men. After a lot of discussion extending over a number of weeks, Alf appeared to be able to tell women from men

Exercise 7.3 Finding out about awareness

Try to find out how aware a person with learning disabilities is. You will probably have to find this out indirectly by spending time with the person in a number of different situations. If there are any particular situations where there is a particular difficulty, concentrate on these, but do not forget to look at different situation too: this will tell you whether the person has not developed awareness or is not using awareness in particular situations. Ask yourself throughout how you know this.

Self-awareness
Behaviour   Does she know what she does, how and how often?

Thoughts   Is she aware of own thought processes and the content of own thoughts?

Values   Does she know on what basic values own decisions, preferences, actions, reactions, etc. are based?

Likes/dislikes   Does she know own likes or dislikes?

Posture   Is she aware of how she sits and stands, holds head etc.; know what that posture suggests to others?

Feelings   Can she describe own feelings or does she confuse emotions?

Speech   Can she recall and monitor what she says?

How does person's awareness differ from that of peers?

In what ways does person become aware of self?
Body: state of muscles, fingers, feet, etc.; state of blood vessels, breathing, etc.; can person recognize self in the mirror, in photographs, when hearing own voice, etc.?

Continued

Emotions: Can bodily changes be detected? Can they be labelled?

Senses: Impairments in these (touch, smell, sight hearing) can constrain the sense of self.

Others: Feedback from others is important in constructing self-awareness. Does she use reactions, comments, criticisms, etc. of others in becoming aware of the kind of person she is?

Social awareness

What things external to self is she aware of?

Feelings of others When doing different things, does she know how others feel? Is she sensitive to own impact on others?

Interests of others Does she have any idea of what others might want or need? How realistic is this idea?

Thoughts of others How aware is she of what others think, particularly in relation to own behaviour? Empathy?

Social roles Is she aware of how she fits in in terms of age, sex, child/adult, acquaintance/friend/lover, person who needs help/helper, son/daughter, etc.?

How easy was it to get information in these different areas of awareness? Were some areas more difficult than others? Why? What kinds of information did you use? Did you rely on anyone else to give you information? If so, who and what kinds of information? If you have identified any areas where awareness is low, do you know whether this affects the person's social capability? How?

---

consistently. He also knew he was a man. One day when a student was walking up to the market with Alf, he pointed to a red car and said he fancied stealing that one. The student told him that would be silly as he would get caught and then be in trouble with the police. "Oh no, I wouldn't" replied Alf thoughtfully, "I would put on glasses and then they would think I was a woman – no one would know it was me".

OBSERVATION

Interacting with other people requires a constant set of adjustments to what they say or do. Knowing how to present oneself in a way acceptable to others requires sensitivity to the way others present themselves and their reactions to you. Observation of the social behaviour of others is basic to this process of adaptation. Without observation there is no way of knowing what is socially appropriate, what others expect nor how they are responding to what you do. Without good observation, opportunities to learn to become more socially competent may be missed, leading to a vicious circle of social incompetence.

In the following example, Diane does not notice when people indicate, through words, gesture or "body language" that they have had enough of the topic of conversation. She will be impervious to any signs that they may want to contribute to the conversation, and it is likely that most interactions with Diane will be one-sided. People may, therefore, become bored and stop wanting to talk to her.

Diane enjoys having conversations with other people, and often initiates conversation with relative strangers. She talks about Manchester United football team and about "Neighbours". She tends to repeat herself. Unfortunately she becomes so engrossed in what she is saying that she does not realize when other people have had enough and it is time to finish the interaction.

If we cannot observe, we cannot pick up subtle and not so subtle cues from other people that are vital for effective interactions. We will not be able to respond to feedback others give us, and we will make few distinctions between other people and their relationships with us. Poor observation leads to lack of social competence. In Exercise 7.4 we offer a framework for asking questions about the extent to which people with learning disabilities observe the social world around them, including the people and their behaviour.

Exercise 7.4 Finding out about observation

Try to find out how observant a person with learning disabilities is. You will probably have to find this out indirectly by spending time with the person in a number of different situations. If there are any particular situations where there is a particular difficulty, concentrate on these, but do not forget to look at different situations too: this will tell you whether the person is not observant or is not being observant in particular situations. Ask yourself throughout how you know whatever you have said about the person.

Observation

Attention Does she attend at the right times and for the right periods?

Seeing and hearing Does she notice things nearby – the presence or absence of others; changes in company as people come and go; social cues (non-verbal and speech) provided by others; environmental cues that give ideas of what the situation is and how to behave?

General observation Does she notice what people are wearing; how they are behaving; what sex and age they are; what job/role they are doing or playing; what the situation is?

Process observation While interacting with others, does she notice what they are doing and saying; notice what else is going on – people stopping talking or listening, people arriving or leaving, etc.?

Outcome observation Does she notice the effect of own actions?

Continued

How easy was it to get information in these different areas of observation? Were some areas more difficult than others? Why? What kinds of information did you use? Did you rely on anyone else to give you information? If so, who and what kinds of information? If you have identified any areas where observation is poor, do you know whether this affects the person's social capability? How?

It can be particularly difficult with many people to disentangle whether or not they are able to be socially competent, or whether they are just not using their competence in a particular situation. (Some writers use the terms competence and performance for these two things.)

Nora lives in a small staffed house in a busy area of a large town. Her house is near the main road. Nora does not speak, and the staff and her family say she notices very little about her surroundings. It is not even clear that Nora recognizes different members of staff. Nora is not allowed out alone as it is feared that she will not manage roads or even know where she is. One day Nora found the front door open and out she went. Some time later the staff found her missing. No one knew how long she had been away. The police were called. Some two and a half hours later Nora's sister brought her home. She had not known Nora was missing but had accidentally come across her in a nearby park (the other side of the main road), sitting on a bench eating an ice-cream. Nora waved the ice-cream at Peggy when she saw her approaching.

This incident shocked Nora's staff considerably, as she demonstrated far higher levels of social competence that day than she had ever previously shown. It seemed to them now that Nora had powers of observation about both her surroundings and about people that had not previously been evident. (No one ever found out how Nora got an ice-cream!)

INTERPRETATION

Interpreting the actions, intentions and feelings of other people is important if we are to adjust our behaviour appropriately to take account of what the other person does. However, interpretation of people is often linked to our understanding and interpretation of situations. This is well illustrated by what happened when Malcolm went out for a meal:

> Malcolm went with his father to an Italian restaurant where they had
> been before several times in the summer. The proprietor came
> towards them to take their coats, with his arms outstretched.
> Malcolm took one hand and shook it.

Malcolm's mistake made him look inept in that particular social situation, embarrassing both his father and the restaurateur.

Interpretation rests upon knowledge of social customs, social rules and typical patterns of behaviour (social norms). We interpret the behaviour of others using our broader social knowledge. Malcolm may have been unaware of the practice of taking coats from patrons since he had previously been to this restaurant in the warmer weather. In Exercise 7.5 we offer a framework for finding out about how competent people are in interpreting things around them.

Interpretation is not usually something that we can see or hear. So how is it that we know how someone else might be interpreting things? We can ask them, but many people with learning disabilities will not be able to answer this question. Generally, we need to infer from how people behave that they have made certain interpretations. But we need to be careful as, whenever we make inferences about other people, we stand in danger of introducing our own biases of observation and interpretation. Chris and Peter showed by their own actions that they had misinterpreted the intentions and thereby the characters of their neighbours.

> Peter and Chris share a house, and are supported by visiting staff.
> Their council house has a small garden bordered by a privet
> hedge, on the other side of which is a busy road. There is a gate
> with a rather difficult catch and they share this entrance with
> another house. Recently Peter had a big shouting match with the
> family who live next door. The row was about Peter and Chris
> leaving the gate open all the time. Peter was not going to shut the
> gate "for those bloody nosy people" – they were just interested in
> making life a misery for himself and Chris. Peter and Chris did not
> think that the neighbours might have a good reason for wanting the
> gate shut.

Peter and Chris were unaware of the legitimate interests of the neighbours, interpreting their request as petty and an unwarranted interference in their life. However, if we knew that Chris and Peter had been harassed for several months by these same

Exercise 7.5 Finding out about interpretation

Try to find out how a person with learning disabilities interprets the behaviour, feelings and intentions of others. You will probably have to find this out indirectly by spending time with the person in a number of different situations. If there are any particular situations where there is a particular difficulty, concentrate on these, but do not forget to look at different situations too: this will tell you whether the person is not interpreting or is not interpreting in particular situations. Ask yourself throughout how you know whatever it is you have said about the person.

Interpretation

Behaviour   Does she know what different combinations of behaviours mean in different situations and in different roles?

Intentions   Can she make inferences about people's intentions, feelings or thoughts?

Social rules   Does she know what is expected of different people in different situations; understand the notion of social conformity, local customs, different social roles played in different situations and the consequences of breaking social rules?

Self   Does she understand the reasons for own actions and understand the concepts of choice and agency?

How easy was it to get information in these different areas of interpretation? Were some areas more difficult than others? Why? What kinds of information did you use? Did you rely on anyone else to give you information? If so, who and what kinds of information? If you have identified any areas where interpretation is weak, do you know whether this affects the person's social capability? How?

neighbours, we would not, perhaps, have thought their interpretation unreasonable.

PLANNING AND STRATEGY

In most social situations, we know alternative ways of doing things for the same result. Not only do we know of alternative strategies, be they verbal or non-verbal, but we can choose between these alternatives and monitor whether they have been effective or not. Whilst not every competent social activity is planned explicitly, planning is helpful in establishing new patterns of activity and behaviour and in solving problems that face us. A plan or strategy requires that we know what we want or ought to do, that we can generate a variety of alternative ways of achieving our goal and that each of these can be broken down into a sequence of steps for us to take. Vera did not have a plan, nor a range of alternative behaviours to try, when she took something back to a shop.

> Vera had bought an aerosol deodorant from the chemist. On getting it home she found that it was in fact hair lacquer. Having discussed it with her advisor she took the aerosol back. On arriving at the shop Vera stood with the aerosol near the back of the shop, whilst several other customers came and went. Eventually an assistant asked if she could help. Vera then went and put the aerosol down on the counter. Luckily the assistant guessed that there was something wrong with the aerosol and after some questioning she exchanged it.

Vera was told that if she took the aerosol back the chemist would change it, but she did not plan what to do and say when she arrived at the shop, nor did she try a different tack when standing at the back of the shop did not work. In Exercise 7.6 we offer a framework for finding out how people with learning disabilities plan and adjust their strategy according to the situation.

Exercise 7.6 Finding out about planning and strategy

Try to find out how a person with learning disabilities plans and makes decisions in social situations. You will probably have to find this out indirectly by spending time with the person in a number of different situations. If there are any particular situations in which there is a particular difficulty, concentrate on these, but do not forget to look at different situations too: this will tell you whether the person does plan and problem solve or is not planning in particular situations. Ask yourself throughout how you know whatever it is you have written about the person.

Plans and strategies

Goal   Is she able to make own goals clear and what she wants from different situations and people?

Plans   Can she plan how to achieve these goals and plan time?

Knowledge of alternatives   Does she identify different courses of action for achieving particular goals and know how to carry out different alternatives?

Consequences   Does she anticipate what will happen if particular courses of action are followed?

Choice   Is she able to exercise choice and make a decision that is based on knowledge of consequences?

Priorities   Is she able to plan a sequence of steps to be taken in pursuit of own goals; able to decide which are the most important things and where to start?

Monitoring   Can she monitor own progress and reflect on the outcome of a course of action?

Implementation   Is she able to do these things when faced with a problem in real life?

How easy was it to get information in these different areas of problem solving? Were some areas more difficult than others? Why? What kinds of information did you use? Did

Continued

you rely on anyone else to give you information? If so, who and what kinds of information? If you have identified any areas where planning and strategy are low, do you know whether this affects the person's social capability? How?

Even when people have a range of different things they can do in a particular situation and have a good understanding of the situation, failure to plan can reveal a lack of social competence, as Trevor found.

Trevor had an accident on his bike. He left the bike with someone at the market when he was taken to hospital to have his cuts dressed. The next day he returned to reclaim his bike. He did not know where the bike was likely to be so he just started asking passers-by. Nobody seemed to know so he asked some stallholders. Someone suggested he go to the police station. The police suggested he go to the market supervisor, who happened to be the person who had agreed to look after the bike.

Trevor had no plan for locating his bike, but instead used a blunderbuss strategy of asking everybody he met where it was, which, after a lot of asking, eventually brought the result.

SOCIAL BEHAVIOUR

Social behaviour is often seen as the essence of social competence. However as we have seen, other aspects of social competence can contribute to or detract from social capability. Nevertheless, if people say and do nothing when they are in the company of others, most of us would not think of them as socially competent. Social behaviour includes what people say or communicate in some other way and what they do – that is their verbal and non-verbal behaviour. One problem in evaluating whether someone has a problem with social behaviour is that there are few "right ways of behaving". Take Joan, for instance:

When Joan talks to people she stands very close to them. Most people find this rather uncomfortable, particularly as her breath often smells.

Joan does what many socially successful and competent people do, but, whereas they have interesting things to say and pleasant breath, Joan has (on the face of it) little to compensate for breaking the unwritten rule about how much distance to put between herself and others. In Exercise 7.7 we offer a framework for finding out the nature of peoples' social behaviour.

Exercise 7.7 Finding out about social behaviour

Try to find about the social behaviour of a person with learning disabilities – do not forget to look at both what is said or communicated and how it is said. You will probably have to find this out by making some direct observations of what the person does with different people in different situations and in different circumstances. Whilst behaviour rating scales may be of some use in some situations, descriptions of what you saw or heard will be of more use. Try to notice what preceded (antecedents) and what followed (consequences) particular behaviours.

You will, therefore, have to spend time with the person in a number of different situations. If there are any particular situations where there is a particular difficulty, concentrate on these, but do not forget to look at different situations too: this will tell you whether verbal and non-verbal behaviour is lacking, or whether it is not used appropriately in certain situations. Ask yourself throughout how you know whatever it is you have said about the person.

Non-verbal behaviour Does she have a range of non-verbal behaviours; are these combined in meaningful ways; do they replace or support speech appropriately; are there some non-verbal cues that are seldom used or misleading; are there some situations in which the non-verbal behaviour is more appropriate than others?

Movement Can she place self within conversational distance of others; does she have any physical barriers (such as mobility equipment) that prevent other people getting near; does she use and respond to touch appropriately; is she able to control limbs?

Continued

Verbal behaviour Does she communicate through speech/ signing in ways that can be understood; is verbal behaviour accompanied by non-verbal behaviour; have a variety of ways of saying the same thing; have a range of topics of conversations; is she able to speak in more than one word utterance; can she talk about themselves and what they think?

Turn-taking Does she recognize, ask and respond to questions; recognize cues for starting, interrupting and ending conversations; understand what it is like to be the other person in a conversation?

Timing Does she talk for appropriate lengths of time; use pauses to keep conversations flowing; let other people speak and express their opinions?

Specific strategies Is she able to make own wishes understood; exercise choice over whether or not to voice an opinion; make and refuse requests; pick up cues in which other people are interested/uninterested; understand the meaning and practice of small talk?

How easy was it to get information about verbal and non-verbal behaviour? Were some areas more difficult than others? Why? What kinds of information did you use? Did you rely on anyone else to give you information? If so, who and what kinds of information? If you have identified any areas where social behaviour was inappropriate, do you know whether this affects the person's social capability? How?

Behaviour depends for its social effect on the characteristics of both the person and the situation. Some of this can be quite subtle: one person has an unusually loud voice, but its tone and the content of what is said somehow mean that it does not jar on most people's ears; another person has a voice that is no louder but something about the tone and the repetitive content makes for a combination that others find irritating. In a noisy pub, however, there is no problem – everyone is talking in loud voices.

It is essential to look at the impact of people's behaviour if we are to make any judgement about its importance. Liam, for example, asks questions as questions should be asked – on the surface, but the context in which he asks questions is not always appropriate and this means that he is thrown back on staff for company, and the impact of his questions isolates him more.

> Liam is lonely. At some time he has learned that he can get staff to talk to him by saying things like "Are you OK? – I'm depressed", "I'm an idiot aren't I?", "How's your dad?". When he tries this with non-service people he gets rebuffed and so he continues to try and seek contacts with service people. These are not always success-ful – he really upset one of the day-centre staff when he asked her "Did you have sex last night?".

Liam misunderstands the nature of relationships, roles and situations. He either does not notice or misinterprets the reactions of others to his questions, and he has relatively few strategies for opening conversations. So, whilst on the face of it he is able to ask questions and wait for replies, the ways he does this are inappro-priate and reveal his lack of competence. In Liam's case it is clear that people are put off by his approaches. This may not always be the case, even when it looks to us as if people lack certain aspects of social competence.

Does social behaviour matter?

Throughout, our approach is based on the assumption that social behaviour is only one part of social competence for social capa-bility and integration. So-called cognitive aspects of social com-petence, viable opportunities and community competence all contribute to social capability. However, in many ways social behaviour plays a central role. Behaviour is the pivot between the environment with its opportunities and constraints and the per-son's experience, knowledge and effort to negotiate that environ-ment. Without behaviour there is no social skill and social integration remains one-sided. Figure 7.2 shows how social be-haviour links social environments (situations and communities) with their opportunities and constraints with cognitive aspects of social competence.

Social behaviour is not only central to social competence, it is also complex. We have found it useful to consider separately behaviours that are linked to facilitation of interaction and those linked to assertiveness, as in many ways they function quite differently.

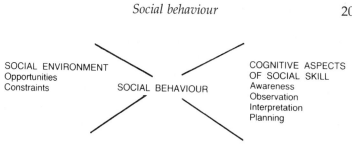

Figure 7.2 Links between cognitive aspects of social competence, social behaviour and social environment.

Facilitation is concerned with developing and sustaining a rapport with another person. In contrast to assertiveness, it is not necessarily "goal directed", but may simply be concerned with making the interaction comfortable or enjoyable.

Facilitation requires us to listen to other people during interactions and to help them communicate effectively. It therefore involves the use of the other skill areas that we have covered, particularly observation and interpretation, in order to keep track of what other people may be feeling.

We can be passive or active when we listen. In active listening we show that we are listening, by nodding, interjecting "mm's", "yes", "really!", etc. and by asking questions or reflecting the content (often emotional) of what has been said – "you must have felt very angry".

Facilitation, however, is not just a matter of listening, for this would make a very one-sided interaction. It also involves self-disclosing, whether of information or of feelings. Obviously the extent to which this is appropriate depends on the particular context and interaction – something that can be difficult to get right, as Karen and Tom found to their cost.

Karen got a cleaning job. By the end of her first day she had told her colleagues all about her boyfriend, including the details of their sex life, her recent abortion and the reaction of her father.

Tom had been to court following incidents when he grabbed women's bottoms in the swimming pool. He had overcome this problem, which was one of impulse control. When he went to a social skills group he told everyone about what he had done, with the result that people avoided him.

Practically, for many people with learning disabilities the main gap in facilitation skills is having something appropriate to say or to share with others. This can reflect limited experiences of ordinary life, so often the most effective approach is to connect the development of facilitation skills to the development of opportunities to experience a variety of activities, places, and social contacts.

Assertion is concerned with controlling the course of an interaction, and achieving other goals through social interaction. When we are being assertive, it is in order to achieve something. What it is we are trying to achieve may be clear to all concerned (for example when we are refusing a request to lend someone something) or not so clear (when we are trying to get out of a commitment we made some time ago). Assertiveness can be described as the **art of confident, clear, and direct communication whilst retaining respect for other people**.

We can distinguish between an assertive act, an aggressive act and passive inaction. If we are not assertive, we can oscillate between passivity (most of the time) and occasional aggressiveness.

Anne lived by herself but was visited often by Greg. Greg rarely had any money and always wanted to go and buy some beer. He would insist that Anne lent it to him. She usually did, but complained bitterly to her community support worker when she ran out of money. One day Anne's alarm clock was missing. She was very fond of the clock. Next time Greg came, Anne asked him about the clock. Casually he said he had it at home. This was the last straw and Anne hit him angrily with her arm. Greg's nose was broken. Greg did not contact Anne for several months.

To a large extent it is different situations that require us to act in assertive or facilitative ways. If there are confusions within the context, or we misunderstand the context, we will not be socially skilled or competent.

SOCIAL CONTEXT

Our own and other people's behaviour is determined in large part by the context in which we act, think and feel. If we are to make sense of other people's behaviour, or know, ourselves, how we should behave in different situations, we must be able to understand the social context and use this understanding to guide our behaviour. If people do not adapt their behaviour according to the situation they are in and the roles they are playing, they will not be seen as socially skilled or competent. Similarly, if they misattribute other people's behaviour to them as people and not to their roles and the situations they are in, they will not be considered socially skilled or competent.

Terri attends the day centre. There is a cafeteria for lunch and members take their trays to a table in the main dining-hall to eat. Terri nearly always takes her tray to the office and tries to sit there to eat. She has to be guided out and back to the dining-room. Terri does not recognize the physical boundaries to the dining-room, nor does she respond to all the props that tell her that one room is the office whereas the other is the dining-room.

Another clue to the fact that Terri does not easily distinguish the meanings of different situations and spaces is given by her behaviour at home. A year ago Terri moved from a hostel, where she always shared a room, to a small family run care home. Here she has her own room. Whilst Terri likes to collect small ornaments and pictures, she keeps them hidden under her clothes in her drawer. She refuses to display them and does not understand that the space in her bedroom is her own. She has never learnt to use personal and private space.

If we cannot distinguish between different situations by responding to physical features of the setting, our social competence will be severely hampered.

It is not only understanding the physical aspects of situations that contribute to social skill and social competence; it is also understanding the social aspects. Once again, if we fail to understand our own and other people's roles we can make mistakes in how we act and the sense we make of how other people act. Most of the roles that people with learning disabilities occupy are relatively informal roles, and in many ways these are harder to learn. Formal roles (such as committee chairperson, luncheon club assistant) will frequently have explicit (even if informal) rules associated with them. We can learn what we should or should not be doing when playing those roles. Less formal roles, however, have less explicit rules associated with them, although the consequences of not following them may be just as serious in their deleterious effect on our social competence.

Colin was very pleased with the flat he had recently acquired. The view from the windows was nice and the neighbours pleasant enough. Although Colin was helped by a community support worker with some of the day-to-day tasks of living independently, he had the weekends and evenings to himself. Over time, Colin's community support worker was stopped as she was waiting at his door by one or other of Colin's neighbours, who were getting very irritated by him. On several occasions Colin had knocked his neighbours up at one or two in the morning to ask for something relatively trivial, like to borrow a hammer or for advice on which washing machine programme he should switch on. Colin had not fully understood the "rules" of being a good neighbour. He got very annoyed when his support worker tried to tell him he should not call up his neighbours in the middle of the night, and why.

Shaun had grown up in a hospital where he had lived since being a very small child. Gradually, as he had got older, he had helped out with the younger children in the hospital. Shaun is now 27. He still likes the company of children and gets on very well with them. Shaun does not always distinguish between children he knows and others. Whenever he sees a group of children playing football or rounders in the park or on the waste ground behind the flats in which he lives, he happily tries to join in. Sometimes they laugh at him or call him names and ridicule him, while parents view his interest in children with concern.

Both Colin and Shaun are misunderstanding the rules linked to their informal roles in the community. They also misunderstand other people's roles in relation to them. It is not clear whether Colin and Shaun misunderstand the roles *per se*, the rules associated with them, or the role–rule contexts of their own and other people's behaviour. Exercise 7.8 presents opportunities to think through a person's understanding of roles and associated rules, and also offers a framework for asking questions about the extent to which people understand the social contexts in which they find themselves.

If people with learning disabilities are not able to distinguish different situations and the demands that both physical and social aspects of the situation place upon them, their social competence will be limited.

Understanding the extent of people's social skill and social competence is, then, complex. However, the advantage of looking at it in this way is to be able to identify particular aspects of social competence with which we can assist people in developing. If we do not break it down into component parts, we stand in danger of generalizing too much to be able to offer specific forms

Exercise 7.8 Finding out about contexts

(a) Try to find out how much a person with learning disabilities understands about physical contexts. If there are any situations the person finds particularly difficult, concentrate on these, but do not forget to look at other situations too. Ask yourself throughout how you know this to be the case. For each situation, fill in the following chart.

Situation:

Physical aspect of the situation	Current understanding	How do you know?	What needs to change?	Why?
Boundary				
Relevant props				
Modifiers				
Spaces				
Portable environment				
Other				

(b) Try to find out how much a person with learning disabilities understands about social contexts. If there are any situations the person finds particularly difficult, concentrate on these, but do not forget to look at other situations too. Ask yourself throughout how you know this to be the case. Fill in the chart for each situation.

Understanding of role

Write the role you think a person with learning disabilities occupies in the large circle (Figure 7.4). Write in what this role means to the person. In the smaller circles write how the person understands her or his role partners. We have included (Figure 7.3) a worked example for Colin, in the example above.

Continued

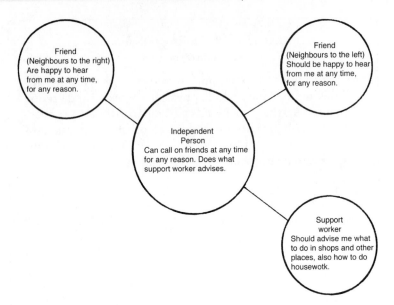

Figure 7.3 Exercise 7.8; understanding of social role, a worked example.

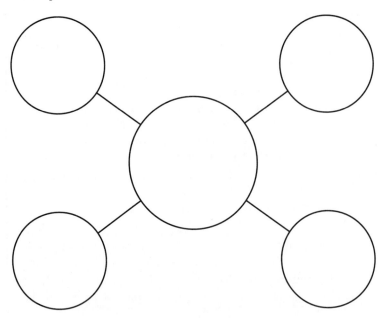

Figure 7.4 Exercise 7.8; understanding social roles.

Understanding of rules

Take a particular situation with which a person with a learning disability has particular difficulty. What does the person understand the rules of the situation to be? How do you know? We have included the example of Shaun, above.

Situation: Children playing in the park

Rule	Evidence
Anyone can join in games in the park	Shaun just joining in without an introduction or any preliminary conversation
It is OK for children and adults to play together	Shaun's reluctance to consider there is anything unusual about his behaviour
Everyone should accept everyone else	Shaun got upset and did not understand why the children laughed at or ridiculed him

Situation:

Rule	Evidence

Were some situations easier to find out about the extent of someone's understanding? If so, why is this? What kinds of information reveal people's understanding of situations? Can you get this information in different ways? If so, what ways? What kinds of information did you need in order to know how the person understands roles and associated rules? How clear were you about the roles and rules yourself? How much general agreement do you think there would be about the rules associated with different roles? What is the origin of the different rules associated with different roles? To what extent do the rules associated with different roles vary with different situations?

of assistance. We then fall into the trap of saying to people "You need to be able to get on with people a little better"; "What you need to do is behave more appropriately and fit in better"; "Try not to draw attention to yourself" and so on. These general statements are not helpful as they do not offer people any analysis about what it is that they could strengthen or try to lessen or, indeed, how. Nor do they give any idea about which things really matter and which do not. Exercise 7.9 summarizes the different components of social competence and skill for a particular person, and invites you to prioritize the areas that would make a real difference to the person's social capability if they were to change.

METHODS FOR INVESTIGATING SOCIAL SKILL AND SOCIAL COMPETENCE

So far we have not suggested methods for finding out about each area of social skill and social competence. If you spend time with the person, many methods will suggest themselves to you.

1. Someone might always talk about herself as "a girl" and not seem to distinguish between adults and children in terms of their activities, interests, responsibilities, etc. From these observations you might suspect that she has a poorly developed identity or sense of herself as an adult.
2. A person might very rapidly become angry and not seem to notice that he begins to breathe quickly and tremble some time before his verbal outburst. You therefore suspect that he is not very aware of the bodily dimensions of his emotional states.
3. For some people with learning difficulties there will be very obvious problems in observation, e.g. a general failure to look up or look at the other person in an interaction or look around at what is going on in a setting. Others may do all this but still seem to fail to notice what is going on.

In all these cases you would want to do some checking of your hunches and carry out further investigation to clarify your understanding of the nature and extent of the difficulty. A variety of methods is available, none of which gives entirely reliable information. Therefore it is worth using several different kinds of information together so that you can be reasonably confident of your conclusions. Here we present a few methods that may be less familiar. Whatever methods are being used, always keep in

Exercise 7.9 Summary of social competence and social skill

Think of the person whose competence you have described in the exercises above. Summarize the areas of competence that could change; then try to predict what difference such a change might make for the person in terms of overall social capability. Finally, mark the area that you guess would make the greatest difference with (1), the area which would make the next greatest difference with (2) and so on.

Area of social competence or social skill	How might this change?	What difference would it make if this were to change?	Rating in order of priority

Awareness:
   self
   others
 Observation
 Interpretation
 Planning and
   strategy
 Social behaviour:
   facilitation
   assertiveness
 Context:
   physical
   social			

How much overlap is there between the different areas of social competence? Is it possible to prioritize component parts of social competence for change? How easy is it to predict what difference any change in social competence might make for the person's overall social capability? Are the issues in prioritizing areas of social competence for change the same for all people with a learning disability? If not, how might they differ?

mind these questions: Might there be another explanation for this? What do I need to know to be able to choose between the different explanations?

Questioning the person

Open-ended questioning

Questions like "Tell me about that last time you got very angry?" or "Tell me about what you did at the weekend?" can provide leads that can be explored later with more specific questioning. Such questions can also be woven into the ordinary interactions with the person that you have set up so far. Unfortunately, some issues are difficult to access in this way, and some people do not talk sufficiently freely to provide much information in response to open questions.

Illuminative questioning

Some fairly simple questions can be used to illuminate aspects of the person's self-awareness: "Which person is most like you?"; "Who would you most like to sit next to?"; "Why do you think the children laughed at you?".

Asking the same question in different ways

This is important in checking that the person is giving consistent answers and understands the words used, by illuminative questions such as "Which is the person that you are most like?", "Which person do you like to be with most?", etc.

Use of non-verbal methods

Such methods are particularly useful where the person is not very talkative, where you want to check the person's knowledge of terms or not rely on language which can be misleading or intimidating; for example "Point to the . . . (using pictures, photos, etc.)" or "Which person is sad (using photos of facial expressions)?"

Closed questions and restricted choice

It sometimes helps to restrict the person's options for response to a limited set – a person who is unwilling to answer questions may be happy to choose between three or four possibilities, or to answer or indicate "yes" or "no". The use of restricted choice can also help narrow down an issue.

A restricted choice method was used to locate Thelma's position, as she saw it, in the power relations of a group home. Using some cards whose meanings had previously been established, the question "Who is in charge?" was asked and, once answered, the card standing for that person was removed. Thelma was then asked "Who would be in charge now?" and so on. The exercise was repeated with questions like "Who is the bossiest?", "Who answers the door / telephone?", etc. From this and other methods a picture was built up of Thelma's understanding of others' roles and of the power relationships among the staff and tenants in the house.

Asking about recent events

All three types of observation mentioned in Exercise 7.4 can be tapped through asking about recent events, particularly if the questioner was also present or has some detailed information about what happened. "Were there many people there?"; "What were they doing?"; "Who else was there?"; "What was the man with the big moustache doing?" etc. are examples of questions about general observation. "Tell me about the evening you had with Geoff"; "What did she say then?"; "Did you notice what I was doing when you talked about your track suit again?" could give information about process observation and some about observation of consequences.

Interruption questioning

Here a sequence of interaction (which might be a role-play) is interrupted to ask a question about what is going on: "Can you tell me what Susan just said?"; "What was Dave doing when you started shouting?"; etc.

These questioning strategies can be used singly or in combination.

Joint exploration

The focus here is not on what the person does or has noticed but on what the person understands by what has been observed. The various ways of questioning described above can also be used to explore the person's understanding.

It will be useful to take the person beyond the first interpretation to find out what the person is capable of interpreting – try to help to speculate on what the person in question meant by that behaviour.

YOU: Why did Fred shout at his mother?
PERSON: Because he was cross.
YOU: What was he cross about?
PERSON: He was cross because she told Sue about the secret.
YOU: Yes. What do you think Fred was trying to do by shouting?
PERSON: I don't know.
etc.

This type of investigation might involve some leading, but then we are not just interested in what the person ordinarily does by way of interpretation – we want to understand the balance between habitual ways of interpreting behaviour and those interpretations the person is capable of making with a minimal degree of encouragement and guidance, which will help us to decide what to do by way of intervention.

Real life settings

It can be useful to explore a topic together in a real setting. We did this in a local market, discussing what people were wearing, what age they were and how they looked. Of course this is a learning experience, too, but it is rarely possible to separate finding out from intervening.

Simulations and use of media

Observing role-play interactions and then questioning (in various ways) can be one way of investigating a person's observational skills. It is also possible to use videotaped interactions, even TV soaps to explore what the person notices in a variety of different types of interaction.

Information from others

Others can be useful sources of information about the person's social and self-awareness, but the information will be laced with bias, interpretation and assumptions: use it in conjunction with your more direct investigations. Examples of things to ask include: "What is important to him?"; "What is she interested in?"; "What would she do if . . . ?"; "Whom does he seem to identify with?"; etc. You can also try out your hunches on those who know the person well. Not only does this check the plausibility of your emerging picture and possibly elicit other relevant information, but it can also help pave the way for the development of a shared way of understanding the person.

Watching others

Also watch how others interact with the person. You will have done this generally, but now do so in relation to your hunches about social and self-awareness. For example, if the person is having difficulty identifying self as adult, are people feeding this confusion by treating the person as a child? Are people failing to give accurate but constructive feedback on a person's inappropriate assumptions about friendship, or failing to respond to questions about social rules and mores?

Use of stimuli

It is possible to bring materials and equipment into the situation to explore the person's self-awareness – mirrors, tape recorders and video (although watching themselves on video can be a traumatic experience for many people) can be used to explore whether the person uses external checks and reference frames for their awareness of themselves: do they recognize themselves in these media; do they avoid looking in mirrors (like the man who disliked his prominent ears and therefore rarely checked his appearance).

Photographs of the person and other people can similarly be used to explore knowledge of both self and others and the relations between them.

Beyond the data: thought experiments

Thought experiments do not provide new information, but they can suggest further lines of investigation or ways of organizing and interpreting existing information.

1. What kind of reaction is this person likely to produce
   - dressed this way?
   - talking this way, about these things?
   - behaving this way?

What, then, does this suggest about the person's self- and social awareness, and what does it suggest about the person's opportunities to improve competence in these areas?

2. It's as if
   - he was the only person that mattered.
   - she felt . . .
   - he thought . . .
   - she was never treated as worthwhile.
   - he felt he could never succeed at anything.

   Again, what does this suggest about the person's social skills?

3. Ask a lay person. You can provide a description of the person's behaviour, without mention of the learning difficulty. Ask something like: "If you met someone like this, what would you think was going on?" (or a more specific question).

Once we have identified the areas of social competence or social skill that might make a real difference to a person's social capability, we can begin to think how we might assist the person to change or develop. The next chapter looks at some of the ways we might help people develop their social skills and social competence.

FURTHER READING

There are no comprehensive texts that can be used to understand issues about assessing social skill and social competence fully. However, we have included readings that may help extend the ideas we have offered for describing a person's social skill and social competence. The material can be read in conjunction with that cited at the end of Chapter 4.

American Association on Mental Retardation (1992) *Mental Retardation: Definition, classification, and systems of supports*, 9th edn, American Association on Mental Retardation, Washington, DC.

Baldwin, S., Baser, C. and Harding, K. (1990) *Multi-level Needs Assessment*, British Association for Behavioural Psychotherapy, London.

Becker, R.E. and Heimberg, R.G. (1988) Assessment of social skills, in *Behavioral Assessment* (eds A.S. Bellack and M. Hersen), Pergamon Press, New York, pp. 365–95.

Cartledge, G. And Milburn, J.F. (1980) *Teaching Social Skills to Children*, Pergamon, New York.

Chadsey-Rusch, J. (1992) Toward defining and measuring social skills in employment settings. *American Journal on Mental Retardation*, **96**, 405–18.

Curran, J. and Monti, P. (eds) (1982) *Social Skills Training: A practical handbook for assessment and treatment*, Guildford Press, Guildford, NY.

Gowans, F. and Hulbert, C. (1983) Self-concept assessment of mentally handicapped adults: a review. *Mental Handicap*, **11**, 121–3.

Greenspan, S. (1979) Social intelligence in the retarded, in *Handbook of Mental Deficiency: Psychological theory and research*, 2nd edn (ed. N.R. Ellis), Erlbaum, Hillsdale, NJ.

Greenspan, S. and Granfield, J.M. (1992) Reconsidering the construct of mental retardation: implications of a model of social competence. *American Journal on Mental Retardation*, **96**, 422–53.

Healey, K.N. and Masterpasqua, F. (1993) Interpersonal cognitive problem solving among children with mild mental retardation. *American Journal on Mental Retardation*, **96**, 367–72.

Hollin, C.R. and Trower, P. (eds) (1986) *Handbook of Social Skills Training: Applications Across the Lifespan*, Vol. 1, Pergamon, Oxford.

Hollin, C.R. and Trower, P. (eds) (1986) *Handbook of Social Skills Training: Clinical Applications and New Directions*, Vol. 2, Pergamon, Oxford.

Kagan, C. (1984) Social Problem Solving and Social Skills Training. *British Journal of Clinical Psychology*, **23**, 161–73.

Kagan, C., Evans, J. and Kay, B. (1986) *Interpersonal Skills for Nurses: An experiential approach*, Harper and Row, London.

Simeonsson, R.J. (1978) Social competence: dimensions and directions, in *Annual Review of Mental Retardation and Developmental Disabilities* Volume 10 (ed. J. Wortis), Brunner/Mazel, New York.

Spence, S. (1980) *Social Skills Training with Children and Adolescents: A counsellor's manual*, National Federation for Educational Research, Windsor.

Spivack, G. and Shure, M.B. (1974) *Social Adjustment of Young Children: A cognitive approach to solving real-life problems*, Jossey-Bass, San Francisco.

Trower, P. (1984) *Radical Approaches to Social Skills Training*, Croom Helm, London.

Trower, P., Bryant, B. and Argyle, M. (1978) *Social Skills and Mental Health*, Methuen, London.

Wilkinson, J. and Canter, S. (1983) *Social Skills Training Manual: Assessment, Programme Design and Management of Training*, Wiley, Chichester.

8

How could social competence or skill change?

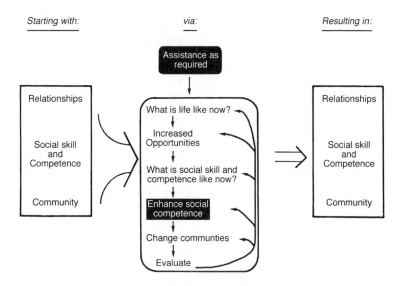

We have looked at the complexity of social competence in terms of different, interrelated aspects of competence. We have explored ways of finding out about how competent people are in these different areas and as a whole: we should by now have a pretty good idea of people's strengths and weaknesses. How, then, do we decide what aspects of their social competence will be worth working on to strengthen further? In order to put people's current social competence into perspective and see how it contributes to their overall social capability, we have to keep asking: "So What?" In other words:

is this actually a problem for the person or for others? If so, to what extent? How does the presence or absence of this aspect of social competence affect the person's day-to-day social interaction; act to perpetuate segregation or marginalization; detract from social opportunities?

We need to ask "So what?" every time we think we have identified a difficulty and think we have identified priorities for change. If our answer to "So What?" is "It doesn't make any real difference, and changing it is unlikely to make any real difference", then there may be little point in making a great effort to alter this aspect of social competence. If, on the other hand, our answer is "It gets in the way of the person being able to do things that matter to them, for such-and-such a reason, and changing it is likely to make a real difference", then it makes sense for us to work with the person to enhance or help widen the repertoire of social competencies.

We can check the potential impact of any change in advance, by estimating how the proposed changes might:

- help move nearer to a person's desirable future (see Chapter 6) – how will community presence, autonomy, respect, participation or capability be affected for the better by the proposed change in social competence;
- increase social opportunities that help move the person nearer to that desirable future;
- strengthen other areas of social competence – how will overall social competence or any other aspect of social competence be affected for the better by the proposed change.

We are suggesting, then, that we need to clarify why we think some aspect of a person's social competence could and should change, and anticipate the overall difference this will make for the person. There is little point in working with people to change if it is unlikely to make any difference in helping them towards greater social capability. In Exercise 8.1 we suggest a framework for checking the decisions we make about what should change and why.

Once we have checked the importance of any weakness in social competence and have assessed the likely impact of any changes in social competence, we have to decide which area of social competence is worth beginning to work on. The decision-making process outlined already in respect to choosing between objectives for change in Chapter 6 is useful here, too.

Exercise 8.1 Identifying relevant change in social competence

Take each proposed change in any aspect of social competence and assess the impact change is likely to have on (i) advancing progress towards a desirable future; (ii) increasing opportunities; (iii) different aspects of social competence and (iv) different people.

Proposed change in:

	Awareness	Observation	Interpretation	Planning and strategy	Social behaviour	Understanding context
(i) Progress towards a desirable future						
Presence						
Power						
Respect						
Participation						
Capability						
(ii) Increased opportunities (examples)						
(a)						
(b)						
(c)						
(d)						
etc.						

(iii) Impact on other
aspects of social
competence
Awareness
Observation
Interpretation
Planning and strategy
Social behaviour
Understanding context

(iv) People likely to
benefit
Person with learning
disability
Family member
Staff member
Management
Other

Table 8.1 Outcomes of expectations that are too high or too low

Expectation	Outcomes
Too Low	Person trivialized and competence not properly recognized
	Little change in competence
	Frustration and disappointment
	Waste of person's time
Too High	Non-achievement of change or perception of future or only partial success
	Waste of person's time
	Waste of trainer's time
	Frustration and disappointment

In deciding on the aims for our work with a person we have to work at a suitable level of expectation. If our expectations are too low, then we are likely to make only trivial gains in the person's social competence. If we set our expectations too high, then we will not achieve change, creating frustration and disappointment for us and for them. Table 8.1 summarizes the effects of unsuitable expectations.

Unfortunately, selecting the right level of goal or intervention is something of an art. It may help, however, to consider the idea of orders or levels of skill.

LEVELS OF SKILL

We can identify different levels of skill, increasing in complexity, particularly in terms of how the skills are applied.

First level: Learning to perform in a predictable range of social situations, without making adjustments to the routines of behaviour we use.

Second level: Learning to perform in an unpredictable range of social situations, using a set of cognitive tools to make adjustments to our action routines.

Third level: Learning about new kinds of social situations that involves broadening the cognitive repertoire we have.

Ideally we would like to achieve progress in all three of these areas, however, what can be done will depend on the person we are working with. Table 8.2 gives a very rough guide to what might be expected of people at different levels of skill.

Table 8.2 Suitable expectations of different people in terms of different levels of skill

Personal characteristics	Main concerns	Most likely levels of learning and performance
Person unlikely to be in unsupervised situations for any prolonged periods	Reasonably effective and comfortable negotiation of frequently occurring and familiar situations	Level one
Person largely reliant on others to structure social situations, but also negotiating familiar situations independently	As above, plus the ability to negotiate a variety of fairly predictable situations (shops, transport, work environment, etc.) alone	Level two
Person largely independent from others, encountering a variety of social situations in a variety of settings	As above, plus the ability to deal with unexpected situations. Significant danger of being picked on and exploited by others. Likely experience of the "competence trap"	Level three

The three categories are not meant to be rigid. While the more able person will be found in the higher order categories of performance, there is a wide variation in the circumstances in which people find themselves, so that environmental demands cannot be predicted simply from the person's degree of learning disability.

Whatever the level of skill we are aiming for, it is going to be useful to build on what is already known when helping people learn more.

WHAT HELPS LEARNING?

Learning social competence is like learning any other skill or social behaviour. A great deal is already known about universal human learning processes, but much of this knowledge is lost in the specialist psychological literature, often untapped even by professional psychologists. At the same time, much of this knowledge is too specialized to be of much practical help. In many ways, there is "nothing new under the sun", and in what follows we will review key principles and issues that are of practical help in assisting people in learning.

Learning on the boundary of the known

For most of us, learning takes place on the boundary of "the known". It is the mismatch between what we already know and what we encounter out in the world that creates learning, whether that is simple association of an action with a reward, or something as complex as understanding a philosophical concept.

> Barry learnt to use the word "tea" for the drink he had following meals. When he was given a biscuit after his dinner at the day centre, he said "Barry, tea", but was told that no, this is "biscuit". As a result he learnt a new label "biscuit", but what is just as important is that he learnt to revise his idea of what "tea" referred to. If we wanted to teach Barry the meaning of the word "biscuit", we would do well to teach him the distinction between "tea", which he already knows, and the new concept "biscuit".

In this example, Barry's learning takes place on the edge of what he already knows. Sometimes, though, when we teach people things we try to teach them things that bear little relation to what they already know; we try to teach them things outside the realms of their experience. To suggest that learning is best placed on the boundary of the known is to imply that we should **build learning on the basis of what the person already knows**, even when that knowledge is inadequate to the demands facing the person. An application of this important principle can be seen in the way that Izza learnt how to greet people appropriately.

> Izza had learnt to offer his hand in greeting to people. Unfortunately he did this indiscriminately, which led to many rebuffs. The next step was to teach him that he should offer his hand when meeting new people, meeting friends that he has not seen for some time, or perhaps when congratulating someone. It was not a case of trying to get Izza to stop extending his hand on greeting people, but rather to channel this behaviour differently.

In working with a person we need to build up a very good idea of what their current understanding is. It is, for example a waste of time providing someone with an explanation about why they should not do a certain thing if they cannot understand the negative "not".

Learning with low anxiety

All of us generally learn better when we feel comfortable in the situation; it is difficult to learn effectively when you feel anxious. It helps, then, to help people feel calm and in control in the learning situation. It is a waste of everyone's time trying to help people learn when they are feeling wound up or anxious. (We would be better off helping people reduce their anxiety in these circumstances.)

Anxiety is often overlooked when video and audio tapes are used in training. In recent years, for example, it has become common for video feedback to be used in social skills training sessions; however, most people feel very threatened by seeing themselves on video, and its use can be quite counterproductive for this reason. Not only do people become anxious when they see themselves on videotape or hear themselves on audiotape, but sometimes their self-esteem plummets too.

> Alex is a man with many capabilities but some unusual mannerisms that other people found frightening, so they tended to avoid him. Alex had a student working with him to help him gain insight into his own behaviour and how others might react towards him. Alex enjoyed the sessions with the student a lot, and when it was suggested to him that he be videotaped, he was keen to participate. However, when Alex saw himself on the film he began to get agitated and insisted that the film was stopped. Alex was miserable for several days and was very short with the student. He no longer cooperated with the sessions. After several days Alex was able to say why he had reacted like this. He had never realized how other people had seen him until he had seen himself on the tape. Now he said he knew why people did not like him – and no wonder, he would not like to talk to him, himself!

Seeing ourselves as "objects", or as others see us, often leads us to make negative judgements about ourselves, which in turn leads to lowered self-esteem. This is not to say that there is no place for the use of video and audiotape in helping people learn, and we will explore this further in the next section on feedback.

A different kind of anxiety can be aroused in people with difficulties in understanding complex speech who are on the receiving end of complex spoken communications. Many people who work with people with learning disabilities use too much speech; speech that is often over-complex in both structure and content and too many questions. All of these things can make people feel overloaded and stressed: it is difficult to learn in this state.

On the other hand, too low a level of arousal can lead to lack of interest, motivation, or willingness to learn. If learning is to be effective, then, we have to be able to notice the signs of low arousal (yawning, looking out of the window, making excuses to do other things, etc.) and anxiety (tenseness revealed in posture, tremor, voice production; agitation; attempts to change the subject, avoid or escape the situation), and to do something about this (increase interest or motivation or help people relax).

Learning through feedback

We have seen how the discrepancy between what is known and what we experience is the basis for learning. This learning, however, has to be cemented or strengthened in some way, and we can attempt to do this through the systematic use of "feedback".

Feedback is the channelling of information about people back to them. It can be the channelling of information about their behaviour (what it is they are doing), their appearance (how they come over to others), the impressions others get of them (how others understand them), about their own bodily changes (noticing when they are becoming agitated, pleased and so on) – about anything, in fact.

Most of us receive, accommodate and respond to feedback all the time as we go about our daily business. As we saw in Chapter 4, we pick up cues from other people and the way they react towards us that contribute to our feelings about ourselves; that help us take part in conversations, knowing when to speak and when to listen. We pick up cues from the situations we are in that tell us how we should be behaving or why other people are there. When we help other people learn, feedback is vital as a means of strengthening the learning, as well as understanding how things may have changed as a result of new ways of doing things, or as a means of understanding how much may still have to be learnt.

Feedback can take a variety of forms, from helping people listen to themselves and notice their own behaviour, to information giving and helping the person experience the results of a particular way of behaving. It really should be as close as possible to the kinds of feedback people experience when performing the skill in natural situations. Whilst this may seem obvious, it means that the learning situations should be the actual situations people are going to have to deal with, wherever possible. If simulated situations have to be used, they should be as close as possible to the real. Taking this seriously would mean putting a stop to those artificial activities that still happen, such as encouraging people in a social education centre to learn to use money by buying mock items with cardboard replicas of coins, or teaching hospital residents to learn the skills of using a cafe in the hospital staff canteen that they will never be allowed to use again.

Both of these teaching contexts involve feedback that would be sufficiently different from the real world context to make the learning less than relevant to the real situation. In the case of the pretend coins, the person would have to learn to handle metal money with its distinctive feel and appearance all over again, while in the hospital canteen the reactions of those playing the part of the cafe staff and public will be different from those of their real-life counterparts. In both cases, why wait; why not learn in real situations from the start?

> Jack had a habit of saying things to women in order to produce a shocked reaction. This was particularly pronounced with the adult education teachers at the college where he went for pottery classes – in the middle of an ordinary conversation he might say "I play with myself". It had been found that he would soon learn not to do this to a person if (a) he was asked not to once, and (b) no response was then made to his statements. Not everyone who came into contact with him did this, however, and some people thought he was becoming a nuisance. It was explained to all the staff why Jack did this, and everyone (even the sceptics) agreed to try the request to ignore the approach for a trial period of three weeks. Jack quickly learned that his behaviour did not pay off, and at the same time learned that people were more interested in him when he did not try to embarrass them.

As B.F. Skinner observed, if you ask for the salt in perfect French in a classroom you get a good mark: if you do the same thing in France, you get the salt. Our task, then, is to try to make feedback as natural as possible.

As we have seen in the previous section, videotape and audiotape feedback can help people gain insight into how they appear to others; it can also help them monitor the progress of changes they are learning. Used sensitively, these forms of feedback can be useful, but due regard for how people react to them must be made.

> Una liked to meet people and to be with them. However, she was generally stiff and stony-faced, with little facial expression or movement. She, herself, gave others very little feedback when they were talking to her. They did not know whether she was interested, bored, enjoying the conversation or what. Una could say when she liked what someone was saying, but she could not communicate it in other ways. People found her difficult to talk to and did not make much of an effort to talk to her. This meant she did not have as much contact with other people as she would have liked.
>
> In working with Una, it was agreed that it would be useful if she could learn how to give non-verbal feedback to others, to show that she was interested in what they were saying. Part of what she was learning was how to be less stiff and to nod her head and look at people when she was interested in what they were saying. It was quite difficult to get her to loosen up, but when she did begin to nod she nearly always began to giggle. She said she could not do this when she was talking to people as bowing to them would be stupid. She did not believe the staff who worked with her when they said she was not bowing. They tried to show her what she looked like in a mirror, but this was difficult as she could not really see herself properly. So the staff videotaped her having two conversations with her sister – one where she was her usual stiff self and one where she was more relaxed and nodding and smiling at her. Una thought she would look ridiculous in the second conversation. When she saw the tape, she could see that she just looked much more ordinary in the second conversation – she did not appear to be bowing, although this is what it still felt like.
>
> Una was learning two things via different forms of feedback. Firstly she was learning, via the video feedback, how she might appear to others according to different ways she behaved. Secondly she was learning, via a combination of bodily feedback and video feedback, what different body movements signalled to others.

Sometimes the term reinforcement is used to describe feedback in a learning situation. However, reinforcement is an overused concept and, whilst useful as part of training and learning specific tasks and behaviours in specific situations, attempts to reward appropriate social behaviours have often led to the use of arbitrary feedback different from that of the situation where the skills will have to be used. This means that it is often difficult to help people transfer their learning to natural social situations, relying on natural feedback: they become dependent on the artificial forms of feedback (reinforcement) we have provided. It is not always easy to support learning in the setting where the skills will be used.

Learning in the skills setting

If we are successful in supporting learning in the setting where skills are to be used, we are also more likely to get spin-off benefits in other areas of people's lives: learning to use buses in real buses does more than teach bus-behaviour, it also exposes people to different choices (which bus and to where?), situations (crowded or empty buses), different people and so on. Because of this, and the fact that the learning is likely to be more meaningful and to stick more strongly, we would suggest that unless there is a good reason, **learning should take place in the setting where the skills will be used**.

Not only does this enable appropriate feedback on the performance of the skill, but it also does the following.

- It allows the person teaching to observe the person's progress, gathering information about other learning that might be necessary; it is difficult to work out where people's problems are without being with them as they try to negotiate social situations. Remember that social competence is not just the performance of set routines of behaviour, but, as we have seen in the previous chapter, it involves cognitive actions concerned with awareness, observation, interpretation and planning, all in relation to the context.

- It helps the learner to anticipate such situations in future. Simulations are always pale images, lacking some aspects of the real thing. As teachers we can miss critically important aspects of the situation, thereby failing to equip the person effectively. In real situations people may take as their cues, for what to do when, features that we have not even thought of including in a simulated setting. Moreover, many people with learning disabilities have difficulty making the conceptual leap from the simulated situation to the real one. For people with limited ability in handling symbols and representations simulation might just not work.

- It helps the teacher to understand what the real situations facing the person actually are. Throughout your work you will be refining your understanding of the person, context and the way the social world actually works: none of us stop learning about that.

One way of seeing how important it is to use natural situations in helping people learn is to try to separate out the features of any natural social situation that guide and support social competence in that situation. Exercise 8.2 suggests a way of doing this.

Exercise 8.2 Social situational cues for social competence

Take any social situation and describe the different steps or episodes most people would go through in this situation (this is somewhat arbitrary, but you can get some sense of this by discussing with other people who are also familiar with the situation the different steps or episodes involved in handling it). For each step identify the physical and social cues in the situation that support us in handling that step competently. Identify the natural social consequences if these cues are not picked up. An example is given of cashing a benefit order at a post office.

Social steps	Natural physical cues	Natural social cues	Natural social consequences (of not responding to cues)
Go to post office	Red and yellow sign; post box outside; goods in window	People going in and out; people posting letters	Would not get benefits
Enter post office	Door; open sign displayed	People going in and out	Would not enter post office

continued

Social steps	Natural physical cues	Natural social cues	Natural social consequences (of not responding to cues)
Go to post office counter	Glass-fronted counter; weighing scales on counter; leaflets and forms displayed	Post office worker behind counter	Would go to shop counter instead
Wait for turn	Space in which to queue	People queuing in line	May offend people if push in
Greet post office worker	–	Seeing post office worker is ready to serve	Not friendly
Make request	Slot in glass front through which conversation can be heard; benefit voucher presented	Post office worker's questions	Do not cash voucher
Hold conversation	–	Questions	Not friendly
Receive money	Money put under glass grill on counter	Post office worker takes money from till and gives to customer	Do not collect money
Depart counter	–	Post office worker says good-bye	Not friendly
Exit shop	Door	People coming in and out	Do not exit post office

continued

Situation: _____

Social steps	Natural physical cues	Natural social cues	Natural social consequences (of not responding to cues)

How easy was it to identify the steps and associated cues? Can you think of any situations where it would be more difficult to distinguish the steps and cues? Why is this?

Natural social situations are, then, extremely complex in that the cues we respond to tell us what the situation is, what other people are doing there and what we should be doing. When trying to disentangle how best to help people learn, it can be helpful to distinguish between different modes of learning.

DIFFERENT MODES OF LEARNING

We can distinguish two broadly different kinds of learning, although of course they do shade into one another.

Learning about

Learning about (or learning that) involves the assimilation of information that guides action. Most of the areas covered in the sections on the "cognitive" aspects of social competence in Chapter 4 are to be learned about. Learning about is concerned with understanding.

Exercise 8.3 Modes of learning in different situations

Think of three quite different social situations. Identify what we need to **know how** to do, and what we need to **know about** in order to be socially competent in each situation.

Situation	Things we should know how to do	Things we should know about
Situation 1 (describe)		
Situation 2 (describe)		
Situation 3 (describe)		

Was it easier to identify things we should know about or things we should know how to do? Why was this? What would happen in each of these situations if we knew **either** about aspects of the situation and our social competence, **or** how to do things in this situation? Would people who are older, younger, from different cultures or of different sexes be expected to know different things in these situations? If so, what sorts of things?

Learning how

Learning how involves learning the actions involved in a skilled performance, rather than the reasons for the performance. In highly skilled social performance we generally pay little attention to the "*whys*" of the performance: we just do it. However, when things go wrong we revert to a performance that involves using our understanding to alter the action sequences that for some reason have failed to work in this particular context or on this occasion. We may be very good at small talk with relative strangers: we just do it without thinking. This works well until we find ourselves in conversation with someone who answers everything we say with, "That's not the best way of thinking about that". In this circumstance, we resort to careful thought in order to decide what to do next. In other words, we shift from the **doing** to the **thinking about** aspects of social competence. If we carry on regardless, without changing our tack, we will have a most unfulfilling conversation. In these circumstances and unless our reasons for keeping on with the conversation were particularly compelling, most of us would probably try to end the conversation as a way of resolving our discomfort. Because social interaction is so complex, we switch from one mode to another continually drawing all the time on both types of learning.

> Velma is the chairperson of a People First group. Her adviser, Noreen, has given her some information about how meetings can be organized, for example about agendas, minutes and the various aspects of the job of the chairperson. In the early days of the group, Noreen had to keep reminding Velma to check whether what people were saying was relevant to the matter under discussion. Now she does this without any prompting. Velma knows **about** the job of a chairperson, she also knows **how** to do it. Occasionally she meets a problem and uses her knowledge **about** meetings to decide what is wrong and what to do.

In helping people with learning disabilities to learn effective social repertoires we should be aiming to give them the confidence to perform in social situations by **learning how,** *and* at least some tools for making the necessary adjustments when things go wrong by **learning about.** We will not often be there when things go wrong, so we need to equip people to make adjustments to their behaviour themselves, and in so doing to continue learning about social interaction and social competence. The distinction between learning how and learning about is made in Exercise 8.3.

There are a number of different techniques or methods that can be used to help people learn how to become more socially competent as well as learn about social competence. Different methods or combinations of methods may be required to help people learn about different aspects of social competence (awareness, observation, interpretation, planning and strategy, social behaviour, understanding social contexts). Whatever the method, we should not forget that the real world is the place where much training should be done and to which all training should be related. Furthermore, training should be geared to things that are relevant to, and that will make a real difference in the person's life.

A CATALOGUE OF METHODS

In our discussion of methods, we are not presenting a manual of teaching or training methods, nor are we offering a manual of psychological techniques. Instead, we are selecting and combining approaches which we have found to be useful in working with people on aspects of social competence contributing to their overall social capability. These methods are not superior to attempts to increase opportunities (see Chapter 6) or working to enhance the competence of the community (see Chapter 9). They are related specifically to those aspects of social capability that are linked to people's own social competence, and they take account of our exhortations to use real situations and to work on things that will make a real difference to people's overall capability.

The methods described below are based upon available knowledge. However, the combining of these approaches into a catalogue of promising approaches is distinctive, as is our emphasis on using the real world as the place where much training should be done and to which all training should be related.

Feedback

The principles behind the use of feedback have been discussed above . Feedback can be positive or negative. Negative feedback should be used with caution as it can contribute to feelings of inadequacy. People with learning disabilities are often bombarded, in different areas of their lives, with injunctions not to do things and with rebukes for not doing things properly. Further negative feedback in the context of social competence may well be counter-productive. Positive feedback, too, is not without its difficulties, particularly for those giving the feedback. We live within a culture that values modesty; it can, therefore, be difficult for us to give people positive feedback, lest they "get a big head" or become "overconfident". Nevertheless, positive feedback contributes to self-confidence and positive self-esteem and it strengthens learning.

Our feelings about giving feedback often prevent us from giving good feedback, even though to do so may lead to change. There is a useful mnemonic that can help us give good feedback – CORBS: **C**lear, **O**wned, **R**egular, **B**alanced, and **S**pecific.

Clear   We should try to be clear about what the feedback is that we want to give. Being vague and faltering may increase anxiety in the person and the feedback not be understood.

Owned   We should give our own perceptions and not make it appear as if what we are saying is an indisputable, ultimate truth (it is not). Thus, feedback of the ilk "it seemed to me that you . . ." rather than "you are . . ." will be more helpful (so long as the person can understand the more complicated grammar of the first statement, i.e. if the feedback is clear to them).

Regular   Feedback that we give regularly is likely to be more useful than occasional feedback. We should try to give feedback as close to the event as possible and in time for the person to do something about it. It is not, for example, a good idea to wait until someone gets home before saying that one should stand aside for people coming out of the library before entering it; this is too late.

Balanced   We should try and achieve balance between positive and negative feedback over time. Nothing but positive feedback may lead people to wonder why it is they should be trying to change; nothing but negative feedback can lead people to feel undermined.

Specific   Generalized feedback is hard to learn from. We should try to give feedback that indicates what it is that people can do differently, should they so choose. Thus, "your attitude towards your parents is wrong" is unhelpful: it tells the person neither why it matters nor what they could do about it. However, "when you look away from your mother when she arrives it makes her feel bad" not only tells the person why it matters, but also what it is that they might be able to do differently.

Timing of feedback

As we have indicated above, feedback is more effective the sooner we give it following an action. However, it is not always possible to provide immediate feedback. When delayed feedback is given it is worth enhancing it in some way, for example by helping relive the situation and the person's action in it, perhaps by describing key aspects of it. If possible build on the person's own description of what happened:

> Will, who flies off the handle easily, is trying to learn to put up with his house-mate, who can be very irritating. One day he was not

able to keep his temper and he threw his cutlery at Graham. Later, he was talking to his key worker who is helping him learn different ways of controlling his temper in different situations. "I got cross with him didn't I?", said Will. "Yes you did; you threw you cutlery at him before he had time to explain why he hadn't poured your drink", replied his key worker. On another occasion, Will managed to get Graham to return the waste-paper basket he had taken out of his room. He said to his key worker, "I got it back OK, didn't I?", who replied "Yes, you kept very calm and explained why you needed it. Even when he started shouting, you kept calm".

Tone of feedback

As we have said, generally, receiving positive feedback is most helpful to people because it makes it clear that they are doing something well. This builds confidence and an understanding of what is required. Occasionally it is necessary to give someone a piece of negative feedback to discourage them from doing something. Here are some guidelines for giving negative feedback.

- Keep it brief.
- Keep it specific, so the person knows exactly what not to do, or what they did not notice/appreciate. This also makes it less likely that you will be seen to be criticizing the person rather than a specific act of theirs.
- Give at least four times as many pieces of positive feedback as negative, and space out the negatives.
- Give the person an idea about what they should do instead.

Sally is outgoing and gregarious. She likes to have a lot of company, but when she is with other people she irritatingly pokes them and often pinches them too. Not many people like Sally. The day-centre officer, Chris, is trying to work with Sally on more appropriate ways of relating to people. He has a tendency to tell her constantly what it is she is doing to irritate people and rarely gives her any positive feedback about her conduct. Nor does he give her any ideas about what she might do differently. In Chris's own supervision sessions, he is being helped to learn to give negative feedback constructively. Taking as an example an incident where Sally had poked someone soon after dinner, it was suggested to Chris that he say something like "instead of poking him in the stomach and laughing, ask him if he enjoyed the meal".

Specificity of feedback

Feedback can focus on a particular element of an interaction or it can be more general. If we want people to notice a particular aspect of a situation or their part in it, then we must use a specific approach.

> Elizabeth lives in a hostel with nine other people. Although it gets crowded, they all have their evening meal together. Any visitors that come also join in the evening meal. One day a member of the management committee was visiting the hostel round about supper time. She was invited to stay for supper. She was making conversation and asking another resident, Sue, about her recent holiday. Elizabeth suddenly snapped "You're very nosy aren't you?" Later, one of the workers said to her, "She was trying to find out if Sue had gone on holiday". On another occasion, Elizabeth was walking to the market with one of the staff; Elizabeth grabbed hold of the member of staff's arm and continued walking, pulling her close to her. She was told, "Elizabeth, try not to pull me so close, it looks a bit odd when you hold on to me like that" When Elizabeth adjusted her distance, she added "That's about the right distance to walk".

Sometimes we have to give more general encouragement, for example if the person has found something difficult.

> Julie uses a wheelchair. She gets very excited when May takes her to the cinema, as she does about once every two weeks. In her excitement she often loses control of her arm and several times has hit May accidentally, but hard. Last week she was as excited as ever, but managed to spin herself away from May as she hit out. May noticed this and said "Gosh, Julie, I think you did really well to avoid me then." Julie's house-mate, Eve, usually ignored May. One day, though, she stayed in the room when May arrived and smiled at her as May talked to both her and Julie. When May and Julie left for the cinema, Eve's support staff said to her, "I liked the way you joined in the conversation there, it couldn't have been easy for you".

Different ways of giving feedback are explored in Exercise 8.4.

Exercise 8.4 Different kinds of feedback

Outline the feedback you might give the person with learning disabilities in the following scenarios.

continued

1. Pete has got into trouble on several occasions because he likes to touch women's breasts. He touches women he knows well (friends of his at the Gateway Club; his sister; staff in the short-term care hostel) with the exception of his mother, as well as those he does not know well. You have been talking to him about why he should not do this. One Saturday you are waiting to pay to go into the cinema with Pete and Mary, his friend who also has learning disabilities, and he quickly touches Mary's breast. What feedback might you give him?

2. Gill is the first to greet people who come into the hostel. She does this by going up to people and linking their arm, putting her face up close and saying, "Hello, I know you". Visitors have complained to the Officer in Charge about this as Gill's breath usually smells very bad. What feedback do you give Gill?

3. Nikhel is a young man who does not like close company. He does not speak but seems to understand what others say to him. He likes to walk to the market and to sit and have a drink in the open-plan cafe there. He often surprises people by suddenly darting over to their table and taking the sugar off their saucers. Sometimes he has helped himself to their drinks as well. Invariably the people say to you, a member of staff accompanying him, "It doesn't matter – poor thing must be hungry/thirsty". When Nikhel does this yet again, what feedback do you give him? What feedback might you give the person whose drink he has taken?

4. You are out with Lee, a young man with Down's syndrome, on a trip to town to buy walking boots. Afterwards you decide to go for a coffee. The waitress gives Lee a cake, although he had not ordered it, and says "This is for you, dear". Lee blushes and replies "Thank you very much, but I would rather be treated just like anyone else". What feedback would you give Lee?

What kinds of decisions did you make when thinking about the different kinds of feedback? How easy was it to suggest either positive or negative feedback? What other ways

continued

might you have given feedback? How important is (a) the situation you are in, and (b) the relationship you have with the person in deciding what kind of feedback to give? How might you help any learning that came from your feedback to be consolidated?

Information giving

People with learning disabilities are disadvantaged in our information-dependent world. Often, merely having a piece of information can make a great deal of difference to their chances of making something happen in their social world, and thereby increase their social capability.

> A group of people using a traditional Adult Training Centre wanted to complain about their "incentive pay". They had tried complaining to the Centre manager, but he was given his budget from above. They thought of raising the matter with "the Government". When the existence of a Chair and Director of Social Services was brought to their attention, their way forward became clear. They invited the Chair of the Social Services Committee to their meeting, which eventually resulted in some changes to the system of pay. It also led to learning about a variety of other issues, including the problems of making decisions on behalf of others and the choices between increasing incentive pay and employing more staff.

Other relevant information includes basic knowledge about the norms and rules of social interaction. Sometimes this might involve gently contradicting the person's erroneous beliefs.

> Winston sincerely thought that if he talked to women who were on their own at the bus stop, this would lead to forming long-term relationships with them. He also thought that the woman who helped out in the corner supermarket, and who always asked how his day had been, fancied him. Once Winston was given information about how relationships developed and about how different kinds of people talked to other people, he was able to understand why he was constantly disappointed and began not to make so many incorrect interpretations of other people's behaviour. He had never been told explicitly before.

There are other types of information we may want to give people, that help them understand why the social world is as it is and why they should do certain things, as well as how they could do things differently. Examples of such information include: "most people are happy to talk about the weather with someone they don't know well"; "stand about this far away when you are talking to someone"; or "since that little girl was attacked people are suspicious of men who like to play with children".

Most of us learn about how the social world works and how we should operate in it during the course of our lives as a result of the different experiences we have had. People with learning disabilities may have missed out on this implicit learning and now need to be told certain things explicitly. There is a danger, though, in giving people information about how the social world operates – we may be wrong. Our own biases and distortions may creep in to the information and advice we give. If in doubt, we should check out our understanding with other people. Some of the issues concerned with giving information are included in Exercise 8.5.

Giving information is not simple. There are a number of useful points about giving information to bear in mind, and these can be summarized in terms of different stages of the process of giving information. Before we decide what information to give, we must know why it is we want to give it: we should clarify the need for information. There is not much point in telling people things they already know or telling them things that they cannot understand. So it is useful to get some idea of what it is they know already about the situation under consideration. Once we know this, we can plan what points we want to make and how we should make them, building on people's prior understanding of the situation wherever possible. Once we give the information we should then check that the person has understood and what it is that has been understood. This means going beyond asking "Do you understand what I have said?" (which invariably gets a "yes" or "no" reply) to finding a way of discovering exactly what the person thinks we have said. It is only when we know this that we can clarify any point if necessary or move on to something else. Many a misunderstanding has occurred because we are reluctant to check exactly what it is that people have understood about what we have told them.

Liam lived in a house with two other men. They shared a driveway with their neighbours, Ellie and Steve and their three-year-old

---

Exercise 8.5 Giving information

In each of the following situations, identify the information that is needed by people if they are to be socially competent. How would you give the information?

Social situation	*Information required for social competence*
Using a fee-per-session tennis court in the local park	
Using a pedestrian crossing on a busy street	
Refusing to give a teenager money when asked in the street	
Taking lifts in cars that are offered by people who are not well known	
Buying new shoes	
Introducing a friend to another friend for the first time	

Would you give different information to men and women in these different situations? How might you check whether your information had been understood? How might you modify the information given to people who understand more or less than those you had in mind when you completed the chart? Would your colleagues agree with you about what information was important to know in these different situations? What disagreements might there be?

---

daughter, Stephanie. Stephanie often left her tricycle and other garden toys in the driveway. There was frequently paper rubbish in the front garden, as it collected there from being blown off the street. Liam's social worker was particularly keen that Liam and his house-mates were seen to be good neighbours. He spent quite a lot of time talking to the men about how people acted in the neighbourhood and why it was important they tried to fit in with other people.

One day the social worker was telling the men that other people cleared up their front gardens by putting rubbish that was lying about in the wheelie-bin. Liam took this to heart and cleared all the rubbish away, including Stephanie's toys. Luckily, Ellie rescued the tricycle from the bin just before it was emptied. Liam did not distinguish between street rubbish and Stephanie's toys. The social worker had not even considered the possibility that Liam might include the toys in his clearing up. But then he had not asked Liam what he had understood about the information about the neighbourhood that he had given.

The process of giving information is summarized in Figure 8.1. It is not just through information that we learn how things should be done and why. Most of us have had many oppor-

Needs	Why is the information required? Has the person requested the information?
Checking	What is the extent of the person's knowledge already? What terms does she or he understand?
Planning	What points do I want to make? How should I make them? Will I speak/show/draw or what? What might stop the information being understood?
Presentation	Have I made a clear and accurate point, given clarification, checked understanding, given further clarification as necessary and elaborated if relevant?
Conclusion	Have I summarized? Will I leave a permanent reminder? If so, what sort? How will I check the person has remembered it properly? When will I return to discuss it again?

Figure 8.1 Process of giving information.

tunities to practise different ways of doing things and of learning by our mistakes.

Rote learning and repetition

When people have learnt new ways of doing things, we may want to help them to be able to use their new repertoires when we are not there to remind them what to do. We may be trying to help them act appropriately without any form of supervision. This means that they will have had to learn the appropriate action or skill very thoroughly indeed. Often this means using rote learning and repetition.

There is nothing artificial about supporting people in rote and repetitious learning: we all have to do it if we aim to improve upon and perfect our skills. There are a number of things, though, that we should bear in mind and that should guide our support when we encourage the use of rote learning, and we list these below.

- Decide what will count as adequate performance.
- Get the person to practise the performance.
- You might have to give a lot of prompts early on and gradually remove these.
- Repeat several times, introducing slight variations each time.
- Test for unsupported performance.
- If the person performs adequately in terms of the criteria set above, leave a delay, at first several minutes, and later from one day to another, before testing again.
- Once the person can retain the performance over several days, you can be reasonably certain that it has been learned sufficiently to be able to be carried out unsupported. However, it does not follow that it will be.

Kenton had recently found that it was possible to telephone the operator without paying. This was much easier on his pocket than using the chat lines to which his friend Nelson had introduced him. Of course the operators alerted the police to the obscene calls they were getting and, as it was such fun for Kenton, he was still there when they traced the calls to the telephone box near his house. Kenton had already learned some problem-solving and self-control skills, but he still found that the telephone box was too difficult to resist. His support worker, in consultation with his probation officer and psychologist decided to use the real world situation to take Kenton through the process of walking past the phone box, crossing the road if necessary, and even picking up the phone and putting it down again emphatically.

These practice sessions were carried out on five days over two weeks, with each routine (putting down the phone, walking past, crossing the road) practised up to 12 times on each day. Three different locations were used, each with a telephone box. Later in the sessions, Kenton's support worker stayed at a distance or went into a cafe while Kenton went through the routine again. At the end of this, Kenton felt confident that he was so used to interrupting his sequence of making a nuisance telephone call that he could now control himself. Kenton made no more nuisance calls.

Repetition and rote learning may not always be possible in natural situations, and there will sometimes be a case to be made for supporting people in learning new behaviours and understanding in simulated situations.

Role-playing, simulation and micro-teaching

We cannot always be there in the situation where the person will need to be socially capable. Moreover, we cannot always carry out training in the natural situation: it might be too stigmatizing for the person or it might be impractical, given the nature of the situation – its sensitivity, unpredictability, speed, or its potential for changing into something else when a "trainer" or a "professional" is present.

We may, therefore, have to rely on role-playing and simulation, which has the added benefit of allowing us to interrupt behaviour sequences, to probe for understanding, to slow things down and to repeat things (as above), in other words to do some teaching on a more "microscopic level" than we can in the natural environment.

Here are some guidelines for the use of role-playing and simulation.

- Ensure that the person understands that this is "just practice", particularly if the situation involves conflict and you are going to play a role that involves provoking the person (or testing the person's strategies for self-control). It is useful, particularly if you have doubts about how well the person has understood the special nature of the role-playing situation, to mark the beginning and especially the ending of the session very clearly, for example with an exaggerated greeting and farewell.

- Only use video if you cannot think of a better way to give specific feedback. It can be very unnerving to see oneself on video, particularly if people are sensitive or ignorant about how "different" their behaviour or appearance looks. On the other hand, some people really enjoy it and it can be a useful motivator to "be on TV", work the camera, etc. In our experience it gets in the way of social competence training more often than not.
- Plan your sessions in general terms, e.g. with a list of things to cover, but do not stick rigidly to the plan if other things crop up or the person has particular difficulty with something.
- Do not just focus on social behaviour, but cover all the areas in the model of social competence; for example simulations can be useful in gauging powers of social observation or skills at interpreting the actions of others.
- Keep sessions short enough so that the person does not lose interest. An hour is the absolute upper limit. However, mini-sessions can be separated by breaks to do other things, or informal time over a drink, which can give you more information on how the person is responding to the training session. Allow time for the person to become comfortable in the setting before getting into the hard work: someone we worked with used to take about 25 minutes to make a drink, go to the toilet, smoke a cigarette and exchange pleasantries before being ready to accept the more formal training session, which in this case was concerned with problem-solving strategies.
- Relate the content of the sessions to what is real for the person. We have found it helpful to come with some examples of situations that the person has encountered in the last few days on which to base the training.
- Do not leave too long a gap between sessions: consider, at least for the early ones, concentrating sessions together, e.g. on consecutive days, and spacing them out later, once you have established that the person is retaining the learning from one session to the next.
- Involve other relevant people in the role-plays and simulations; befrienders can assist in role-plays if they are in a position to support people in their natural settings too, and if they can provide appropriate role models for people.

- Take great care in defining boundaries if you are working with people in simulated and real settings. Try to ensure that everyone involved is clear about the expectations of different settings.

Bethany found that she was exploited by young children living near her because, in her desire to be friendly, she was unable to tell them assertively that they could not keep cigarettes in her flat and come in and smoke them. This got her into considerable trouble with the children's parents. Bethany went out a lot with Bernice, a woman of her own age, who used to take her shopping and to the labour club. Bernice could see that Bethany's inability to be assertive got her into a lot of difficulties in a number of different situations. A support worker, Andy, was given the task of helping Bethany learn assertive ways of refusing unreasonable requests that others made of her.

Andy was about 20 years younger than Bethany, and being a man believed that he would not be the most appropriate person to model assertive behaviour for Bethany. Instead, he asked Bernice if she would be willing to help. The three of them practised lots of examples of assertive behaviour, with Bernice modelling different ways of doing things for Bethany. Bernice was also able to give Bethany valuable feedback about how well she was doing practising her new skills in the different situations they were together. The role-play sessions had taught Bethany alternative ways of doing things and let her practise them in the safety of her own flat: Bernice was then able to help Bethany consolidate the learning in natural situations and give her valuable support when she found things difficult.

Minimal prompting

Once new behaviour or understanding has been learnt, it may be necessary to remind people what it is they should be doing or why. If any training is to be effective, the person being trained must be an active and willing participant. This involvement cannot just be assumed, however, and often has to be worked at in its own right.

Whenever learning has been taking place over a period of time, people will have to recall events, both real events in everyday life and the content of previous training sessions, in order to work on alternative strategies for dealing with them. They will have to rehearse actions (which can be from any of the six areas of social competence – awareness, observation, interpretation, planning and strategy, social behaviour and understanding of situations) in order to get used to them and to become proficient: as we have seen, rehearsal of actions or of information by repetition is necessary if retention of learning is to take place.

Both remembering (or recalling) and rehearsing (practising) new learning can be facilitated by the use of prompts. These can take a variety of forms: specific or prescriptive prompt, for example "do this . . ."; suggestive prompt to which a number of possible responses could be made, for example "what's next?"; and prompts can involve the trainer speaking, gesturing, showing the person something or using physical guidance.

While prompts are inevitable, it is also essential that they are not used unnecessarily. This can be a particular problem with verbal prompts which are difficult to fade out and whose overuse can lead to people becoming dependent on them, pausing between action sequences and waiting for the next prompt. We should only use prompts where necessary and give the person time to respond: many of us underestimate the time we should leave for people to respond and jump in to prompt before they are even ready to respond. We mistake delay in response for lack of knowledge, understanding or ability. Remember also that people are likely to take longer to respond in unfamiliar settings or unfamiliar tasks.

Sometimes it will be necessary to demonstrate or model different ways of doing things.

Demonstration and modelling

Imitation is a very powerful way of acquiring new behaviours, being a capacity most of us acquire early in life. We build upon this ability when we show somebody how to do something, by demonstration or "modelling": it is often easier to show than to tell.

If using modelling check that the person is paying attention, show them what to do and then have them practise the act for themselves. More complicated actions can be demonstrated in smaller parts before putting them together into a sequence.

"Interim" activities

In whatever capacity we are helping people develop their social competence, we cannot be with them round the clock, helping

Exercise 8.6 Designing suitable interim activities

Outline suitable interim activities for the following people in their different circumstances. What additional information would you require if you were to make the most of naturally occurring situations in supporting the people in these activities?

Situation	Suitable interim activities	Useful additional information
Mark has been learning to fill in forms. He understands what is required of different kinds of forms, but now has to discover how useful they are. He lives at home with his mother and adult brother.		
Heather uses a wheelchair and does not speak, although she can communicate her wishes clearly. She attends a day centre and has shown a lot of interest in compiling a personal history book and in making contact with people she has known in the past. She wants to include photographs of her family that she keeps at home in the hostel.		
You are Patsy's key worker in the house where she lives with three other people with learning disabilities. Patsy is impatient and you have been working with her on how to listen and give other people time to talk. You are going on holiday for two weeks and would like Patsy to practise listening whilst you are away.		

continued

> To what extent can you plan for interim activities over which you have little control? What ethical issues are raised in deciding whether or not to involve other people in helping people learn aspects of social competence? Are these issues different if the other people are non-professionals? If so, in what ways?

them move forwards. Yet social situations are always presenting themselves, and it is wasted opportunity if we do not somehow try to use those situations that arise between our times with people to help people learn. We can make use of these opportunities if we agree tasks or activities to be completed before our next meeting.

We have noted that it is not always possible to be present when the person needs to use the skill that has been learnt. One way around this is to get the person to practise the skill in the context where it should be used.

Often we will not be able to rely on people remembering to carry out the agreed activities, or whatever it was that they were supposed to be doing in between our sessions with them. In these cases it is often possible to involve someone from some other part of people's lives to act as a human *aide-mémoire*.

Bob attended a special class at an education centre where some youths at another class would sometimes make fun of him. Bob had got into several fights as a result, and was getting a reputation as violent. He was taught a way of avoiding responding to taunts by a combination of counting and walking away. As he had difficulty remembering to do this, two of the tutors agreed to watch out for incidents and prompt Bob to use his self-control strategy. Bob agreed to practise this when reminded. As a result both the fights and the taunts were much reduced by the end of term.

Try and identify suitable "interim" activities for people in the circumstances outlined in Exercise 8.6.

Providing labels

It is important to give people as much control over their learning and understanding as possible. In order to do this, we often have to supply labels for actions and social episodes that have been missed in their learning to date. Those of us who are socially competent use a variety of labels to identify aspects of our behaviour and feelings, and the situations in which these occur. If we can identify something we can then take action to alter it if necessary, but if things remain unidentified or not described, we cannot really begin to make adjustments and changes. Having appropriate labels, then, is essential if people are to take any kind of control of either themselves or the situations they encounter.

Broadly speaking, we can help people use three kinds of label.

**Exercise 8.7 The place of labels in
social competence**

Take any social event that has recently occurred. This could be in real life or from a television programme. Describe it briefly in terms of people's behaviour; the feelings of the main actors; the situation and social episodes within the situation.

What was the situation?

Behaviours of different actors:

Feelings of different actors:

Overall situation and social episodes within the situation:

How easy was it to identify the different labels for the behaviour, feelings and situation within this social event? Would the labels have been different if the actors had been much older, younger or from different cultures? Why? Would the labels have been different if the overall situation had been different? How much agreement would there be between you and your friends over the labels best used to describe what was going on? Why?

For behaviour

By labelling behaviour, it can be isolated from the stream of events, allowing the identification of the critical element which can then be encouraged or reduced as necessary. Similarly, by having ways of describing the behaviour of others, it is possible to identify what it is that requires a response or creates a problem.

For feelings

Learning labels for emotional states is particularly difficult for all of us. This is largely because, as we saw in Chapter 4, identifying particular emotions depends to a large extent on the way we interpret the context in which we experience them. So, when we point to a kettle and call it a "teapot", others can correct us because they know and can see to what we are referring. But if we feel anger and say that we feel hungry, it is more difficult for others to know what it is that we are referring to. This is likely to be a particular problem for people who are already disadvantaged when it comes to learning.

In fact, we often find that people with learning disabilities do not distinguish well between different emotional states, and that they have difficulty in identifying how they feel in a particular situation. We can help people do this by drawing their attention to internal feelings when we know what the external triggers are, for instance when something sad has happened or when the person has been thwarted.

For situations

There are some situations that crop up again and again – going into a shop, meeting a new person, being ignored, sharing time with friends are all examples of situations that are like "templates" for a variety of related events and incidents. Being able to identify and label the more important and common of these reduces the complexity that the person has to deal with. While there are no formally fixed rules for most social situations, there are common characteristics and broad do's and don'ts that make situations easier to handle, if followed.

Exercise 8.7 offers the opportunities to explore the different labels that help us to be socially competent.

Linking teaching to aspirations, interests and identity

The whole point of helping people develop their social competence is as part of enhancing social capability, or the ability to get things done that matter. All learning should, therefore, be linked to people's own hopes and aspirations. Keeping the learning and teaching relevant to the person, then, is a general principle in our approach: it also suggests some techniques for maintaining attention and motivation.

> Alison complained of being bored at weekends. In conversation she mentioned going out to the park for a cup of tea and a cake with her sister, some years ago. We thought that Alison might be able to do this with a friend who lived locally. In helping Alison plan these outings, we were able to remind her of her previous experience in several ways: in planning where and when to go; in deciding what to take; and in helping her keep interested in the exercise. Not only did Alison (and we) find that she remembered quite a lot about going out to the cafe in the park, but the memory of going there made her enthusiastic about everything connected with the outings, including planning and problem solving.
>
> Les, whom we mentioned before, saw himself as a friendly, helpful person. However, he would refuse to carry out reasonable small requests, such as holding open a door for a person laden with shopping, because he thought people were trying to take advantage of him. Appeal to Les's preferred identity meant working with him to identify the characteristics of a "helpful person" and comparing his actions with that description. In so doing Les had to "take the attitude of the other", as well as developing his sense of self and learning to perform some more socially appropriate behaviour.

Review of recent situations/episodes

We continually stress the importance of relating everything to the person's life in the real world. Without this, the assessment and intervention can easily become irrelevant to the person's needs. One way of keeping the person's everyday experience in focus is to use events that have recently been experienced as a basis for training. Often a recent episode that has gone badly illustrates one or more areas that people could usefully work on in improving their social competence. Similarly, reviewing recent episodes that have gone well serves to sustain motivation and enthusiasm, as people can see that change in social competence can make a real difference to them.

We all vary in how well we can recall and describe events (and this in itself is an index of social observation, interpretation and awareness). For some there is little difficulty, and simply asking "How has the last week been?" brings forth a variety of valuable scenarios. For others, it may be necessary to prompt – "What did you do yesterday?", "What happened at the party on Saturday?" etc. – rely on your own observations or even on third-party information. In most cases a combination of these ways of obtaining information will be used.

The information on recent events can be used to update your analysis and understanding of people's social competence (and more broadly their social capability) – we continue to learn as we continue to work with them. It can also be used as a basis for generating different ways that the person could have acted in the situation in question. Here, other methods discussed in this section, such as role-playing and feedback may be used. In so doing, you will work not just on the person's manifest social behaviour, but on the other less observable areas of social competence: your shared understanding of "what went wrong" might involve a failure to notice an important social cue, or a mistake in interpreting another person's motive.

Making distinctions

In helping people to become more "literate" in social interaction we are often concerned with enabling them to notice differences and distinctions, for example between:

- friends and acquaintances
- assertion and aggression
- anger and excitement
- advice and instructions
- feedback and reprimands
- public and private situations
- friendliness and over-familiarity, and so on.

In the training situation, we sometimes need to teach the person to make "discriminations" like these quite systematically. Again, the method used will depend on the person and the circumstances, but here is an outline of a typical procedure.

1. Identify the distinction that the person needs to be able to understand.
2. Familiarize the person with the two (or more) categories involved (e.g. assertion/aggression) by providing examples (e.g. from real life or on videotape).
3. Provide more examples, but now ask the person to guess

which category applies – this can be made into an enjoyable game, and considerable help can be offered in the early stages.

4. Once the person has learned the discrimination, return periodically to it and actively use the concept so established to build understanding of real social events and situations.

In order to learn to discriminate, we must be able to help people direct their attention to the appropriate things in their social worlds. This may involve us in helping to remove distractions.

Removal of distraction and focusing attention

One prerequisite for both learning and the exercise of competence is the ability to direct attention on the relevant aspects of the situation of interest. People with learning disabilities often have significant difficulties with this, but considerable progress can be made, both in terms of attention within a specific situation and in the general ability to sustain and direct attention. We suggest three ways of helping with this.

1. Removal or reduction of extraneous stimulation
Choose somewhere to work that is quiet, with little in the way of interesting objects that could grab the person's attention. In more formal training sessions, it is worth developing what is almost a ritual of beginning, middle and end, with the middle reserved for the serious business of training, the beginning including such events as getting a drink, talking about the weather, etc. and the end being for the unwinding of the session. This means that there is "somewhere to put" the distracting small talk that might otherwise interfere with the training, and helps with the general learning of how to match behaviour and conversation to the social situation.

2. Focusing or redirection of attention to task
In keeping with the above it is important to be calmly insistent on bringing the person back to the topic under consideration. While there has to be opportunity for people to introduce ideas, issues and concerns of their own, it is important to keep the work focused on a small number of learning points and to prevent interruption by relative irrelevancies. Do not be afraid to interrupt and redirect people – this is often more respectful than

letting them pursue an irrelevancy without them realizing it. Sometimes changing the subject can be a way of avoiding emotional or intellectual effort, likely in people not used to such "work".

Sometimes people consider their situation in very generalized terms: "Everyone is horrible to me"; "Nobody likes me"; "I don't like going out". It is important to help the person break down the problem into its parts: "Who was horrible to you yesterday?" "What did they do?" "What happened just before that?" etc. You will have to draw artificial boundaries around issues: "Let's talk about that in a minute: just now I want to know more about what Geoff did."

Here, as throughout this work, humour can be valuable in defusing what otherwise could become a rather teacher – pupil-like relationship.

3. Practising paying attention
Where there is a particular problem of maintaining attention it may be necessary to devise ways of helping the person practise paying attention.

> Lauren had difficulty in paying attention to what other people were doing. It was decided that some practise might help. Barbara would do three simple actions in sequence and Lauren would try to say what she had done. At first this was difficult, but soon it was possible to move on to more complex actions, such as the things people said. With this practice, Lauren became more accurate at observing what was going on in an interaction, something necessary for the work on observation and interpretation that was a particular need of hers.

Social problem solving

This is a technique developed by D'Zurilla and Goldfried (1971) (see Chapter 4): it makes explicit the steps to take in solving a problem. A sequence of steps can be identified to follow.

1. Recognize that there is a problem to be solved and identify it.
2. Define what is to be achieved (the goal).
3. Generate a set of alternative means for reaching that goal.
4. Anticipate the likely consequences of each.
5. Decide which course of action to follow.
6. Put this decision into practice.
7. Review its effectiveness.

In practice, we can take people through each of these steps, for one or more problems. Additional help may be needed for particular steps, and the person's performance will yield more information about the nature of their social competence. Many people with learning disabilities have difficulty in generating a list of alternatives until they have had some practice at this. Lack of knowledge of social rules, roles or relationships may mean that they find it difficult to anticipate the consequences of a particular course of action.

We have found that just exposing some people to the idea that there may be more than one way of doing something, or getting them to think ahead about the consequences of their social actions is enough to yield real improvements in their social competence.

The full social problem-solving process is not something we would expect people to use routinely, but it is useful to take people through it in regard to real problems, and some parts of it may be worth using on their own – for example working on the specific identification of a problem can be helpful when someone reports a global undifferentiated problem such as "Nobody likes me", "I've got nothing to do" or "Nothing I do goes right".

Just as we can help people develop strength in social problem solving, so we can help them develop skills of observation in social situations.

Guided observation

Sometimes people's knowledge of the real world can be the limiting factor in their social competence, and this is best worked on as much as possible in the real environment. We have to be careful that we do not, ourselves, make incorrect assumptions about the social world, which is after all in a constant state of change, when we are helping people with learning disabilities to greater understanding.

Mr Jessop dressed appropriately enough for someone of 18; unfortunately he was 54. Having discussed the issues around choice of clothes (he is a very articulate man, but one who spent most of his life in a remote institution), he agreed to test out our suggestions about who wore what. We went to the local shopping centre and (from a distance) identified people of similar age to Mr Jessop. We discussed what they wore and identified people wearing similar clothes to himself, noting their probable age. This allowed Mr

Jessop and ourselves to relate our training to the social reality of the local community. Incidentally it also led to two other pieces of work.

We found that Mr Jessop had a limited understanding of age (using height as a way of estimating age, which of course only works for children). We also had discussions wherein we explored the differences between social norms and individual rights to self-expression: Mr Jessop could wear what he liked, and there was nothing to say he should dress like everyone else, but, if he did, he should be aware of what other people might think and how they might judge him and treat him if he dressed in ways that appeared bizarre to most people.

As a way of testing out a lot of the things he had learned, Mr Jessop had us take a number of photographs of him in different kinds of outfits he tried on in a large department store. When these were developed he could see for himself how he looked, and compare these images with what he saw round about him. Indeed, he took his photographs down to the shopping centre and spent several hours sitting on one of the benches, comparing people who passed with the pictures of himself. He was locating himself within the social world about him for the first time.

Anxiety reduction techniques

We mentioned earlier that people cannot learn if they are anxious. Social anxiety blocks learning social competence. Sometimes a gap in social competence arises not from a lack of skill, as is often supposed, but from a failure to use that skill. We have already considered some of the constraints imposed on skill use by the person's environment: another reason for not using skills is because the person is anxious. Much anxiety about social situations can be tackled through work using the methods we have considered, so that the person has a repertoire to use in a variety of social situations. However, sometimes the person can be so anxious that the anxiety needs tackling directly and, indeed, other training may not be possible before anxiety has been reduced.

Anxiety reduction techniques include various forms of relaxation (with behavioural relaxation training being the most useful for people whose verbal understanding may be limited), meditation and related approaches, systematic desensitization and graded practice with increasingly demanding situations. It is worth noting that many of these approaches depend upon people's expectations that they will improve, and upon their confidence in the person offering help. Professional advice may be useful in assessing and treating anxiety: psychologists are trained in the analysis and treatment of anxiety and anxiety-based disorders, while occupational and physiotherapists are usually familiar with relaxation and related techniques. Useful sources are listed at the end of the chapter.

WHAT CAN GO WRONG?

A number of things can weaken the likelihood that training in different areas of social competence will be successful. This does not necessarily mean that the person cannot learn social skills. It is most likely that something will have been wrong about what we were trying to achieve, about the extent to which we understood the level of learning already, about the situations people found themselves in, about our methods of helping them learn and so on. It is useful to bear in mind that:

> **the person is right**   i.e. we should rethink our plans and techniques of help if people have not learned; we should use our analysis of why it is that learning did not occur as a source of information in rethinking;
>
> **and so is the person teaching**   i.e. those of us who are helping people develop their social competence have to make decisions; we are leading the process, acting as guide or facilitator, and we should take care to avoid being misled by people's immediate wants into working on things that will not make any overall difference to their social capability (see the Caroma window, introduced in Chapter 1).

Common problems in changing social skills and competence

Failure of "motivation"

Sometimes the person does not want to change or to put in the effort required to effect change. It is easy to assume that the cause of this lies "within the person", and perhaps in some cases the person simply does not have the energy or the habit of expending energy, required for learning and change. Most of the time, however, a lack of motivation is a result of something else, such as lack of a clear outcome that the person can anticipate as a result of learning and change. In these cases, re-examine what you are doing: is it relevant to the person's current concerns and aspirations? If it is, but the person does not see this, ask how the link might be made.

Failure of generalization and maintenance

Sometimes the things we teach do not "generalize" to other times or places, or if they do they soon stop happening there. The person shows understanding or performs social behaviours appropriately in the training context, but outside it there is no noticeable gain. We tackle this potential problem in this book

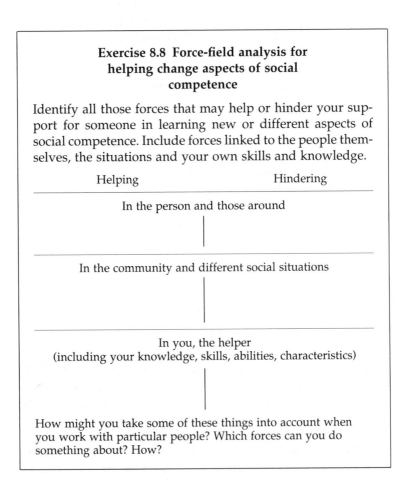

**Exercise 8.8 Force-field analysis for
helping change aspects of social
competence**

Identify all those forces that may help or hinder your support for someone in learning new or different aspects of social competence. Include forces linked to the people themselves, the situations and your own skills and knowledge.

Helping   Hindering

In the person and those around

In the community and different social situations

In you, the helper
(including your knowledge, skills, abilities, characteristics)

How might you take some of these things into account when you work with particular people? Which forces can you do something about? How?

primarily through our emphasis on understanding social competence in relation to social capability more broadly: how do we expect this learning to benefit the person, and how will those around the person provide supports for this.

We recognize that increasing competence by itself will often be insufficient to produce change. Likewise we emphasize understanding the real social worlds of the people we are working with and carrying out training there where this is appropriate. Problems of generalization are often a result of carrying out irrelevant training in inappropriate, isolated ways. In the remaining cases (for example where the person's community supports are limited or we cannot be there to train in the real social context), there is little substitute for persistence, both on the social competence front and on the wider community competence front.

Sabotage by significant others

Sometimes what we are attempting to do is threatening to significant people in the social network of the person with a learning disability. If a person becomes more competent, maybe there will be less need for the help of some staff or family members. Sabotage is rare and can be made less likely through proper analysis of the person's social situation, but it is worth being aware of the possibility.

Problems as information

If we find problems in what we are trying to do, we should not despair: this is an opportunity to increase our understanding of the person we are working with, his or her context and social capability generally.

Exercise 8.8: invites you to conduct a force-field analysis on helping people change, identifying all those aspects of the learning situation that may help or hinder improvement in social competence.

FURTHER READING

Many of the techniques for helping people develop their social skill and competence draw on general principles of learning. We have included some of these general techniques in the list of further reading, as well as more specific techniques in areas that cause particular difficulties. We have also included review papers on social skills training with people with learning disabilities.

Bregman, S. (1984) Assertiveness training for mentally retarded adults. *Mental Retardation*, **22**, 12–16.

Dickson, A. (1982) *A Woman in your Own Right: Assertiveness and You*, Quartet Books, London.

D'Zurilla, M.R. (1986) *Problem Solving Therapy*, Jossey-Bass, San Francisco.

D'Zurilla, M.R. and Goldfried, M.R. (1971) Problem-solving in behaviour modification. *Journal of Abnormal Psychology*, **78**, 107–26.

D'Zurilla, M.R. and Nezu, A. (1982) Social Problem Solving in Adults, in *Advances in Cognitive Behavioral Research and Therapy* (ed. P.C. Kendall), Academic Press, New York.

Edmonson, B., Leland, H. and Leach, E.M. (1985) Social inference training of retarded adolescents. *Education and Training of the Mentally Retarded*, **5**, 169–76.

Ellis, R. and Whittington, D. (eds) (1983) *A Guide to Social Skills Training*, Croom Helm, London.

Gresham, F.M. (1981) Social skills training with handicapped children: a review. *Review of Educational Research*, **51**, 139–76.

Hazel, J.S., Schumaker, J.B., Sherman, J.A. and Sheldon, J. (1982) Application of a group training program in social skills and problem solving to learning disabled and non-learning disabled youth. *Learning Disability Quarterly*, **5**, 398–408.

Jackson, H.J., King, N.J. and Heller, V.R. (1981) Social skills assessment and training for mentally retarded persons: a review of research. *Australian Journal of Developmental Disabilities*, **7**, 113–23.

Kanfer, F.H. and Goldstein, A.P. (1984) *Helping People Change: A Handbook of Methods*, 2nd edn, Pergamon, New York.

Ladd, G.W. and Mize, J. (1983) A cognitive-social learning model of social skills training. *Psychological Review*, **90**, 127–57.

Marholin, D., O'Toole, K.M., Touchette, P.E. *et al.* (1979) "I'll have a big Mac, large fries, large coke, and apple pie" . . . or teaching adaptive community skills. *Behavior Therapy*, **10**, 236–48.

Mcloughlin, C.S., Garner, J.B. and Callahan, M. (1987) *Getting Employed, Staying Employed: Job Development and Training for Persons with Severe Handicaps*, Paul H. Brookes, London.

Mesibov, G.B. (1986) A cognitive programme for teaching social behaviors to verbal autistic adolescents and adults, in *Social Behavior in Autism* (eds E. Schopler and G.B. Mesibov), Plenum, New York.

Poplin, M.S. (1988) The reductionistic fallacy in learning disabilities: replicating the past by reducing the present. *Journal of Learning Disabilities*, **21**, 389–400.

Poplin, M.S. (1988) Holistic/constructivist principles of the teaching/ learning process: Implications for the field of learning disabilities. *Journal of Learning Disabilities*, **21**, 401–16.

Priestley, P., Maguire, J., Flegg, D. *et al.* (1978) *Social Skills and Personal Problem Solving: A handbook of methods*, Tavistock, London.

Robertson, I., Richardson, A.M. and Youngson, S.C. (1984) Social skills training with mentally handicapped people: a review. *British Journal of Clinical Psychology*, **23**, 241–64.

Shure, M.B. (1979) Training children to solve interpersonal problems: a preventive mental health program, in *Social and Psychological Research in Community Settings: Designing and conducting programs for social and personal well-being (eds*, R.F. Muñoz, L.R. Snowden, J.G. Kelly and Associates), Jossey-Bass, San Francisco.

Shure, M.B and Spivack, G. (1978) *Problem-Solving Techniques in Child Rearing*, Jossey-Bass, San Francisco.

Spivack, G., Platt, J.J. and Shure, M.B. (1976) *The Problem-Solving Approach to Adjustment*, Jossey Bass, San Francisco.

Stokes, T.F. and Baer, D.M. (1977) An implicit technology of generalization. *Journal of Applied Behavior Analysis*, **10**, 349–67.

van Ments, M. (1983) *The Effective Use of Role Play: A Handbook for Teachers and Trainers*, Kogan Page, London.

Zarkowska, E. and Clements, J. (1994) *Problem Behaviour and People with Severe Learning Disabilities: The STAR Approach*, Chapman and Hall, London.

9

Increasing the competence of the community

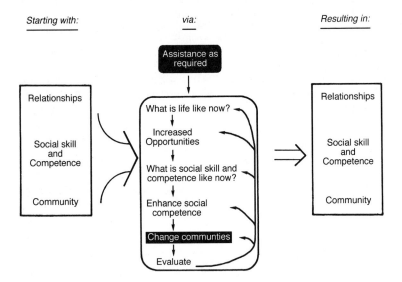

Starting with:

We have looked at what life is like now for a person with learning disabilities, how opportunities might be increased and how social competence can be enhanced. As we saw in Chapter 1, Figure 1.2, social capability is inextricably bound up with the competence of the community. We use "community" to refer to the places and social networks in which people live and move and to which they contribute (see Chapter 3). Thus the community for people with learning disabilities includes the people they do or could meet; the behaviour, attitudes and values of the people they do or could meet; the social networks to which they do or could contribute; the places they do or could frequent; the neighbourhoods and social situations in which they do or could participate; the interests they do or could have; and the services they do or could use. All of these parts of community are influenced by legislation, social attitudes and political priorities. Our work to help increase the competence of the communities can be directed at all or any one of these aspects of community.

There are some aspects of increasing community competence that can be seen as part of our existing work practices, sometimes requiring us to prioritize or to emphasize different things; some require us to extend and develop our work practices in various directions; others can better be addressed by our engaging in non-work-related activities. If we take seriously our commitment to helping people with learning disabilities to greater social capability, we cannot split any professional obligations apart from our obligations as citizens and part of our own communities – which are also those of people with learning disabilities. We are, at one and the same time, workers assisting people to develop their social competencies and part of communities that may or may not welcome people with learning disabilities to full membership. We have, therefore, included some strategies for increasing community competence that may be outside the realm of paid employment.

In building community inclusion, and thereby social capability, we are trying to move towards something that only exists now as a set of fragments. Not surprisingly the full vision of a competent, inclusive community is difficult to describe, and we often fall back on a "service image" of what is required. So some workers' descriptions of steps towards social integration include use of the post office, dentist, attendance at a health centre or at a college. While these are in themselves valuable, they might not become a focus for the development of authentic relationships, friendships, purposeful associations, meaningful roles, social group solidarity or the other basic building blocks of community. This can lead to what is almost a delusion on the part of service providers that people are becoming part of the community, whereas all that may be happening is that while they repeatedly pass through its archi-tecture, they are never part of its society.

Social capability, then, does not just imply change for the way services work: it also means change in the way that communities function. It is the right of people with learning disabilities to be included in communities, and if this really happened then communities would become rather different – we believe enriched, but also more competent at accommodating difference and difficulty in their members. It is in all our interests as citizens to bring this about.

To date, much of the emphasis has been on the service *"pushing"* the person with learning difficulty into the community, often with a bit of the service in the form of a worker, but with little effort to help the community to *"pull"* the person with learning difficulty into itself. If we see the task of our services as in part to assist communities to include people, then the work might be tackled more effectively.

PRINCIPLES FOR STRENGTHENING COMMUNITY COMPETENCE

Wherever the focus of our work in helping communities to become more competent, whether it be on people, knowledge, values and attitudes, places and activities, services or general cultural issues, there are some common issues we should keep at the forefront of our minds. If we omit to follow these principles, change is likely to be neither sustainable nor very independent from formal services.

- Always ask WHY? a particular piece of work or strategy should be adopted. If we cannot give an answer to the WHY question in terms of the impact it will have on the lives of people with learning disabilities, we probably need not spend time on it.
- Find out what the current situation is – how competent is the community already?
- Identify the current concerns of people within the locality and the potential for stimulating interest and commitment.
- Build on the existing strengths of the community. Even if new relationships, networks, activities and so on have to be developed, try and link them to existing ones. There is a danger here that services will take over or colonize existing community networks, and this should be avoided.
- Make alliances. Deliberately try to forge links between networks, activities, places, interests and so on. Seek for things in common, such as ideas, vision, shared interests and mutual advantage that strengthen existing and new networks.
- Work through other people or at least hand over power and

control as soon as possible. Avoid charismatic leaders. Develop and support commitment from others. When involving other people, build in support so that people can cope – do not rely on them totally.

- Be opportunistic as well as strategic. Plan for change and involvement, but also be ready to jump at opportunities as they arise. Take care to look for how things could be sustainable.
- Anticipate and plan to overcome resistance: try to focus on the issues, not the people. Why are X and Y opposing you – are their issues at all legitimate? Can you devise ways in which everyone gains?
- Make compromises if these lead you further on. Volunteers, for instance, may be patronizing to people with learning disabilities, but do not pass up the opportunities and contacts that they would offer for some kind of ideal purism today: instead, work to increase understanding for tomorrow.

We cannot become capable in any walk of life without resources. If we are considering ways to increase the competence of the community in order to strengthen people's social capability, we must clarify those resources in and of the community with which we might work.

UNDERSTANDING COMMUNITY RESOURCES

We, ourselves, bring to the neighbourhoods in which we work the resources of our agencies, which include staff (with their working hours, knowledge and expertise) and sometimes buildings. The very work we do brings additional resources, linked to the service system, including technology, management practices, staff recruitment, training and supervision, policy and procedures and so on. These things are common to all organizations and will be found in one form or another in all formal and informal bodies in any locality. However, these types of resources, underpinned as they are by budgets and available finance, are not the only ones we can draw on in communities. Community resources include:

- *places*: spaces and buildings with or without a specialist purpose;
- *money*: some that is already committed and some that can be mobilized through local fund-raising;

- *services and facilities*: formal and informal services, including caring, health, welfare, utilities (water, gas, electricity, transport);
- *activities*: many different human activities, including leisure, work, recreational, hobby, educational, cultural, social, domestic and caring activities, some of which are aimed at people of different ages, sexes and cultures;
- *energy*: the commitments of time and labour by people, groups and organizations to particular activities and practices;
- *interests*: in people, things, areas of knowledge;
- *commitment and obligation*: to activities, groups, individual people, social causes;
- *solidarity*: the strength of people as social beings, the sense of community, of togetherness. This togetherness is captured in common campaigning and social development phrases, such as "The people, united, shall never be defeated", or "All for one and one for all", and "We shall overcome". The community can be more than the individuals within it: it can embody concern and unconditional commitment to one another;
- *reciprocity*: people with mutual dependencies on each other, each having their needs met from within the community and offering help, support, advice and commitment in return;
- *roles*: formal and informal parts people play that are recognized by others; these may be within organizations or networks of people, or not;
- *expertise*: people with different kinds of knowledge, skills or time which may be used for their own purposes or for others.

One thing to notice about this list of resources is how many of them are not linked to money: they are free. Any or all of these resources may, however, have to be unlocked to enable people with learning disabilities become more socially capable. We have to "open up the community" to those with learning disabilities. Whilst all these resources will be available in one form or another in all localities, we have to get to know just how they are deployed in the areas in which we work. We have to understand the pattern and interlinkages within local resources.

Understanding local resources

To understand local resources we must spend time getting to know about how people in the neighbourhood live their lives and about how the particular neighbourhood locality or community "works". We must find out what resources there are locally and how these are used at the moment. This includes, most importantly, finding out about local people, their actual and potential activities, interests and organizations. Without this knowledge and understanding we will not be any position to help people with learning disabilities develop their social capability.

Informal methods

If we live in the area in which we work and the area in which people with learning disabilities live, we will have a head start in understanding the community. Even so, it is a good idea to stand back and take another look at our communities – are there parts (or layers) of the community about which we know very little? If we do not live locally, we will have to do more to get to know the neighbourhood.

It is never a good idea to try to change anything in communities quickly. What we have to do is understand the community as a dynamic entity – one that is in constant flux. This means that there will be some things about any neighbourhood that are consistent and resilient: others that are temporary and constantly evolving and changing. We need to give ourselves time to understand these dynamic aspects of a community; to see which things or people are likely to be stable and permanent, and which are not. Some communities, for example, will have a long history of successful collective neighbourhood action, such as tenants or residents groups, parks committees, civic forums and so on, whereas others will not. We will only find out these things over time. If we do this, we will avoid the pitfall of being seduced by the person or issues of the moment, which might not have any lasting impact on the community. Key people, activities, concerns of a community are often not those that quickly come to the attention of an "outsider" trying to understand the community for the first time. To make lasting changes, we have to find out and work with those things, people and networks that form the heart of a community, not the relatively superficial surface.

One way to find out about the localities in which we are supporting people with learning disabilities is not to use a car in our work. If we walk, cycle or wait for the bus, we will meet more people and talk to them. We will also be seen around the locality and be more likely to be accepted as part of it.

Formal methods

There are formal ways of finding out about communities. Some ideas about finding out about the nature and resources in a neighbourhood are given in Chapter 3. At times, we may want to base our understanding on more organized and reliable information. In particular, if we wish to find out about a specific aspect of local activity, we may want to undertake some preliminary research.

> There seemed very little to do, in one area of a large town, for people with learning disabilities who had been resettled from hospitals, as well as those living in their family homes. Although most people attended the adult training centre, based in the locality, they did little outside its opening hours. A small. locally based random sample, door-step survey was conducted, to get a picture of how people of different ages spent their leisure time. This was useful in understanding the different types of activities that people of different ages and at different stages in their "family life cycle" did.
>
> Young adults did little. They occasionally had friends around and sat at home listening to records or tapes. Older adults with young families did even less. They described their leisure activities as largely revolving around the interests of their young children: the rest of their time was spent at home watching television. Older adults, whose children were older or who had left home, or those who had never had children, spent more time out of the house in pubs or clubs, with friends. These older adults made greater use of church activities and (mostly the men) worked the local allotments. The survey revealed useful information about how people spent their time, and also identified gaps in the resources available for single adults of different ages. This led to work that not only linked particular people in the locality with individual people with learning disabilities to share some very specific leisure activity, but also led to the development of more community groups in which people with and without learning disabilities could participate.

Undertaking a piece of research of this sort can have a number of advantages. It can be useful as a way of presenting information to employers and funding bodies as a means of persuading them to support particular community developments. It can also be a way of stimulating local interest in the area under study. Several people who took part in this research, for instance, commented on how they had never realized how little there was to do in the locality before. Some of these people later became active in pushing for the development of local facilities that would be of benefit to the whole community. What the research had done was stimulate collective responsibility within the locality for the well-being of all people living there. The issues to take into account when contemplating a piece of fact-finding research are considered in Exercise 9.1.

**Exercise 9.1 Researching
communities**

Identify an issue in the community about which you might want to gather accurate information. Work through the questions given. (If you cannot think of an issue for yourself, work through the questions in relation to the following question: How much time do people spend at home on different days of the week?)

Issue:

Why do you want to
know this?

Who has been or
should have been
involved in deciding
what questions
should be asked?

Are there any
supplementary
questions that need
to be asked (for
example do you want
to know about people
of different ages,
sexes, cultural
backgrounds)?

What kind of
information do you
want (descriptions,
numbers, people's
accounts)?

How might you collect
this information?

Continued

Whose advice might
you seek in collecting
this information?

What will you do with
the information once
you have collected it?

Whose advice might
you seek in making
sense of the
information you have
collected?

Who will have access
to the information?

Who will you tell
what you found?

Who else should
know?

How will your
findings help you in
your purpose (stated
in answer to first
question)?

Do you really want
to collect this
information in this
way?

What other ways
might you find out
what it is you want
to know?

Any other comments?

How can you be sure that the information you collect in this
formal way will help you achieve whatever it is you are
trying to achieve? How many choices did you have over
how the information should be collected? Do you have the
expertise to undertake this work?

Once we have a good idea about what already exists in a community we can identify gaps and work to try to fill them, or identify existing resources that we can harness or strengthen.

MOBILIZING COMMUNITY RESOURCES

As soon as we begin to try to mobilize community resources in one way or another as a means of enhancing the social capability of people with learning disabilities, we have to begin to think strategically: we have to identify our goals (what it is we hope to achieve and why); our tactics (including personal, interpersonal, group and organizational tactics); the people we can draw on; the alliances and networks we can stimulate; the opposition we might face; the compromises we might have to make; the safeguards we want to introduce; the supports we can contribute and the ways we can withdraw. Figure 9.1 illustrates a strategic approach to increasing community competence.

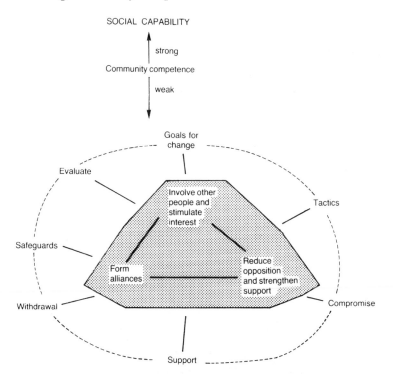

Figure 9.1 Strategic approach to increasing community competence.

Focus of work with the community

Working with communities to increase their competence in order to enhance the social capability of people with learning disabilities may involve work which focuses on awareness and understanding; information, education and knowledge; skills; access (physical and social); participation and involvement; role development and expansion; procedures, policies and legislation. We can work with different parts of the communities in which people with learning disabilities are located, including families, relatives and friends; support staff and professionals working in different direct services; people, places, activities and organizations in localities and neighbourhoods; people, places, activities and organizations more widely; social systems (including social attitudes) at regional, national and international levels. Figure 9.2 illustrates these different components of people's communities.

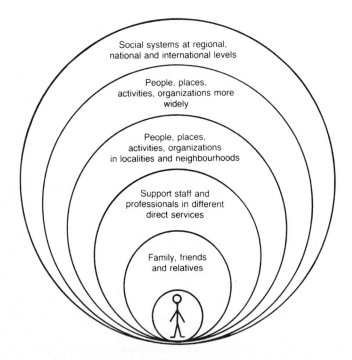

Figure 9.2 Communities of people with learning disabilities.

Table 9.1 Focus and nature of work with communities to strengthen community competence

Focus on:	Family, relatives and friends	Support staff and professionals working in different direct services	People, places, activities and organizations in localities and neighbourhoods	People, places, activities and organizations more widely	Social systems (including social attitudes) at regional, national and international levels
Working on:					
Awareness and understanding					
Information, education and knowledge					
Skills					
Access (physical and social)					
Participation and involvement					
Role development and expansion					
Procedures, policies, agreements, guidance, rules or legislation					

Table 9.1 sets out these different areas of work in a grid format. This grid can be used to help clarify the focus and nature of our work with communities.

There are many different kinds of ways we can begin to enhance the competence of communities, and before we look specifically at how community resources might be mobilized it is worth listing some of them. Some examples include:

- interweaving different areas of welfare need: as in the case of a young person who needed somewhere to live sharing accommodation with a person of similar age with a learning disability, who has the rent paid in return for some support to the person with the learning disability; finding link families who can offer short-term care for young people with learning disabilities;
- building on the service's own connections to the community: often it is the lower status, local staff member who is a mine of information about the local community and how to get into it;
- working with specific groups to create integrative opportunities: such as the development of a new cycling proficiency course for adults, to which two or three people with learning difficulties might go; a city farm which might involve 30 people, two of whom also have learning difficulties;

- using inter-agency knowledge and understanding: other service organizations can be closer to the community than the health and social care sector, and they may be able to help in relation to issues such as benefits, employment or housing;
- developing relationships with agencies such as the media before you need them;
- not being afraid to ask: like the staff member who had been providing transport for a client attending an Asian sewing class and who felt in the way of the client's interactions in the class now that she was settled in – on asking the tutor whether anyone might be prepared to provide the transport, she found that someone had already wanted to offer but had not wanted to usurp the staff member's role;
- putting service system money together with other contributions to set up integrative options such as a community centre, a housing cooperative or a small business;
- getting the "pull" model established in service procedures and structures, e.g. job descriptions, policies, supervision and appraisal and other practices;
- learning the community's rules wherever possible and following them, rather than expecting the community to behave as if it were part of the service system; starting where the community, its sections and people within it are at the moment and moving forward from there;
- helping family and friends gain access to understanding, knowledge and skills;
- building roles for people with learning disabilities that enable them to take up positions that are satisfying to themselves and of service to others;
- using existing community facilities in imaginative ways so that all involved can benefit, such as the local community support team that negotiated being able to use a night-club as a meeting place for people during the day when it was not in use;
- forming alliances and coalitions to generate a critical mass of support for change in a locality;
- celebrating success.

All of the above ideas are based on things that have been done somewhere. It is important to share our best ideas and examples of good practice with others so that together we can learn how to move into the next phase of community-based provision – true integration by communities that include all their citizens. To do this we have to mobilize those resources that are already in the community.

METHODS FOR MOBILIZING COMMUNITY RESOURCES

Linking and networking of activities, people, and organizations

The research project mentioned above brought local people into discussions about the lack of leisure facilities and they became involved in trying to get something done about it. There are other ways in which we can work to stimulate local interest in developing resources in the community. In particular, we might be able to build on existing facilities or organizations in order to stimulate and create a willingness for people with learning disabilities to be included.

> A thriving community action project existed in the suburb of a small town. Volunteers helped people who were housebound to shop, get to and from church, hospitals and to visit friends. Cathy, a community support worker for some people with learning disabilities living in staffed houses in the area, had noticed that many of the gardens in a few of the streets were unkempt. On talking to the coordinator of the community action project, Cathy discovered that these gardens were those of housebound people, in the main. Cathy suggested that the community action project broaden their remit to include gardening, and also suggested that some of the people with learning disabilities who lived nearby might be able to contribute to this activity. The community action project management committee thought this would be a good idea, but thought housebound people would be reluctant to have the "mentally handicapped" doing their gardens. They also did not have the resources to supervise such work.
>
> Cathy was able to attend a meeting of the management committee to argue her case. She took George, who had worked on the gardening team of the ATC for many years with her. He brought along a folder in which he had collected pictures of his gardening achievements. Before Cathy could speak, George told the committee why he did not like being called "mentally handicapped". He went on to suggest that the gardening scheme could work with teams of people with and without learning disabilities, and that this might allay people's fears, as well as deal with the matter of

supervision. Cathy agreed to get together a group and try it out. By the end of the meeting, members of the management committee had met a person with learning disabilities (most of them for the first time!), learnt something about language and its effects on people with disabilities, found a way to broaden their activities and found a way to include people with learning disabilities in their activities. Had Cathy not known the coordinator of the community action project in the first place and seen for herself something about what was needed locally, this may not have happened.

Over time, people with learning disabilities became involved with other aspects of the community action group's work; management team members came to know individual people with learning disabilities and to include them in some of their other activities (many members of the community action management committee were active in other community groups).

What Cathy was able to do here was to work with an already strong and well-established community group in order to expand their activities without diluting their existing activities and weakening their overall purpose, and was able to highlight two sets of needs which were, hitherto, unmet. Firstly, she drew attention to the needs of housebound people to have their garden maintained; secondly, she raised the need of local people with learning disabilities to be able to contribute to their communities. If neither of these needs was identified, the other group would not have been able to have their needs met. We have here an example of reciprocal need: once this is noted, a solution can be found.

Once a reciprocal solution is found, the mutual dependence of one group upon the other will make it more likely to be sustained. The success of Cathy's strategy lay in (i) having picked up things about the locality and the people living in it; (ii) being able to identify reciprocal needs; (iii) making contact with the coordinator of a well-established community group with an interest in diversifying; (iv) clarifying a desirable end position for people with learning disabilities, housebound people and the community group; (v) negotiating a compromise solution to the ideal end point; and (vi) offering some support to the plan in order to make it happen. George's meeting with the management committee was vital in helping them see what might be possible. Some of the issues relevant to building on existing organizations are explored in Exercise 9.2.

Whilst Cathy was able to build on people, activities and organizations, other networking may emphasize links between people

---

Exercise 9.2 Building on existing organizations

Identify any local community or commercial organization in a particular locality and answer the following questions about it:

Organization:

To what extent does the organization include people with learning disabilities now?

If people with learning disabilities were more included in the work of the organization, what would it look like
  for the organization?
  for the people with learning disabilities?
  for the people without learning disabilities?

Can you identify any need within the organization that greater inclusion of people with learning disabilities might meet?
  How might you help the organization and those within it see this need exists?

Who is in a position of influence within the organization?
  Do you (or does anyone you know) know him/her/ them?
  How might you make contact with him/her/them?

What compromises might you be prepared to make as the organization opened itself to people with learning disabilities?

What supports could be offered to better enable the organization to include people with learning disabilities?

Continued

Any other issues:

To what extent would the issues to take into account differ with the type of organization? In what ways? How might you involve people with learning disabilities themselves in opening up community organizations to include them? What threats to positive inclusion of people with learning disabilities might there be concerning any of these issues?

in order to increase the participation of different people in the lives of people with learning disabilities.

Veronica is 20. She lives at home with her mother, Sarah, and father Paul. Her brother, James, finished university in a nearby town last year. He is currently unemployed, doing voluntary work. Veronica has a complicated week attending a day centre for three sessions, college for five sessions, and the rest of the time she is at home. Sarah works part-time and Paul works full-time.

Since Veronica left school, Sarah has become increasingly concerned about the reliance on her to do things with Veronica when she is at home. Whilst Sarah does not mind doing this, she thinks it is not good for Veronica to spend so much time with her at the stage in her life when she should be beginning to think about moving out from home. Sarah and Paul have discussed with Veronica and her social worker how they might secure a more varied week for Veronica, leading to greater independence (whilst recognizing that Veronica will always need considerable support). The social worker suggested to Sarah and Paul that they involve other family members in the discussions, and also anyone else they knew had a good relationship with Veronica and was interested in her well-being. Sarah was reluctant to involve the rest of the family, friends and people who knew Veronica as she did not want to pressurize them into thinking they had to help out.

Eventually Paul persuaded her that they might as well give it a try – they need not ask anyone to do anything, just to have a discussion and come up with ideas. So they invited James and his girlfriend (and James brought along Nigel, an old school friend who lived and worked locally and who has known Veronica all her life), Paul's sister, Maria, Mrs Warburton from next door, Veronica's support worker, Sue, Veronica's friend, Elaine, and her mother round for coffee and a chat one Thursday evening. Much to Sarah and Paul's surprise, everyone was very pleased to be invited and they all had a lively discussion about what might be possible. Veronica did not fully understand what was going on, but seemed delighted that so many people were at home in the evening.

Not much was decided that first evening, but they all met up on a number of occasions and gradually came up with lots of realistic ideas about what Veronica might be able to do and how. In particular, all the different people were able to come up with some ideas about what they, themselves, and people they knew well could do with Veronica. These ranged from Maria saying she would love to have Veronica to stay with her for a weekend every two months (interestingly, she also said that she would have liked to have Veronica to stay regularly for a long time, but had not liked to suggest it in case Paul thought she was accusing him of not being able to cope), to Nigel suggesting that he could drop Veronica off at college two mornings a week to save Sue having to come and collect her from home: this would mean Sue would have an extra hour and a half a week to spend with Veronica. Mrs Warburton could not think of anything at the moment, but in the summer her niece was leaving her dog with her while she travelled to Australia for three months and then Veronica might like to help her exercise the dog, as she knew that Veronica was fond of dogs. (In the event, Veronica not only exercised the dog but took it to a dog-training class, where she met several other people who were also dog lovers).

Over time, this circle came up with other ideas and membership expanded and contracted as people's commitments changed. Certainly, Sarah and Paul were extremely surprised at how willing people were to take an interest in Veronica and to commit time and energy to helping her live a more fulfilled life. They began to think, "If only we had asked before . . .".

Linking people and strengthening the personal support networks around people with learning disabilities takes time. It is likely to be more successful, though, if we start with people who already know each other and who already have an interest in the person with a learning disability. It is this interest and commitment to the person that will help ensure that the network is a strong and continuous one. Some key issues to bear in mind when stimulating and supporting personal support networks include:

- do what you can to encourage people who show an interest in a person with a learning disability as a person;
- let people know what is possible and what it is they could offer: do not underestimate the barriers that many people see between them and the person with learning disabilities, barriers that are often erected by services;
- do not be afraid to ask people to do things or to become involved – often people find it easier to offer when asked than to volunteer in the first place;

- make it clear that people need not commit themselves to large-scale involvement: they should be encouraged to spend as much or as little time as possible, and to understand that their commitment can change over time;
- try to ensure that all those who are willing to spend time with a person with learning disabilities know that others are also willing to spend time (this helps to alleviate any fears people have that taking an interest themselves will require a greater commitment of time and responsibility than they may wish to contribute);
- give help and support when needed in knowing the best ways to communicate, assist and discover what motivates and interests a person and so on;
- help families and service support staff who may fear the un-certainty of the involvement of other people in supporting a person with learning disabilities to discuss and explore this concerns.

In Exercise 9.3 we ask you to identify potential personal support networks of a particular person with a learning disability.

We have seen, then, two ways in which activities, people and organizations can be linked in order to make it more likely that communities will be competent and people more socially capable. Sometimes strategies are needed that involve even more nego-tiation, and sometimes campaigning activities are required.

Community activism: campaigning and negotiation

Local facilities are not always accessible to people with learning disabilities because of some physical aspect of their design or because there is a poor "fit" between the situation and behaviour expected. In order to enable communities to include people with learning disabilities, we may have to negotiate with the powers that be over particular features of the setting.

Jane had recently moved from her parents' home to live with her brother, Iain, and his wife, Michelle. Iain and Michelle were particu-larly keen for Jane to learn to travel independently: they thought she had been over-protected at home. All three of them talked with the Deputy Officer in charge of the day centre, Ken, who agreed that they would begin working with Jean to teach her to travel by bus to the day centre, as a start. From Iain and Michelle's house to

Exercise 9.3 Personal support networks

Identify a person with a learning disability. Write the person's name in the centre of the diagram below, and in the circle nearest to the centre write the names of those people who have significant contact with the person just now. In the next circle write the names of people who have significant contact with those in the previous circle and so on.

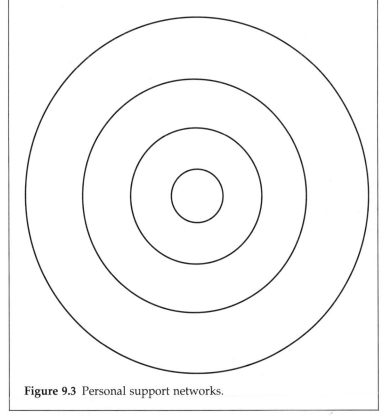

Figure 9.3 Personal support networks.

the bus stop to the centre, Jane had to cross a busy road and walk several hundred yards along the roadside. When she alighted from the bus, there was a pedestrian crossing which took her to the centre. Travelling home, Jane could walk from the centre along a pavement to the bus stop, and the bus dropped her off outside Iain and Michelle's driveway.

Jane could manage it all in safety except the 200 yards with no footpath to the bus stop taking her to the centre. A pavement needed to be built. Ken wrote to the Council about the pavement, but received a curt reply telling him that as no residents living near that stretch of road had made any mention of the need for a pavement it was unlikely to be a priority. Ken talked this over with Michelle, who took it upon herself to petition people living near her in order to put pressure on the Council.

As Michelle began to do this, she explained to people why she wanted to get a pavement built. This meant that she had to explain to her neighbours that Jane was now living with them. Quite to her surprise, several neighbours were interested in meeting Jane. They had not known she was living there. Jane ended up making particular friends with a middle-aged woman who lived alone with two dogs. Although Jane had never known any dogs, she became attached to these two and looked after them when their owner went on holiday. In turn, Jane stayed with this neighbour when Iain and Michelle wanted to go out or away by themselves. The council built a footpath five years later. Meanwhile, although Jane had not been able to travel to the day centre totally independently, she had gained considerably, as had her neighbour.

Ken had done relatively little, except begin to get the Council interested in building a footpath. He also negotiated with Iain and Michelle about how they might get the footpath built in the end. Clearly, the work of getting local support for the footpath was more effective as Michelle had taken it over than it would have been if Ken had tried to get the support. Nevertheless, without Ken's writing to the council and negotiation with Iain and Michelle, little would have changed for Jane. There had been a poor "fit" between independent travelling behaviour and the environment, which eventually was made better. Sometimes there is no fit between a setting and people with learning disabilities, such as when buildings or facilities are not physically accessible.

Sumira had very little opportunity to go out and share her interest in classical music with anyone. One term her support worker, Palvi, noticed a "Music Appreciation" class at the local adult education college on Tuesday evenings. Sumira uses a wheelchair and relies on help to get herself from one place to another. To their dismay, they found that the class was on the third floor of a building with no lift. Palvi went to see the adult education manager to ask that the sessions be moved. She was told that this was impossible as the class was held in the music room which had specialist facilities, such as high quality speakers. Palvi did not give up. Instead she wrote to the district adult education coordinator explaining the problem and requesting that the class be moved. She wrote back saying this was impossible as they could not accommodate valuable music equipment on the ground floor, for fear of theft.

Palvi still did not give up. She decided to see how many other people who used wheelchairs had wanted to attend things at this college but had been unable to. She contacted local disability groups and the other workers in her service, as well as voluntary organizations working with elderly people. She discovered that several people had wanted to attend classes at the College over the past few years, but had been unable to because they could not get access. The Director of the local Age Concern group knew one of the local authority governors of the college.

Over the next year, concerted pressure was put on the governing body of the college to improve access. This resulted in the college activities relocating to a primary school which had a lot of ground-floor accommodation. Sumira could now go to her class, which she thoroughly enjoyed. In particular, she enjoyed the concert trip with the class, which the tutor had taken special care to ensure was accessible to her. Three years later, the original college building was fully accessible.

The above examples, aimed at increasing the participation of people with learning disabilities in different settings and increasing the numbers of settings which include people with learning disabilities, show ways of working to increase community awareness and understanding.

One potentially powerful tool to use in local campaigns is the local press, often on the lookout for good local human interest stories. Some journalists will be interested in joining local campaigns, or campaigners can write letters to the paper. Newspapers will give coverage to small local success stories and events, as well as sometimes highlighting injustices. It is worth investing time with journalists so that they understand the situation of people with learning disabilities and do not fall into the trap of exploiting pity, sympathy or heroism in their stories.

Luke, Barry and Philip were all moving into a small house in the locality. Nothing new in this, you might say, except that they had done all the planning, negotiating, designing of supports and employing of staff by themselves with the support of their families and friends. It had taken a lot of doing and a local journalist heard of the story. He wanted to write a piece about the three of them that focused on how they had overcome their difficulties, accompanied by photographs of them which highlighted their disabilities. Luke, Barry, Philip and the others involved did not want coverage that emphasized the men as "heroes" or aroused pity in readers when they saw their disabilities.

After quite a bit of negotiation, they managed to persuade the journalist to write a piece that highlighted the ways in which the house had been renovated, and had moved from being a derelict eyesore to a well-kept property, playing down the "disability" angle. He also wrote another piece that highlighted the advantages to everyone in being a part of the project, concentrating on what the non-disabled members of the community had got from their involvement with people with disabilities, rather than vice versa. In this piece, Philip conducted most of the interviews.

If we are to use the local press to help us strengthen the competence of the community, we might have to monitor the coverage they give to people with learning disabilities and try to help journalists learn the importance of the type of stories they write and the imagery contained therein for either helping or hindering community competence. We may also have to feed journalists positive stories to use so that they move away from highlighting the problems of including people with learning disabilities in community life. Practice in thinking through what is required in challenging the local press about their coverage of people with learning disabilities is given in Exercise 9.4.

Helping people with learning disabilities negotiate with journalists and editors of local media is not only a powerful way of helping them see why different kinds of reporting may be required, it also can give the people with learning disabilities, themselves, more power and control over things that affect their lives and a greater sense of purpose. Similarly, helping people with learning disabilities get involved in local campaigns that affect everyone in the community helps them build and/or expand their roles in the community. Very often, if people are given the chance and helped to understand what the issue or the campaign is about, we can assist people with learning disabilities make useful contributions to local groups which are often, themselves, undermanned.

One of the most difficult things for us as workers is to be able to introduce the people we support to issues and to work on campaigns with which we may not agree.

Flora used her local shop and knew the shopkeeper and assistants quite well. One day she saw a notice on the shop door that had not been there before. She asked what it was about and was told that

Exercise 9.4 Negotiations with the local media

Read through the following situations. How might you take issue with the local media over how they have reported events? Use the questions below as a guide.

1. The local Lions club has held a raft race to raise money for "special needs" holidays. It is likely that some of the money will be given to a local parent-run day centre for adults with learning disabilities. The day it was held, the weather was hot and thundery. The event was reported under the headline of "Balmy boat race to raise money for the handicapped". It was accompanied by a picture of people with multiple disabilities sitting under a tree (it was not clear whether they were at the raft race or not).

2. A new independent hostel is opening in the locality. An advertisement appears in the local paper announcing the opening on 1 April. The advertisement is a large boxed advertisement with clowns around the edge and a picture of the hostel in the centre. It says "Mr and Mrs Eckswise are pleased to announce that All Fools Day sees the opening of 'Seaview Lodge' for the handicapped and disabled". It goes on to give details of accommodation and contact numbers. Your town is nowhere near the sea.

3. A local firm, Sycamores, has taken all the members of the day centre to a fun fair once a year for the last 15 years. You have been trying to get the firm to change its policy on this and to encourage them in sponsoring small group outings instead. This year the trip went ahead as usual and the local paper reported the occasion under the headline of "Handicapped go with Sycamores to Gaiety Park". The article begins: Four coach loads of the handicapped from Parkway Day Centre headed for Gaiety Park on Thursday with supervisors from Sycamores.

Continued

4. The local radio station had a news bulletin that said: Two men, recently released from Pear Tree Hospital for the mentally handicapped, saved a dog that had fallen into Marged Brook late last night. Neighbours describe the men as "quiet men who keep themselves to themselves: they don't seem to mix at all".

What issue would you want to raise?

With whom might you raise it?

What do you want to change?

What advantages might there be for the media if they take your suggestions seriously?

What compromises might you make?

What support could you get for your position?

What forms of opposition would you expect?

How easy is it to identify strategies for dealing with these issues successfully? Did you include people with learning disabilities in your strategies at all? What would be the advantages of doing this? What backing might you expect from the agency for which you work if you were to take issue with the local media? How might you secure backing from the agency for which you work?

there was a petition in the shop for people to sign if they objected to the proposal to build a shopping complex on the edge of the town. She did not understand the issues involved, but told Mary, the principal assistant, that she would like to find out more. Mary told her there was a meeting with people from the planning department in the primary school later in the week. Flora asked the support staff member who would be on duty that evening to take her to the meeting. Although none of the staff disagreed with the proposed development, they agreed that Flora should be able to go to the meeting if she wanted to. They made arrangements to cover the shift in the house so that someone could take Flora.

At the meeting, Flora heard how local shopkeepers and residents were afraid that the proposed development would result in their own shops having to close. Although Flora did not understand, yet, why this would be so, she did want her local shop to stay open. The staff worked with Flora to help her understand the issues and to continue to attend meetings and a demonstration about the development. Flora offered to distribute leaflets in the locality and the members of staff helped her do this. As the campaign went on, Flora took on the task of storing and collecting in unused leaflets and posters. She would not have been able to do this without the support of the staff. The campaign was successful and led to Flora being invited to take part in meetings about other environmental issues in the neighbourhood, which she did. She got to know many other people and they got to know her; she also began to develop different roles in the community.

It is not always easy to find out about local campaigns and issues, and it is particularly hard if we live outside the areas in which the people we are supporting live. It is also difficult if there are well-established cliques within a particular locality, in so far as they may not readily take to the inclusion of people with learning disabilities (or anyone else outside the clique, for that matter!). We can, however, do a lot to:

- pick up on interest shown in local issues by people with learning disabilities;
- find out information;
- contact leaders of campaigns (names can often be found in local papers, either in articles about the campaign or in letters to the editor);
- get people's names put on mailing lists;
- find out the dates and times of meetings;
- ensure the places of meetings are physically accessible;
- find ways of helping people with learning disabilities get their own concerns put on the agenda of local campaigns;

- provide specialist support if required – not just at meetings, but to enable people with learning disabilities to find out about and take an active role in the campaign if they so wish;
- demonstrate how people with learning disabilities can be included in discussions and activities linked to the campaign;
- help other members of local campaign groups include the person with the learning disabilities.

We should not be disappointed if it takes a long time to help communities become competent at including and supporting people with learning disabilities. We should remember that many communities have been in existence for a long time and, like our service systems, have built up structures and processes that exclude rather than include many people. There are times when we may have to work on developing new community resources or organizations, either because existing ones are so resistant to change or because there are large gaps in community resources.

Creating community organizations

Often we will want to work through local organizations, such as the churches, youth organizations, volunteer groups or voluntary organizations (increasingly service providers rather than campaigning organizations). Sometimes an area is relatively impoverished for local organizations, or there is not one that is able or willing to take up community development for people with learning disabilities. In these cases it may be worth creating a new local organization.

A group of friends, associates and colleagues worked in learning disability services, the local Council for Voluntary Service, the Community Health Council, or were active politically in the local council. They shared a concern about the lack of community inclusion of local people with learning disabilities and were interested in stimulating citizen advocacy. They had seen some examples of schemes that involved volunteers in leisure activities, but at that time (the early 1980s) these were mostly segregated pursuits or involved activities for groups of people with learning disabilities in ordinary locations. They decided to set up a different type of initiative and, forming an organization, they successfully applied for a grant to appoint someone who could recruit local people, match them (in terms of shared interests and lifestyles) with people with learning disabilities, provide support and monitor progress.

It was decided that the focus would be one of the Council wards, which comprised a community with some local identity. The worker was based at a local volunteer centre, itself located in a community education centre in a local secondary school.

The project itself was successful in linking people with other people who shared their interests and lifestyles; in extending the friendships and other relationships of the people involved; and in supporting a limited number of instances whereby people's partners acted as advocates in order to improve things for the person and to defend their rights. It also sparked off other developments.

- The worker was able to share local contacts with the volunteer centre, increasing its effectiveness, while saving some of the hard work of establishing a presence in, and knowledge of, the local community.
- The worker persuaded the local community education coordinator to experiment with opening up a variety of evening adult education classes to people with learning disabilities, and arranged support from volunteers and co-students.
- Fund-raising events were held in the local Labour club which, for one night, gave many local people a taste of what it might mean to include people with learning disabilities in the ordinary activities of a night out: this led to several offers of help; people who had not met anyone with a learning disability before asking how they could continue to see certain people they met on that night; and recruitment of further "partners" for local people with learning disabilities.
- The local formal services learned from the model of work and its management: they adopted many features of the scheme, in new service developments of their own (local development workers undertook detached work in the community and befriender schemes) after the project's funding ran out.

The project no longer exists, but ripples from it continue to spread well beyond the initial brief of the project.

Often the gaps we are trying to fill in communities so that they can be more competent at including people with learning disabilities will be short-term gaps, or the resources we stimulate to fill them with will be short term. This, in itself, is not a bad thing. However, we must take great care to ensure that the benefits experienced by the people with learning disabilities are more permanent.

Communities and the resources within them are dynamic entities – they are continually changing. When we embark upon community development work with the express purpose of increasing the social capability of people with learning disabilities, we have an obligation to ensure that the changes for the better are as sustainable as possible. We must, wherever possible, build in safeguards for them; this is particularly so if our work depends on paid staff to support whatever changes we have made. Paid staff move on; their personal and work commitments change, and it is sometimes very difficult for them to maintain their commitment to particular people with learning disabilities. The more we can lock any developments into more permanent community organizations and activities, the more we can hand over support to ordinary people who live in the community, and the more we can work to get our own agencies to encompass work with communities as a legitimate task, the more sustainable any change is likely to be.

Making services face outwards

Existing service agencies often obstruct moves to community competence. Our services may well espouse integration, but this is rarely expressed in assertive terms as the right to inclusion. Instead, we still seem dominated by the model of care as a paternalistic relationship between provider and client. While workers in services still see their roles as fundamentally those of "expert" and "care giver" rather than those of "someone who can learn", "a guide and support to real life", then people with learning difficulties will continue to be excluded, in a real sense, from society, yet powerless within it. Practically, this means that services have to act as bridges, not get in the way of what ought to be the primary relationship – that between people and their society. Two examples will serve to illustrate this point.

> Vic had moved into a small staffed house in a town 15 miles from the hospital where he had lived for most of his 45 years. Since moving, two years ago, staff have encouraged and supported Vic to discover a wide variety of interests and activities. About a year ago Vic began going to church regularly. He was welcomed into the congregation and has spent many days and evenings doing different things with members of the church. A small group from the church, who all knew Vic and who he knew, were going away on a weekend retreat. Vic was invited to join them. He was not permitted to go because there was no staff member who could accompany him, and the people who were going had not been vetted and registered by the authority as bona fide volunteers.
>
> After Mr Black's wife died when he was 45, he felt his life lacked purpose. His GP suggested he got in touch with social services to

offer help: this would give him a chance to look outside himself and do something for others. At the time, most residential services for people with learning disabilities were in hostels or hospitals. However, almost by chance, Mr Black got in touch with a social worker who was looking for an ordinary household in which to place Adam Wilson, a man with learning difficulties and occasional explosive behaviour who could no longer live in his own family home. Fifteen years later, Adam still lives with Mr Black, and several other people have come and gone in the interim period. Mr Black says the last 15 years have been the best years of his life (although not always easy, as on occasion he had to lock himself in his bedroom for fear of inciting Adam to even greater rage). He says "If I had only known what could have been possible, I could have done so much more with my life."

In the first example, existing service practices and requirements blinded the agency to see what is probably patently obvious to any reader – that Vic had been invited to go away with a group of people who had moral and personal commitments to him, and were willing to support him without any professional staff. Service practices and procedures made it impossible to take advantage of the invitation and to hand over care and responsibility to "lay" people.

In the second example, the service let Mr Black into the lives of people with learning disabilities to mutual advantage, and it is clear from what he says that Mr Black would not have been able to enter their lives unless invited. Happily, there are many examples, nowadays, of arrangements such as that offered by Mr Black (adult placements, family link and so on); unhappily, there are still many examples of the barriers imposed by services which prevent ordinary people from entering the lives of people with learning disabilities.

We can take steps to "turn our services outwards". Many of the ordinary operating procedures of our services can be reoriented to the community: we can rewrite job descriptions; change our recruitment practices; expand our performance objectives and goals; redefine the skills needed by workers and the constituency towards whom training and information is addressed; and develop new management systems and procedures. Building a community focus into existing service procedures is highlighted in Exercise 9.5.

Services are not going to change overnight to incorporate a focus on community competence. However, we can all be

Exercise 9.5 Community competence as part of existing operational procedures

Think of your own work practices. For each of the following, describe how a focus on community competence might be incorporated.

Existing system	Changes required to incorporate focus on community competence	Ways in which changes may be achieved
Job descriptions		
Job advertisements		
Recruitment and selection (all elements)		
Staff supervision and appraisal		
Team meetings; review days		
Expenditure decisions		
Documentation of work carried out		
Policy formulation		
Induction and training		
Organization of staff deployment and work allocation		
Report preparation		
Monitoring of the service (informal/formal)		
Production of written guidelines		
Inter-service meetings		

Continued

What are the obstacles to "turning our services outwards"? Are some aspects of the service more easily adapted to incorporate a community focus? If so, which ones and why is this? Even if you cannot do anything about changing the overall service you work in, can you see how you might be able to adapt your own job description and working practices? What would it take to do this?

working towards this in the long term if we really believe that people's social capability is constrained by the competence of the community. It is useful to think in advance what difficulties there may be, as well as what sources of support and strength we can draw upon. In Exercise 9.6 we suggest a force-field analysis as an aid to identifying these things.

It is likely that some of the forces you identified as hindrances to change were your own skills and those of other workers. We have touched on some of the skills required in some of our examples above, but we now draw attention to some specific skills that are used in different areas of working with communities.

SKILLS FOR DEVELOPING COMMUNITY COMPETENCE

If we are to work effectively with ordinary people in the community, with a view to helping communities develop their competence to include people with learning disabilities, we must be able to deploy skills at different levels of operation. At a personal level, we must be committed, ourselves, to opening up communities to include people with learning disabilities; develop attitudes of acceptance and tolerance; accept people with different, sometimes hostile, views and opinions; and be able to tolerate resistance, conflict and frustration. We must have the confidence to work independently, sometimes alone, and to take decisions in full anticipation of the likely consequences of those decisions.

At an interpersonal level, we need to be able to make contact and talk with a wide range of people, some of whom we may not know, and to stimulate interest, enthusiasm and motivation to include people with learning disabilities. This means that we must be able to talk with and about people with learning disabilities in positive and respectful ways without minimizing the kinds of supports and arrangements these people may require in

Exercise 9.6 Force-field analysis:
developing a focus on community
competence within existing services

List all those things that you think will help you move
nearer the objective and all those things that will block
progress. Identify strategies for weakening the hindering
forces and strengthening the helping forces.

Objective: To incorporate a focus on community competence within existing service practice

Nearer to   Further from

You and the service
(including knowledge, expertise and skills)

|

Society
(including social attitudes, beliefs and local people's behaviour)

|

People with learning disabilities, their families and friends

|

Were you able to identify more helping or hindering forces?
Why is this? What kinds of strategies for increasing helping
forces did you identify? How many of these can you do
something about? What else will you have to do to promote
change? What roles do people with learning disabilities
have in helping move towards this objective?

order to participate. We must be able to advocate on behalf of
people, and this includes being able to see where power and
influence is located and use it to better the lives of people with
learning disabilities. We need to be able to negotiate with different people over different kinds of matters, sometimes in the face
of considerable opposition. Nearly all negotiations end in com-

promise of some sort and we should see this not as a sign of failure but of success, if the compromises still help us move forwards in the desired direction.

> Jeanette was the manager of a day centre for 60 people with learning disabilities. She had argued for a long time that the day centre did not meet the needs of the people who spent time there, and that a dispersed day support service would be more appropriate. The social services committee, however, was proud of the centre, which had been purpose-built only three years ago. Jeanette had little local interest or support for her plans, although her managers within the authority were supporting her. The Chair of the committee wanted to keep the centre open; Jeanette wanted to close it and link people who attended more firmly in their local communities. The compromise they reached was that the activities in the Centre would be opened to local people, and the canteen facilities would also be made available. Both Jeanette and the councillors, as well as centre members, families and local people were all happy with the compromise, and all stood to benefit from the solution agreed.

Many situations will require us to compromise, and we should remember that there is never only one solution to any decision or challenge that we face. Compromises, though, can be of different sorts, as illustrated in Table 9.2.

The different types of compromise, with the exception of retrograde compromises and cop-outs, will all help us move in the

Table 9.2 Different forms of compromise

Type of compromise	Features
Neutral	A course of action is agreed that has little to do with the original suggestion
Retrograde	A course of action that results in moving away from objectives
Progressive	A course of action which results in moving towards objectives
Comparative	A course of action which is better than expected
Selective	A course of action wherein one part of the objective is pursued at the expense of others
Cop-out	A course of action which is irrelevant and where little attempt was made to achieve a satisfactory outcome

desired direction. Constructive compromises lead to all those involved reaching a decision or agreement that is to their mutual
advantage. This is an important principle that we should bear in
mind whenever we are negotiating with people. We should not be
aiming to "win at all costs", but rather reach a position of mutual
gain. It is worth bearing in mind, though, that not everyone may
approach negotiations in this spirit. We can look at three basic
approaches to negotiation.

- Both person A and person B are willing to give in order to get,
  and they enter the negotiation with this in mind. How much
  and what they have to give, in order for both to get, is worked
  out during the negotiation. This approach has a high chance of
  success as both A and B appreciate the principle that both
  should be "winners".
- A is willing to give providing something comes back in return; B will only give after something has been received.
  Whilst both A and B understand the importance of mutual
  gain, if they wait to see what they get before offering something, they may reach stalemate. Nevertheless, this approach
  will sometimes be successful.
- Both A and B come to the negotiation determined not to give
  until they have got something. If neither is willing to move
  from this position, stalemate is reached and there is no negotiation. This approach is unsuccessful.

Whenever we meet with others in order to negotiate a change of
some sort, the potential for conflict is there. Provided things do
not get out of control, positive and imaginative ideas and solutions, as well as future working relationships, can arise from
conflict. Conflict becomes unhealthy when it is avoided or approached with the attitude, "I must get my way and this person
must not" (this is known as a win/lose approach). If this happens,
animosities may develop, communications may break down and
we will get nowhere. Furthermore, breakdowns in relationships
with certain members of the community (if we have selected them
because they hold key positions in the community) may have far
reaching effects that we had not anticipated. Strategies for handling conflict vary according to how assertive and cooperative
people are. Figure 9.4 illustrates different strategies for handling
conflict.

Assertive

Win/lose:
confrontational;
must win at any
cost; claims to be
ethically or
professionally
correct

Problem solving/
compromising:
needs of both
parties important;
assertive and
cooperative: maintain
good relationships
and agree there is
more than one
possible answer;
believe in mutually
beneficial solutions

Sitting on the fence:
all parties retain
good relationships
but nothing much
happens; each party
achieves minor
goals

Avoidance:
non-confrontational,
passes over issues,
denies conflict
exists; aims not to
create additional
problems

Accommodating:
agreeable, non-
assertive at the
expense of personal
goals; considered
not to be worth
risking damage to
relationships

Unassertive

Uncooperative 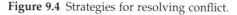 **Cooperative**

Figure 9.4 Strategies for resolving conflict.

A problem-solving, compromise approach to handling conflict will be the most effective and productive, and yet we do not always remember – or even have the skills – to adopt these strategies. It can also be very difficult to stick to this kind of strategy if the people with whom we are in conflict are using one of the others. Nevertheless, if we can remember to avoid the common traps of working towards mutual gain and compromise, whether this is in the context of negotiation, decision making or the handling of conflict, we will be well on the way to gaining cooperation, trust and commitment from people in the community. The common mistakes that are made include:

- focusing on the person rather than on the issues;
- inadequate preparation;
- misunderstanding, not following or forgetting the give–get principle;

- impatience and frustration;
- loss of temper, becoming aggressive or sarcastic;
- not listening;
- emotive argument instead of rational reasoning;
- ignoring conflict;
- misunderstanding starting positions and aiming for too much too quickly.

Even if we have effective skills for working with communities, we will need backup and support. It is essential that our managers understand the reasons for and the nature of our work. The more detached our work is from mainstream team and service activities, the more important it will be to have clear boundaries to our roles, supportive management, clear risk management policies and, perhaps most importantly, clarity of purpose and objectives. Without clarity of purpose we cannot know if we are doing what is required at the right time, in the right place, with the right reasons and for the right purpose. We need to know all this before we can begin to evaluate our work in the community and, indeed, the progress we are making towards social capability.

FURTHER READING

Working with communities for change can be approached from a number of different perspectives. The readings we have included range from work on community development and community work to participative change within organizations, work on social movements and social development and on social innovations generally.

Albery, N. (with Yule, V.) (1992) *The Book of Visions: An encyclopaedia of social innovations*, Virgin Books, London.

Alinsky, S. (1971) *Rules for Radicals*, Random Press, New York.

Association of Community Workers (1979) *The Community Workers' Skills Manual*, Association of Community Workers, London.

Bell, G. (1992) *The Permaculture Way: Practical steps to create a self-sustaining world*, Thorsons, London.

Briscoe, C. and Thomas, D. (1977) *Learning and Supervision in Community Work*, Allen and Unwin, London.

Burton, M. (1989) *Australian Intellectual Disability Services: Experiments in Social Change (Working papers in Building Community Strategies: No.1)*, Kings Fund College, London.

Burton, M. and Kagan, C. (1995) Rethinking empowerment: shared action against powerlessness, in *Marxism and Psychology: Conflict and coexistence* (eds I. Parker and R. Spears), Pluto Press, London.

Cohen, S. and Syme, S. (1985) *Social Support and Health*, Academic Press, New York.

Croft, S. and Beresford, P. (1993) *Citizen Involvement: A practical guide for change*, Macmillan, London.

Croft, S. and Beresford, P. (1993) *Getting Involved: A practical manual*, Open Services Project/Joseph Rowntree Foundation, Brighton.

Dluhy, M.J. (1990) *Building Coalitions in the Human Services*, Sage, San Francisco.

Fisher, R. and Ury, W. (1981) *Getting to Yes: Negotiating agreement without giving in*, Hutchinson, New York.

Freire, P. (1972) *Pedagogy of the Oppressed*, Penguin, Harmondsworth.

Henderson, P. and Thomas, D.N. (1987) *Skills in Neighbourhood Work*, 2nd ed., Unwin Hyman, London.

Holman, R. (1983) *Resourceful Friends: Skills in community social work*, Children's Society, London.

Kagan, C. (1987) *Evaluation of Blackley Leisure Integration Support Scheme: Final report to the Mental Health Foundation*, Manchester Polytechnic, Manchester.

Lattimer, M. (1994) *The Campaigning Handbook*, Directory of Social Change, London.

Maddux, R.B. (1988) *Successful Negotiation*, Kogan Page, London.

Muñoz, R.F., Snowden L.R., Kelly, J.G. and associates *Social and Psychological Research in Community Settings: Designing and conducting programs for social and personal well-being*, Jossey-Bass, San Francisco.

Nisbet, J. (1992) *Natural Supports in School, at Work and in the Community for People with Severe Disabilities*, Paul Brookes, London.

Orford, J. (1992) *Community Psychology: Theory and practice*, (Chapter 11), Wiley, Chichester.

Parry, G. (1988) Mobilising social support, in F. Watts (ed.) *New Developments in Clinical Psychology*, Vol. 2, Wiley, Chichester.

Pearpont, J. (1990) *From Behind the Piano: The building of Judith Snow's unique circle of friends*, Inclusion Press, Toronto.

Perske, B. (1980) *New Life in the Neighbourhood*, Abingdon, Nashville.

Warren, R.B. and Warren, D.I. (1977) *The Neighbourhood Organizer's Handbook*, University of Notre Dame Press, Notre Dame, Indiana.

Wilson, D.C. (1992) *A Strategy of Change: Concepts and Controversies in the Management of Change*, Routledge, London.

10

Evaluating change

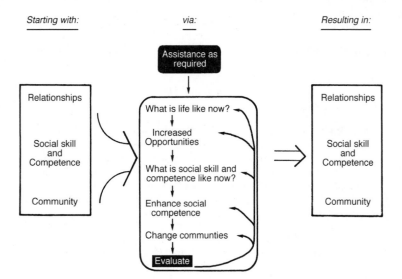

Starting with: *via:*   *Resulting in:*

WHY EVALUATE?

Why evaluate? After all, we do not usually evaluate real life. We have to know whether we are using our effort, time and skill wisely, and whether we are making any difference for people with learning disabilities. We should have good reasons for doing what we do with service users: have we used their time wisely; have we been fair to them in the way we have introduced them to the experiences we have selected? Furthermore, in a society that increasingly demands accountability from its publicly funded services, we must be able to justify the resources that go into this work.

In this chapter we will suggest some issues that need to be considered when evaluating our work on improving social capability.

EVALUATION MODELS

There is a wide variety of approaches to evaluation. The different models emphasize different things, which themselves reflect different assumptions about the nature of the world and the nature of knowledge.

We can distinguish between three main approaches to evaluation, which employ, "technical", "interpretive" and "liberatory" models respectively (Table 10.1).

These models do not necessarily compete with one another. Instead, each can be seen as important at appropriate times and places.

Table 10.1 Three approaches to evaluation

Type	Main characteristics	Typical information	Relation to other people
Technical	Based on natural science; emphasizes being objective, prediction and control	Numerical	Distancing, objectifying
Interpretive	Based on social science, arts and literature; emphasizes shared understanding	Description	Understanding others' viewpoint
Liberatory	Based on liberation movements and therapy; emphasizes reducing mystification and exposing hidden power in order to free people	Exposure of hidden social power	Participatory, shared action

Mr Thomas went into hospital for an operation to lengthen the tendons in his left foot. This was successful: he made a complete recovery, and while previously he limped, he now walks normally. While in hospital he felt frightened because little effort was made to explain what was happening to him at a level that he could understand. It had taken the concerted efforts of his community nurse to get his GP to refer him to the consultant who carried out the operation in the first place: the GP appeared to think that it would make little difference for a person with a learning disability.

In the above example, we have implicitly evaluated Mr Thomas's hospital experience using all three models. Technically the operation was a good one, it produced the desired (mechanical) measurable, effect. On an interpretive level, however, the episode was less successful: Mr Thomas had a bad experience and little effort appears to have been made to understand his feelings and perception of what happened. In liberatory terms, the community nurse was able to overcome the discrimination by the GP and gain access to the medical treatment, which itself reflects the wider discrimination against people with learning disabilities. However, as the experience in the hospital was traumatic, this emancipation was rather compromised.

In most cases the three models are not pure: the methods of one approach may be used to answer a question posed within the perspective of a different approach, but it is helpful to recognize that for useful evaluations in real cases we are likely to need to combine elements from each of the three perspectives.

WHOSE PERSPECTIVE?

Evaluation of social competence is likely to be concerned with several stakeholders, each of whom may pose different questions.

Lloyd lived with his father. He was 25 and went to work on a voluntary basis at the distribution centre of a large voluntary organization. His support worker was working with him to expand his interests and social contacts at weekends, as well as enhancing his social skills.

How could this be evaluated? Different stakeholders had different ideas.

Lloyd	Will I have some friends and things to do?
Lloyd's father	Will he be happy and safe?
Support worker	Will I be successful in making a difference for Lloyd without creating additional problems? Will he become less isolated but less dependent on me?
Support worker's manager	Will I be able to justify the investment of resources in this way?
Psychologist advising the support worker	Do Lloyd's social skills increase? Did the worker use the best available methods? Were these methods responsible for any positive change?
Voluntary organization	Will there be any spin-offs for Lloyd's social skills in the workplace? Will he complain less about being bored at weekends?
Minister at Lloyd's church	Will Lloyd stop coming to church because he is too busy? Will Lloyd's father be any less worried about him?

The perspectives of different stakeholders will frequently balance each other. At times, the stakeholders might have totally different views of what criteria should be used for judging the success of an intervention, but more often what is at issue is where the emphasis should be placed.

In the above example there are multiple perspectives on evaluation, and we have to make a judgement about which are the most important to address. Also note that the list is a mixture of technical and interpretive perspectives: if Lloyd's degree of social inclusion is also part of the picture, then there will be a liberatory perspective too.

With different models and different stakeholders in any evaluation, there is likely to be a large number of possible aspects of change to evaluate. In evaluating change we have to be selective, we have to prioritize rather than trying to answer every possible question. Exercise 10.1 invites you to practise prioritizing.

Exercise 10.1 Prioritizing evaluation questions

For one of the pieces of work with a person that you have identified so far, work through the following.

1. List the things that you expect to change:

(a) in the person's social opportunities

for presence and participation in the community	to be respected	to have some control	to become more capable

(b) in the person's social competence

awareness	observation and interpretation	planning and strategy	social behaviour	understanding context

(c) in the competence of the person's community

family	direct services	people, places, activities, organizations (locally)	people, places, activities, organizations (more widely)

2. Identify the people who are stakeholders, i.e. have an interest in what happens.

   What are the key issues for change for them?

3. What is the view of the person with a learning disability?

4. Review the above material. What two to four themes stand out most strongly?

(a)   (b)

(c)   (d)

Are these themes mutually exclusive (i.e. contradictory) or are they merely different questions? If there is a real conflict, decide or discuss which themes are closest to the needs of the person in question. If this is unclear, consider the next question.

Is there a balance between technical, interpretive and liberatory themes? If not, then review your answers to the above questions.

5. Now settle on two or three main themes. Convert these to questions that could be asked about the changes made.

(a)

(b)

WHAT IS EVALUATED: PROCESS AND OUTCOME

We can also look at evaluation in terms of where in the sequence of change the evaluation focuses. We distinguish between **process**, the how of change, and **outcome**, the what of change. Let us look at our example of Mr Thomas (page 307).

Process:
- conduct of the operation;
- treatment pre-and postoperatively;
- Mr Thomas's subjective experience while in the hospital;
- process of advocacy and negotiation to gain access to this treatment;

Outcome:
- effect of the operation (after recovery) on function;
- side-effects (scars, side-effects of the anaesthetic, cross infection, etc.);
- lasting subjective effects (fear of doctors and hospitals);
- effects on the ease with which other people with learning disabilities gain access and are treated in the future.

Both process and outcome are important. While we want to emphasize the outcomes, especially those that affect the person's quality of life, we also want to know something of the processes by which these outcomes were attained. Without some analysis of process, we will find it difficult to understand what to do next time to secure a better set of outcomes.

We might define desirable outcomes in advance in terms of goals to be achieved. There are some advantages and disadvantages in this way of thinking about evaluation. Goals keep us focused on what we are trying to achieve. If they have been set properly they will be clear, so we can all agree that they have been attained. It is often possible for goals to be agreed in advance among stakeholders, and they can then share in common criteria for evaluation.

On the other hand, setting goals may focus the effort for change on one set of outcomes at the expense of others. Setting goals can pre-empt other changes, imposing an excessively simple model of change and growth. Much of what we have been proposing in this book rests on an alternative view of change, in which we consider the person in context and do what we can with both to make positive changes: the goals emerge from this process of joint exploration, serving the work rather than dictating it. Furthermore, setting goals often tends to limit the scope of the work and force expectations down.

If setting goals too early or too tightly can distort the content and process of the work we want to evaluate, they can also unduly narrow the focus of our evaluation. By focusing on goals we can fail to look for other changes, both positive and negative.

Errol lived in a bed-sit in a large house with twelve other single men. He was friends with nearly every one of them. Errol frequently found himself without money: at least three of the other men used to ask him for money and he would give it to them. At a recent review, Errol and those professionals involved thought it would be a good idea if he were more assertive and refused to hand over his money. Errol's support worker and Errol worked over a two and a half month period on different ways in which he could be assertive. The goal was for Errol to refuse to give money when asked.

The work was successful in so far as Errol did learn a number of assertive strategies and refused to give the men his money. However, most of the men in his building stopped popping in to see him round about the same time. Errol felt he was losing his friends. The evaluation of the assertiveness work did not pick this up. It was not noticed until Errol mentioned at his next review that would rather have had his friends and no money than his money and no friends.

Despite the above cautions, sensible goal specification remains a helpful way of focusing our evaluation efforts. It is not the only approach. We could, alternatively, focus on *evaluation questions; concerns and issues;* tests of *assumptions* about what happens during the process of change; on information gathering for decision making; or around increasing *understanding of the needs* of the person with whom we are working.

TIME FRAME

Our discussion of process and outcome suggested that the distinction is mainly about the time at which we look at the sequence of change. We should extend this idea to note that we may well draw different conclusions depending on when we do our evaluation and over what period of time.

A staff team worked with Antonio who had a history of assaults on other people. A behaviour modification programme was put in place (the details of which are unimportant for this discussion) and the number of assaults counted. The following summarizes what happened.

Before programme introduced	average of 10 assaults per week
Week 1 after programme introduced	33 assaults
Week 2	12 assaults
Week 3	1 assault
Week 4 to week 32	no assaults
Week 33	monitoring of progress ceased
Week 67	Antonio re-referred to behaviour specialist
Week 68	Antonio moved to secure unit

There are, of course, several possible interpretations of what might have happened. What the example illustrates is that our perception of relative success or failure will depend on when and over what period of time we carry out our evaluation. If we stopped at week 1 we would come to a different conclusion from if we stopped at week 2, 13 or 68.

Influential research papers have been written on the basis of shorter range evaluations than the 33 week period in the above example: how confident can we be about their conclusions?

Ripples and slow fuse change

In evaluating our efforts to improve social capability we also need to be aware of the possibility of the phenomena of "ripple effects" and "slow fuse" change.

Ripple effects

Ripple effects occur when an intervention gives rise to changes beyond its original focus. In social capability these effects are likely to be mediated in various ways, through:

- the influence of one skill area on others: for example when an increase in people's capacity to observe has a direct effect on their ability to notice the effects of what they do, so speeding up the learning process in all their social interactions.
- the effects of skill on social opportunities: such as when a person starts meshing more appropriately in social encounters and, as a result, the number and duration of social interactions increases (itself feeding back to the person's learning).
- one aspect of the person's community affecting other aspects: for instance when one member of a social network establishes a relationship with a person who has a learning disability and, as a result, others do, too, thus increasing social opportunities for several people with learning disabilities.

We hope to set in motion as many helpful ripple effects as we can, which means that evaluations of this work will need to at least be open to this possibility.

Slow fuse change

By slow fuse change we mean change that is delayed or whose effects take time to become obvious.

Tracy was approached by Jane who wondered whether she might be able to share some time with Irene who had just moved in across the road. Tracy had just started a new job and said she was sorry that she couldn't. Eighteen months later Tracy was in the same supermarket queue as Jane: she recalled their previous conversation and said that she had thought about Irene a lot since then and wondered if she would like to go to the Irish night at the pub down the road with her and her sister Pat.

Judy was thought vulnerable to sexual exploitation. Her support worker spent time helping her to distinguish between the things she wanted to do and the things she didn't. She also taught her to refuse unreasonable requests. Meanwhile, other steps were taken to reduce the immediate risks from certain men in her social circle. Eleven months later, Judy reported being approached by a man on the way home: she had dealt with the situation effectively, drawing on the things she had learned before.

Again, an evaluation that is too narrow or too short in its time-scale is likely to miss these "slow-fuse" changes.

Once we have decided on the purpose of the evaluation, and considered the time-scale in which the evaluation is to take place, we will have to choose appropriate methods of evaluation.

METHODS

A variety of methods is available, and those chosen will depend on the particular purpose of the evaluation, together with the situations in which they are applied and the resources available.

Methods Amvailable

There are four basic methods of collecting information.

- Observation (direct, indirect, participative, unobtrusive, time sampling or continuous)
- Interview (conversations varying in their degree of pre-planning, and ranging from structured to unstructured)
- Questionnaire (self-report scales, opinion surveys, factual information gathering, etc.)
- Reporting systems (incident forms, analysis of entries in case notes, etc.).

Each of these can be used to produce **quantitative** (numerical) information or **qualitative** information (descriptive: usually in words, but could be in the form of pictures, diagrams or drama). Table 10.2 outlines the key features of quantitative and qualitative methods.

Table 10.2 Quantitative and qualitative methods

Quantitative	Qualitative
More manageable information to analyse and compare; limit information to a restricted set of predetermined categories	Produce rich and detailed information; allow study of issues in depth without the need for predetermined categories for analysis
Attempt to break down complexity into parts	Attempt to present complexity for what it is
Easily summarized and presented; summary data may be misleading unless interpreted with caution	Relatively difficult to summarize and present findings; data often in the form of people's own words; can speak for itself if allowed to

A balanced approach to evaluation combines qualitative and quantitative techniques, using the strengths of each, such as when we interview a person in order to obtain their answers to a questionnaire.

Choosing a method

Before a method can be chosen, we must be clear about what we want to know, i.e. the question to be answered, and how we will use the information gathered in answering the question. Once we are clear about these two things, the following criteria can be used for choosing a method.

- Does it provide the information required?
- Is it compatible with the pursuit of social capability?
- To what extent does it involve the person with a learning disability and his or her allies?
- Is it practical in use?

We will now consider each of these questions in turn.

Does it provide the information required?

Ask what kind of information the method is likely to provide – is it going to be of any use in answering the questions to which answers are needed, and in helping to plan the next steps? The kind of information obtained will depend on the kind of question asked, and of whom it is asked. Detailed descriptive accounts will be needed if quality of life is being reviewed: in this case, qualitative, observational and interview methods would be appropriate. On the other hand, if information is required about the availability of social opportunities, a survey or regular statistical reporting might yield some of the required information.

It is important to have an idea of the extent to which any information gathered will be accurate enough to be useful. Questions such as the following need to be asked.

How accurate is the information? We could deliberately build in to our evaluation checks on accuracy, such as using more than one source of information or asking the same question in more than one form.

How dependable is the information? We could identify those factors likely to improve or reduce the dependability of the information, such as the bias of observer or interviewer; any drift over time in accuracy as boredom or complacency sets in; superficiality of observation; vagueness or ambiguity of questions; and bias of those involved to provide the information they think is desirable.

How serious are any threats to the accuracy of the information?

What further information could be easily collected to check that the picture obtained is plausible?

Is it compatible with the pursuit of social capability?

Methods should be chosen that treat people with respect, only minimally disrupt their relationships or their use of ordinary places and activities and, where possible, enhance their capabilities and reputation. Highly intrusive methods, such as video-recording, can threaten the dignity and respect of people with learning disability and could, therefore, weaken – even extinguish – any positive effects of the intervention on their quality of life. On the other hand, methods that focused on people's own views (where this was feasible) and gave them experiences and assistance that helped them to express their own views would fit well with the pursuit of social capability in its broadest sense.

To what extent does it involve the person with a learning disability and his or her allies?

In evaluating change, methods should be chosen that involve the participation of those with a legitimate interest in the person concerned as much as possible. It is essential that the findings are "owned" by those who will be affected by action that flows from them.

A powerful way of achieving such ownership is through participation in the production of the information. Evaluation should not be monopolized by professionals, although they may have a leading role in carrying it out. People with a learning disability, their families and friends will have a legitimate interest in the evaluation of change and at least some of the methods used should reflect this.

Is it practical in use?

The methods chosen for evaluation of change must be practical to use. It is no use devising a perfect method if it would be too expensive, time consuming or laborious to use. The practicality of different methods is explored in Exercise 10.2.

Exercise 10.2 Practicality of evaluation methods

For the example you used in the previous exercise (Exercise 10.1), make brief notes about how you will carry out the evaluation, then answer the following questions.

1. How will information be collected?

2. How long will this take?

3. Who will be involved in

   (a) providing information?
   (b) gathering information?

Continued

---

4. What materials (forms, audio or videotapes, exercise books, flip charts, felt-tip pens, checklists and question-naires, etc.) will be required?

5. How will information be collated (filing, transcribing, copying, etc.)?

   Who will do this?

6. What storage arrangements will be required?

7. How will this information be analysed?

   Who will do this?
   What methods of analysis will be used?
   How long will this take?
   What resources would be needed?

8. How will findings be summarized and presented?

   To whom?
   By whom?

9. What resources and time will be required?

   Can all this be afforded in terms of money?
   time (of people with learning disability, their allies, staff and others)?

10. Can the same kind of information be obtained, at an acceptable level of detail and accuracy, more economi-cally in terms of time and effort?

Were any of these questions particularly hard to answer? Why was this? Whose help will you have to enlist in order to carry out meaningful evaluations of your work?

Once the above questions have been answered it should be possible to make appropriate choices about the method to be used.

Good evaluations should help us do better work in the future and should, therefore, help us identify what work needs to be done and how. In the case of social capability, evaluation of social capability will often highlight not only what we and the people with learning disabilities have achieved, but also how much more there is to do. As we saw in Figure 1.2, strengthening social skills may lead people to greater opportunities, which then reveal other social and community competencies to be strengthened. We will then be starting all over again.

For many of us, work in the social capability field exposes us to our own limitations in terms of opportunities to develop new and meaningful ways of working, the competence of our communities to support us in working in new and meaningful ways and, last but not least, in our own social skill or competence. We can, therefore, apply the same model of social capability to ourselves and our abilities to get things done that matter. But that is another story.

FURTHER READING

There are many different approaches to evaluation, and we have included here general guides as well as those which stress the participation of those on the receiving end, and sources which discuss issues that we have raised in this chapter. The distinction between technical, interpretive and liberatory approaches to evaluation draws on the work of Habermas.

Burton, M. (1992) *Roads to Quality: A sourcebook for improving services to people with major disabilities*, Regional Advisory Group for Learning Disability Services, Manchester.

Feuerstein, M.T. (1986) *Partners in Evaluation: Evaluating development and community programmes with participants*, Macmillan, London.

Habermas, J. (1979) *Knowledge and Human Interests*, Beacon Press, Boston.

Herman, J.L. and Morris, L.L. (1988) *Evaluator's Handbook*, Sage, London.

Kazdin, A. (1980) *Research Design in Clinical Psychology*, Harper and Row, New York.

Key, M., Hudson, P. and Armstrong, J. (1985) *Evaluation theory and Community Work*, Community Projects Foundation, London.

Patton, M.Q. (1982) *Practical Evaluation*, Sage, London.

Patton, M.Q. (1986) *Utilization-focused Evaluation*, 2nd edn. Sage, London.

Pusey, M. (1987) *Jürgen Habermas*, Tavistock, London.

Rossi, P.H. and Freeman, H.E. (1993) *Evaluation: A systematic approach*, 5th edn., Sage, New York.

Strauss, A.L. and Corbin, J.M. (1990) *Basics of Qualitative Research: grounded theory procedures and techniques*, Sage, Newbury Park.

Weiss, C.H. (ed.) (1972) *Evaluating Action Programmes: Readings in Social Action and Education*, Alyn and Bacon, Boston.

Wood, S. and Shears, B. (1986) *Teaching Children with Severe Learning Difficulties: A radical reappraisal*, Croom Helm, London.

Index